The Cheapskate Millionaire's Guide to Bargain Hunting in the Big Apple

The Best Deals on the Best Stuff

Designer clothes • Handmade shoes • Caviar and gourmet foods • Deluxe hotels •

Charity auctions •

Glassware • China •

The Cheapskate Millionaire's Guide to Bargain Hunting in the Big Apple

Lighting •

• Draperies •

• Venetian blinds •

• Soapstone sinks •

Renting and buying apartments • Sample sales • William Morris wallpaper •

Tracie Rozhon

TIMES BOOKS

RANDOM HOUSE

To Chris

Who fixed my computer, made my telephone calls,
crashed up my car doing errands for me—and brought me
red-and-white striped tulips when the deadlines
seemed unbearable

All rights reserved under International and Pan-American
Copyright Conventions. Published in the United States by
Times Books, a division of Random House, Inc., New York,
and simultaneously in Canada
by Random House of Canada Limited, Toronto.

LIBRARY OF CONGRESS CATALOGING-IN-PUBLICATION DATA
Rozhon, Tracie.
The cheapskate millionaire's guide to bargain hunting in the Big Apple:
the best deals on the best stuff / by Tracie Rozhon.—1st ed.
p.   cm.
Includes index.
ISBN 0-8129-3108-4
1. Shopping—New York Region Guidebooks.   2. New York Region
Guidebooks.
TX336.5.N48R68   1999
380.1'45'000257471—dc21   99-25227

Random House website address: www.randomhouse.com

Printed in the United States of America on acid-free paper

9 8 7 6 5 4 3 2

First Edition

SPECIAL SALES

Times Books are available at special discounts for bulk purchases for sales pro-
motions or premiums. Special editions, including personalized covers, ex-
cerpts of existing books, and corporate imprints, can be created in large
quantities for special needs. For more information, write to Special Markets,
Times Books, 201 East 50th Street, New York, New York 10022, or call 800-
800-3246.

Contents

is a $12.50 martini worth it? Swinging at Birdland. List of
sources.

Chapter 5 Where Are the Chocolates on My Pillow?
Fancy Hotels with Deals   74

During the week. On the weekends. Small boutique hotels and
deals under $100. Talking with Bernard Goldberg, the man
who invented the Cheap Hotel that Looks like a Million. Plan A:
How to make reservations like a millionaire (how to get the
best room—with no fibbing). Plan B: How to change rooms
like a millionaire (for use only after Plan A has failed). List of
sources.

Chapter 6 How to Find Your Dream
Bargain Apartment   85

An insider's glossary for reading between the lines. To rent:
Reading the *Village Voice*. Surfing the Net. Playing the odds.
Surfing the streets: Checking out the signs, greasing the palms of
the doormen and supers. To buy: The real secrets in a hot
market. "Dead listings." The advantages of using one broker vs.
many. The advantages of using no broker: Going direct. The
disadvantages. Bargaining like a millionaire. List of sources.

Chapter 7 Outfitting Your Apartment   108

Furniture: Discount outlets and designers' warehouses. Antique
shops. The 26th Street antiques market. The pier shows. Going
to the Armory (The Winter Antiques Show) *not* to buy. Auctions
in New York City and its environs. The best auctions in
Connecticut and New York State. Brimfield, Massachusetts, and
Renninger's Extravaganza in Pennsylvania. What to look for; how
much to pay. List of sources.

Chapter 8 Fabrics Galore   129

Silk taffeta from the Orient—on 39th Street. Finding
Brunschwig et Fils in Westerley, Rhode Island. Wallpaper for
$2.99 a roll. William Morris from England. Blinds from South
Carolina at half the price of the city's "discount" stores. List of
sources.

Introduction

So you don't have a million dollars. Join the crowd. But you don't want to *be* like the crowd; you want to live, dress, eat, and, well, exist like a millionaire. Or maybe you actually are a millionaire, but you're a cheapskate. It doesn't matter which you are. As long as you have style, this book is for you.

There are plenty of books about bargains in New York City. The problem with them, as I found out a while back, is that most of them give only the cheap stuff—not the cheap *good* stuff. So one guide might have an extensive listing of cheesy boutiques on 14th Street, plus a variety of discount stores and by-the-hour flophouses. But what millionaire would be caught shopping there? Or staying there? And yes, the book might tell you that at a particular store, you can find a man's sport jacket by a famous designer, but the book doesn't tell you that (*a*) it's purple-and-orange plaid or (*b*) it's only in size 38 Short or (*c*) it's the same price as it would be at a fancy store on sale.

The Cheapskate Millionaire's Guide to Bargain Hunting in the Big Apple will tell you how to live like a millionaire—without paying the price. This book will tell you where to find the best designers' clothes at 40 to 75 percent off. It will show you where to find stunning wall sconces for $49—about one-sixth of their retail price. It will tell you where to find fabrics for $5 a yard—fabrics that look like $100 a yard. It will tell you where to find spices for 50 cents a bagful.

It will tell you where to find a gorgeous sapphire ring surrounded by diamonds—for about one-fifth the price of the same ring in a posh Fifth Avenue emporium.

But more than that, this book will show you strategies: how to negotiate with the leather merchants on Orchard Street—and with the antiques dealers at a 26th Street open-air booth! How to get a busy real estate agent to call you back. And how you can save hundreds of dollars on airfares, engraved stationery, and custom-made cabinets.

That's important. Because to a true cheapskate, getting 20 percent off isn't worth leaving one's ten-room (dirt-cheap) Park Avenue apartment for. The game is to buy things for 20 percent *of* the retail price.

This guide will also tell you how to find a cheap rental in a city where the average studio rents for $1,300 and the average one-bedroom goes for $1,800. And if you're going to stay a while and want to actually make some money too, the book instructs you, step by step, in how to find an incredible buy on an apartment in a fancy neighborhood (the Upper East Side—not the Upper End of Hell's Kitchen).

The book is much more than a compilation of listings. You'll be guided through the process of tracking down a bargain on something really desirable, not just a "famous brand name" label stuck on an item everybody else has rejected.

Do you love William Morris wallpaper by the English firm of Sanderson's? If you go into an American store, you'll pay $96 a roll. But what if you know how to send away to England? Oh, right, the English distributors won't ship when there's a U.S. distributor. But the London paint shops will. So with the names of the shops in this book, you can telephone your order, give them your credit card—and get as many rolls as you want for about $35 apiece. The same works for fabrics. So go into the Sanderson's showroom here—or easier still, a Janovic Plaza paint store where they have the wallpaper books—pick out what you want, make a note of it, and call London.

As someone who has worked as a general contractor, buying wrecks in both New York City and Connecticut—as well as being a reporter for the House & Home section of the *New York Times*—I have lots of experience. I also spent a summer dealing antiques, exhibiting and wheeling and dealing at places like the Brimfield, Massachusetts, weeklong antiques extravaganza. I've bought old doors at

United Housewrecking in Stamford, Connecticut, and more than paid for my flight to England with the savings on brass hardware I bought at J. Shiner on Windmill Street. My house in Connecticut has been photographed for *House & Garden*—and it's full of cheap stuff. Besides that, I just bought two apartments, one above the other, in a landmarked mews on the Upper West Side, both for $80,000—in the midst of a white-hot real estate market. How I found them—through a real estate agent's brilliant idea of canvassing "dead listings"—is in the book.

Remember that millionaires are notorious cheapskates. No, that's not *how* they got their money. But it's definitely how they're keeping it.

Note: Most books don't give prices because authors are afraid they'll make the book outdated sooner. I always find that frustrating: just saying a store "offers significant savings on Army boots," say, means nothing to me. So I've peppered these pages with real prices I gathered from the shops, hotels, and services at press time in fall 1999. Take them for what they are, and place them in their proper time frame. But I think they give the reader a good handle on exactly what's being offered, a chance to really size up whether something is a bargain. Cheapskate millionaires rarely waste their time—they have too cushy a life for that!

The Cheapskate
Millionaire's Guide to
Bargain Hunting
in the
Big Apple

Clothing Bargains for Men and Women: Strut Your (New) Stuff like a Millionaire

When you think of shopping in New York City, you may well think of clothes shopping. Maybe you're thinking of a *grand magasin* like **Bergdorf** or **Henri Bendel** or even **Saks.** Or maybe you're thinking of thousand-dollar-a-square-foot Madison Avenue, with its Italian shoe stores like **Tanino Crisci** and **Fratelli Rossetti,** its luxurious children's emporiums like **Bonpoint,** and its fin-de-siècle mansion that **Ralph Lauren** transformed into the world's preppiest showcase. Or good old 59th Street and Lex, where certain people have always been attracted to **Bloomingdale's.** And the shops along 57th Street, including **Hermès,** the den of $2,500 handbags; **Burberrys,** home of plaid doggie coats; **Prada; Louis Vuitton**—down with Vs!—**Turnbull & Asser; Celine;** and more. And **Barneys,** which started out as a cheap men's store but now features some of the most expensive ways in the world to drape your body.

These stores, frankly, are all musts. Take a look through Barneys if you want to see clothes on the cutting edge. Tour Henri Bendel, one of the great department stores of all time, with its Lalique second-floor window, almost destroyed but for one lone preservationist who spotted it underneath layers of grunge. It was the first to create famous-name boutiques within a larger retail setting. A sublime experience. Check out the shearlings and the silky smooth, quilted, tomato red barn jackets at **Searle.** Examine the scarves at Hermès.

(Why not? Everyone else does. Feel them—are they *really* worth $275?) Pay particular attention to the leather in the shoes at Tanino Crisci; the styles at Rossetti—you will see those styles in lesser leathers at places like **Ann Taylor:** Is one worth $284 and the other $149? (I say yes, but it's up to you.)

Then spend a lazy afternoon in SoHo cruising the clothing stores, and end up at **Dean & DeLuca,** the city's ultimate gourmet food shop, where you can check out the produce, the baked goods, and the celebrities. Sit on a stool and drink a cup of cappuccino, for a mere $3. Skip Ladies' Mile, the shopping district along Sixth Avenue in the high teens, unless you're into the great beaux-arts buildings that housed great department stores around the turn of the century. Despite the grand surroundings, the stores have names right out of a suburban mall: **Filene's Basement** and **T. J. Maxx.** The next morning, head back to Fifth and Madison to see if you still adore the expensive moleskin britches and suede jackets you adored the day before.

Sure, you're trolling the shops for bargains—and sales time especially is the time to catch a deal. (More on this below.) But *another* reason you're browsing (besides the fact that it's fun) is to familiarize yourself with colors, textures, and prices. After all, how can you spot a bargain somewhere else—especially with all the cheap stuff found at the designer outlets—unless you know what the real stuff is and how much it costs? When you find a similar suede jacket on Orchard Street and the same Ralph Lauren moleskins in a designer outlet, you'll want to be able to judge both quality and price. Then you can—with my blessing—grab for that charge card, and save a millionaire's ransom.

SHOPPING SURPRISE: ORCHARD STREET

Walking up Orchard Street, you get the feeling that everybody is right: The best days of this famous Lower East Side discount shopping mecca have evaporated up into one of the tenement fire escapes crisscrossing the front of the buildings here.

Oh, it still has its raffish charm. They could—and probably do—still shoot any number of turn-of-the-century melodramas here: not only are the fire escapes still out in force, but so are the old hanging signs advertising notions and underwear and men's suits. There are still some of the old shop windows with the shopkeeper's name—

Beckenstein, for one—in gold script across a large pane encased in mellowed oak. And there are still dozens of sidewalk trays with handprinted signs: "All Silk Ties—$4.86." "All Fabric—$1 a yard." "Any Shoes—$7.99."

At first, the life seems to be gone from the street. It appears bleak. The Lower East Side Tenement Museum is on the block near Stanton Street, and a visitor is struck by a crazy notion that the whole street could be a museum. For the most part, the bargains outside the shops are no big deal. It's the same kind of junk you see along West 14th Street: Those fabrics are worth no more than $1 a yard; the shoes are plastic; the silk ties are acetate.

What would a millionaire be doing here?

Plenty.

A millionaire would be buying leather jackets, suede blazers, and shearling coats—both men's and women's—for starters.

One of the reasons Orchard Street seems empty is the rumor (or report or opinion) that the clothing shops here are rip-offs, that in the words of one woman attorney who used to shop here "they mark up the clothes just so they can mark them down."

That definitely goes on here. If a few of the more famous shops don't actually mark *up* the suits and skirts, then they don't really take that much off the retail price. But to the cheapskate millionaires, it really doesn't matter, because the stores that do that don't have anything they'd want to buy.

Perhaps the most famous shop on Orchard Street is "Forman's of Orchard Street," plus its annex, Forman's Petites. To me, this is the shop that gives Orchard Street its slightly shopworn reputation. After breezing through Forman's, I was convinced the lawyer had been right. At Forman's, I found one of the "Lauren" navy blue blazers with the heavily embroidered, initialed crest (this is actually a secondary line of Ralph's). The original price was $250. Forman's price? $198. The Lauren turtlenecks in preppy colors were marked down from $38 to $29.50. A beefy Lauren button-down shirt was supposedly listed at $50. At Forman's, you'd pay $39.50. Bernardo made a classic red, boiled-wool, hip-length jacket with collar and silver buttons. It was supposed to be $160; here it's $119.50. (**Loehmann's** had a similar jacket for $59.95, just to give you an idea.)

That's not to say the suits are not perfectly wearable and office-ready. If you happen to be down here, you might want to pick up a few turtlenecks or button-down shirts. But bargains for millionaires? I don't think so. You can find the exact stuff at similar prices in the Ralph Lauren outlet stores or at department store sales. So certainly not worth a special trip.

Although I was disheartened, I walked on. More rubbish. Then I stumbled into the small downtown section of Joe's Fabric Warehouse, and things started looking up—see Chapter 8, on fabrics. So maybe it wasn't a great place for clothes, but it sure is for fabrics, I thought.

But then, at 137 Orchard Street, the picture changed. I found **Ben Freedman:** "A Tradition on Orchard Street Since 1927," according to the window. But I didn't see the window at first. I came to a screeching halt in front of the sidewalk trays. "Pants—$8.50," one announced. "Belts—$4.87," trumpeted another. "Ties—$5.87." That was the one that got me—after I saw the ties were really silk. I grabbed a Perry Ellis Portfolio tie: a wonderful wide blue creation with green triangles. (I know it sounds terrible, but it is really very hip.) I grabbed a braided leather belt for $4. (You could easily pay $25 or more.)

I stepped inside.

Right away, on a table with men's slacks piled up, I spotted a really superb pair of light olive chinos, the kind that are sold at **J. Press** and **Paul Stuart** for $65 and up. They came in size 34— only—and there was only one pair. They were $14.95.

I left Ben's with two cheap-looking plastic bags. Inside were six ties—the most expensive, an utterly divine subtle navy blue paisley Italian-silk number that set me back $8.50; the others, Perry Ellis's best for $4.87 and $5.87. I bought several pairs of Perry Ellis suspenders: navy blue silk with an ivory-colored feather motif trimmed generously with navy leather; his name was on the back of the brass clips. I also bought a blissfully un-logoed pique polo shirt in navy, for $12. This place is great for men and men's gifts. I also bought two great belts: one in dark pomegranate red and the other a deep emerald green—absolutely de rigueur for jeans. They had all sizes for $4.87, on a circular rack just inside the front door. (Considering how great they look, I think they look much more expensive than, say, Coach belts—I'm going to go back and buy about a half-dozen for gifts. They had scads of them.)

Okay, now my energy was coming back. Where next?

That was when I discovered the leather places. Now here, the reader has to be a bit of a connoisseur of leather. If you're not, go to **Gucci**—check out the best. Once you've seen it and felt it, you won't make a mistake. Think baby's skin.

Then go to Orchard Street. If you're looking for a rough and rugged look, try **Soha's Leather.** Walk upstairs and look around for anything that catches your eye. Most of the jackets here are cheaply made, with leather that has creases or isn't totally supple. But there *are* exceptions—and if you bargain, the prices are give-away.

If you bargain?

Ah, yes. One quickly finds out. To get the best deals in leather, it's vital to bargain. But don't despair. I've bargained in the marketplaces of Rabat and Oaxaca—this is a piece of cake, *and* you speak the language! What you don't know—and even I didn't until I started working on this book—is that millionaires bargain in Saks Fifth Avenue.

Bargaining: Learning the Ropes

On Orchard Street, you don't even have to start it, and, for me at least, that's the part that is always the hardest. You just bend over to pick up your shopping bags. The shop owner will sing out a lower price. Then you should pick a ridiculously low price; a real price, however; the price you'd pay; the price that would make you feel you got a real steal. Say it. Then just keep saying it as you move to the door. They'll go lower. They'll follow you out to the street, shouting lower numbers every time.

Here's an example—and, incidentally, how I learned the ropes on Orchard Street.

I was looking at a cream-colored, double-breasted, fitted leather blazer. It was very good leather—not the absolute silky finest, but nothing any millionaire would sneeze at. This jacket would be great with the cream-colored flannel pants I had bought the year before at a Ralph Lauren sale for $59. (They also had jackets in stylish colors: hot pink, cobalt blue, tart lime leathers, along with delicious baby calf children's jackets.)

The creamy jacket was marked $275. I tried it on, had them get a bigger size from the basement, and then had them get another that was slightly better leather (the collar on the first one they brought upstairs wasn't as smooth as the body of the jacket). So now they realized I was a serious customer. But no—I wasn't ready to pay $275. I bent down to pick up my plastic Ben Freedman bags. "$175!" said the salesman.

To be frank, I hadn't even thought of bargaining. But now the gauntlet was thrown down. I started to look around. I found a marvelous dark brown, short, fitted, stripped-down motorcycle jacket in that thick, pebble-grain leather, with a zippered front and zippered pockets and tight-fitting sleeves. It was marked $299. I looked at the price and then glanced questioningly at the salesman. "Same price— $175!" he replied.

Hmmmm. I liked both of these jackets, which offered completely different looks.

"What about $250 for both?" I asked.

"Ohhhh, noooo," he said, holding his head in horror.

"Well, okay," I said. "I really like the jackets. I'll think it over."

I started to leave.

He watched me as I walked toward the front of the small shop.

"Wait," he shouted.

I looked back.

The deal was done. I gave him my charge card. He added on the tax, and I walked down the steps.

But wait. As I was confidently strutting up the street, my bargains in yet another plastic bag, I heard him call after another woman who had actually left the store and was walking down the steps. "$90!" he shouted. Since every jacket in the shop was approximately the same price, I realized I hadn't bargained hard enough. Could I have gotten *both* of those jackets for $175? And gotten *them* to include the tax in the price? You try it.

More Bargaining

That said, I was still feeling good. On Madison Avenue, jackets of this quality would have sold for far more: in Barneys or in Searle, a jacket like this could have cost $750.

But next door, at 150 Orchard, in **Arivel Fashions**—also known as Arivel Furs wholesale and retail—I found even better stuff.

First of all, there aren't many furs at Arivel anymore. But there *are* shearlings and suedes, plus some excellent Italian ladies' suits in soft beige tattersalls and fine black wool crepes. The store is not exactly giving the suits away; they cost $499, but they're fine quality—and, as I had learned in the shop before, there's always bargaining.

But none of the suits caught my eye. The first thing that did was a maple syrup–colored suede blazer in size 46. (These run small, so be prepared to swallow your pride and try on a 14 even if you normally wear a 10!) This jacket was top quality, and I had recently seen an advertisement in *Vogue* for a suit that looked similar. Now, when I was a college student—eons ago—I had a suede suit in blond pigskin. It was rough and tough and didn't move much. This was not the same item. This was silky-silken suede, smooth as the skin on the inside of your thigh. The jacket was marked $399. My saleswoman, Rose, said, as I was flinging it onto my back, I could have it for $299.

But there were other leather and suede suits. Where were the matching slacks and skirts for this one? Answer: They didn't order them. Weren't they available on order? Oh, yes, I was told. Didn't I want to buy the jacket and wait to hear? No, I wouldn't buy the jacket unless I got the whole set. Alas! I am still waiting.

But there was more. Downstairs are the full-length shearlings, the crème de la crème. I found two: One was a glorious long (about halfway between knee and ankle) deep olive coat with a bit of a flair and a detachable hood. The lambskin was excellent: The pieces were bound together with matching deep olive leather. (This sounds awful, but it was charming.) The ticket price was $1,499.

But, no, the saleswoman said (now joined by the owner, who, of course, did not know I was a writer), you must see the full-length, deep chocolate brown Russian coat, the color of freshly tilled humus—a real czarina coat. (Could I compete with Julie Christie for Dr. Zhivago's affections? Perhaps.) This was a killer—complete with hood—marked $1,799. But wait—the owner was now running to the back room—look at it with the hat. She produced a charming silky-felt cloche with the same Godiva glow. I checked the price: $145.

Okay, I said wildly (all in the spirit of research): How much for both coats—and the hat?

Rose threw up her hands and glanced meaningfully at the owner.

"Oh, if you take them both . . . $2,000," she said, "And you must have the hat. I'll give it to you for $100."

Well, that was all pretty dirt cheap.

Uptown, a Sawyer coat of comparable or perhaps a little lesser quality will go for $2,500.

But I hesitated. Was the czarina coat, with its wonderful frog closures, a little too 1970s? But the '70s were back. Weren't they? And did I really need to buy the olive shearling, especially when the thermometer was close to 90? I walked out. The salespeople were both dejected.

On the Track of the Dream Coat

I walked down the street. Should I take them or should I not? Almost absentmindedly, I strolled into **Rita's Leather Fair,** an uninspiring place a block north of Arivel. This claustrophobic store is full of leather: on side racks, on overhead racks, on floor-to-ceiling racks. Unlike Arivel, where the quality is consistently high, Rita's has a range of skins, so if you don't know which is which, you might get burned.

But this is where I found my shearling.

There it was, hanging down from one of the overhead racks: a buttery blond creamsicle of a coat, just knee-length, a pants coat or a short-skirt coat—definitely *not* a coat to be worn with longer skirts. What sold me on this coat? Everything: the color, the style, the quality. This was the finest quality—so light, it felt like a whisper (okay, so maybe a loud whisper).

The shopkeepers sounded Russian. They said the coat was a Gianni Versace, or came from the same factory—or something. I didn't doubt it. It was the finest shearling I've seen—with the exception of my friend Carol's champagne-colored shearling wisp of a coat she purchased in Henri Bendel—for a mere $5,500.

But mine was a dream. The only obstacle was the price: $1,595— well worth double that, of course, but I had learned my lesson. I sadly handed it back to the lady, after giving her a brief, tragic, pleading look. "Twelve hundred," she offered.

"Eight hundred," I shot back.

"Oh, nooooo . . ." she said, and renewed her sales pitch about Versace.

"It's not that it's not worth it," I said generously. "It's just that it's out of my budget."

"One thousand," she replied.

"Eight hundred," I said.

We took the matter to the court of last resort: the manager.

"I can't do any better than a thousand," he said, making it sound like the poor saleslady would be whipped beyond recognition for daring to give me such a scandalously low price.

I said I was sorry and started to leave.

"Nine fifty," he said.

"Eight hundred," I said.

"Okay, you're killing me—nine hundred," he said.

"You can put it on layaway," she whispered.

"Eight hundred," I said, and moved toward the door.

"All right," he said, mopping his brow and leaning on the counter for strength.

"Including tax," I said.

But he was a broken man. He nodded. I bought the coat.

SHOPPING THE SALES: WHAT YOU'VE BEEN WAITING FOR ALL YEAR

Although Orchard Street and **Daffy's** and T. J. Maxx have bargains—and they're fun to prowl in any time of the year—the winter sales are the highlight of a year's clothes shopping in New York City. Here's the main reason: Things go on sale here that are *never* seen in a discount outlet! The single-maker boutiques along Madison are the best—you cannot, no matter how you try, find Tanino Crisci shoes in a discount mall. (If you do, please write to me—immediately—I wear size 9.) Or Fratelli Rossetti shoes. Or a rack of dove gray Armani suits behind paneled doors, practically half price.

Even before Thanksgiving, the big shops start with the year's sales, so if you don't already live here, fly into New York for the action. In Bloomingdale's, each designer boutique recently had racks of stuff marked 40 percent off. And in Barneys, there were major reductions all over the place—in both men's and women's clothing. For women, there was a Christian Lacroix fitted coat of black alpaca, mohair, and wool, with a single button, marked down from $2,565 to $1,719. A phenomenal leather Carpe Diem jacket the color of vanilla pudding was similarly marked down. Barneys also has one of the widest selections of handbags, and at the post-Christmas sale, a good many of them were marked down—substantially. I bought two: a big squishy caramel-colored Italian-made shoulder bag had been $325; I bought it for $149. A black harness-leather tote had been

$795; I took it home for $349 and returned it the next Monday. I decided I didn't like the brass trim; if it had been nickel, I would have kept it. But the caramel-colored one still looks great. I get a lot of compliments on it; it's simple but delectable, and it goes with almost everything.

The truly impecunious shopper may decide to wait until the last two weeks of January, when the sale items get their second markdown. This happens again in the late spring or summer, but not with the same consistency. Some stores hold their sales in May, so people will buy their summer clothes; other stores will wait until August and often slash the prices then even more than for a late May sale. For the summer sales, it's always important to call the stores you love in early May and just ask them. I was reluctant to call the first time—I must have been embarrassed—but the salespeople, for the most part, seem to expect the question and quickly fire off their answer.

I offer the following guide to the best sales in the best stores. I have tried to give a pretty broad range, so depending on your tastes, pick the shops that suit your style.

At **Etro,** the Italian company that specializes in heavenly paisleys and fine clothes for men and women, signature silk scarves were marked down to $145 (and were ever so much nicer than those dated Hermès ones with the saddles and bridles, for $275). The problem with Hermès is that the company's wares have been so knocked off for so long that even the most beautiful pocketbooks now look passé—a shame. FYI: The Hermès Christine bag, a simple clutch with a shoulder strap, goes for $2,050, and Hermès is one of the few stores that says it does *not* have a winter sale! Or a summer sale!

But back to Etro. On the second floor are the handsomest women's silk blouses and suits and formal "tuxedo" coats I've seen. Go for a peek anytime—the store itself is worth seeing—but sometime right after the first of January, they're half price. A stunning dark-tweed trouser suit with a kind of hacking jacket and the most delicious bittersweet orange–colored lining tempted me. But the problem is that the price was so high to begin with—$1,340—that 50 percent off was still exorbitant. But that lining was gorgeous!

At 9 East 57th Street, **Burberrys** is a bastion of men and women who like corgis—or at least look like they do. But that's why you can get a great deal on something you find here that *does not have Burberry plaid all over it!*

Yes, believe it or not, there are a few things here that don't show the plaid, and guess what? Nobody wants them, except me. So I bought an Edwardian hat, very swashbuckling and very uncorgiesque, for a mere $49. (My former boss saw me in an elevator and e-mailed me later: "I haven't seen a hat that big outside the Royal Enclosure at Ascot.") Not everyone's cup of tea, obviously. For followers of the plaid, there were plenty of men's and women's storm jackets in cheery yellow, orange, and red with that famous fabric peeking out at the collar, marked down to $229; the famous raincoats were now $569 (from $895—unlined—ouch!). Men's gloves were almost half price, at $59. Some well-coifed woman jumped in the elevator, clutching a raft of scarves with richly colored cashmere on one side, silk paisley on the other. "In London these are a fortune, because I just came back from there and I know," she told her companion, who just grunted, pointed at one, and asked, "Red for granny?"

At the competition, **Aquascutum,** there was a rather inviting collection of men's outerwear, all substantially marked down. And on an upper floor, the store offered riding-style women's jackets—long and tight in the waist, some with velvet collars—nicely sliced from $625 to $399. Matching skirts, which had been $225, were now $149. One of my favorite sales is at **Fratelli Rossetti,** the men's and women's shoe store where I bought my best coat: a long, pencil-thin, double-breasted, graphite gray suede trench coat. Just as autumn wafted into the air, I bought it there for the full price: $1,400. I know that sounds amazing, but occasionally, it pays to do that. I had to have it, and I got almost four months' wear out of it . . . before it went on sale for . . . gulp . . . $835. One reason I paid $1,400 was that I thought the coat actually looked closer to $3,000; at $835, it's a steal. Rossetti also had great prices on their shoes, which are widely imitated but, unlike the cheaper competition, wear forever. Their elegant black, low-heeled, lace-up walking shoes were marked down to $169, from $280; women's brown suede wing tips were $119—and there were comparable markdowns on the elegant, but extremely well-made, men's shoes and leather jackets. (Men's shoes were marked down from $365 to $229.) Their fine pocketbooks were also marked down, to about $230. The sale starts a few days after Christmas. The whole store is rearranged, and just about everything is on sale. It sounds corny, but the clothes and shoes here are really fit for a lifetime of use, if you take care of them.

Down the block, at **Ann Taylor,** the store was selling knockoffs of the Rossetti women's bluchers for $59. This presented an interesting choice because the knockoffs might appeal to more people than the real ones. Where the Rossettis were hard saddle leather with largish luggage-type stitching around the toes, the Ann Taylor shoes were made out of softer leather and were stitched discreetly: Both were made in Italy. Altogether, a difficult choice. While the Rossetti shoe is innately more stylish and will wear forever, the Ann Taylor is one-third the price and is a pretty good shoe. The solution? Buy both, and use the Ann Taylor pair for everyday.

DISTINCTLY FOR MEN: UPTOWN TO DOWNTOWN—A SHOPPING TRIP THAT WON'T BORE YOU

It's easy for men in New York to dress like millionaires—just follow the example of the cheapskate millionaires I know. First, shop the sales in the very best stores, and then, to fill in, shop the special bargain places detailed below. My advice is to stay away from the Brooks Brothers sale: It only brings you down to the level of the Brooks Brothers normal discount outlet prices. And then again, despite recent ad campaigns showing much younger and hipper guys, Brooks Brothers is not exactly at the cutting edge of chic.

The Uptown Scene

If you want a traditional look, but with extra cachet and quality of workmanship, go next door to **Paul Stuart,** at the corner of Madison Avenue and 45th Street. The clothes there make you want to mortgage your house—and indeed when there isn't a sale on, you'd have to. The materials are sumptuous, far more sumptuous than the run-of-the-mill preppy stuff at Brooks Brothers. And the men's shoes are marvelous. So take a look. At the back of the store, there is a special section where Gatsbyesque shirts were marked down 40 percent. The shoes are in the front of the store, and one group was 40 percent off. (Stuart's used to have wonderful women's clothes, but the styling seems to have fallen off in the past five years—so stick to the men's departments, which are the mainstay of the whole place, anyway.)

Now that you have seen Paul Stuart and, earlier, gone through Barneys, both men and women's, try going to the sale at **Davide**

Cenci, between 67th and 68th Streets. This Madison Avenue shop appears smaller than it really is. There are four floors of clothes—almost all of them marked way down for their semiannual sales. While this store is certainly not a bazaar of bargains regularly, the quality of the clothes—mostly men's—is magnificent and the sales are a real event. Besides the markdowns, the reason for shopping here is simple: The clothes are elegant and you won't find them anywhere else, except for the other two Davide Cenci shops, in Rome and Milan. They are private labels, all made in Italy.

The sale is artfully arranged. Almost as soon as you enter, you see a table full of bargains: There are some excellent values here, including Italian silk ties for $10. (And unlike the street vendors allegedly offering the real thing, these *are* real silk and very fine silk at that.) There is also a selection of belts, hats, and other accessories, at similar prices—all top quality. But then there are some indescribably luscious offerings, including a pair of men's flannel pajamas for $235, less 40 percent. I know that sounds ludicrous, but these pajamas—charcoal gray with a tiny yellow windowpane plaid—are a killer. In case you're shaking your head, nearby is a group of cashmere sweaters, reduced 70 percent (some fall below $100), and upstairs there is a rack of men's sport coats, marked down 60 and 70 percent. There is a camel-hair blazer and a cashmere hopsack jacket in normal sizes: 60 percent off. A charcoal gray, wool-and-angora coat, in a balmacaan style—both stylish and traditional—is 40 percent off $1,250. (On the women's floor, some of the shoes are 50 percent off. And there is a 60 percent off bargain table, with one to-die-for black-and-white tweed suit with a fitted jacket and a sleeveless dress, reduced 40 percent from $1,250. This is, of course, expensive—but well, you'd have to see it. You would seriously get a lifetime of wear from it, as you would from the men's clothes here.)

Cenci has reduced two of what Mr. Cenci called his "signature" items for men: his quilted microfiber barn jacket, a chocolate brown (or black) silky thing that was reduced 40 percent off the regular $750 to $450 (although this seems high, I saw a similar one of lesser quality in a lesser shop for $975) and his Entrefino suede toggle coat, which is still, alas, not cheap: $1,660.

Another happy surprise is the transformation of **Saint Laurie,** now at 350 Park Avenue at 51st Street. When last spotted (and patronized), Saint Laurie was a big warehouse-type operation on Broadway and East 19th Street, in business since 1913. Then, it was primarily a men's discount outfitters, featuring racks and racks of suits of medium quality—for very cheap prices. Back then, you could get a Ralph Lauren Polo knockoff suit that didn't really fool anybody, but was tasteful and well made, for about $150. In the 1980s, the company introduced women's suits and trousers, and I bought an extremely well-made lipstick red (remember Nancy Reagan? Remember the 80s?), double-breasted suit with white pearl buttons and a straight skirt for about $200. Well, with the incredible rise in property values of the 19th Street location, the Saint Laurie people decided to sell their building—a health club now fills the ground floor space—and start afresh. Where before, the factory and the salesrooms were in the same building, they are now separate. The tailoring factory has moved to West 39th Street, in the garment district, and the salespeople have moved up—and so has their merchandise.

Where previously, you bought the suits off the rack, now Saint Laurie custom-makes them at bargain prices. According to Arthur Oliver, a youngish salesman arrayed in the company's own handmade jacket and shirt, Saint Laurie is one of the few remaining stores (versus a hole-in-the-wall tailor's shop) that specializes in totally handmade suits. It is even rarer that all the work is carried out in New York City, not shipped off to Hong Kong or South America.

The experience is delightful. Upon entering the sunny Park Avenue shop, you see large tables covered with different types of men's suit and jacket materials and a price tag indicating how much it will cost to complete the item just for you. To add to the education, each bolt has an excellent description of the material, including its weight. For example, one particularly handsome bolt on the sport jacket table read "100 percent Wool whiskey and camel Glen plaid. Harris Tweed. Woven in Scotland. 13 ounces per yard." Another finer, softer, tinier plaid read "Reid and Taylor. Scottish saxony. 11 ounces per yard." There were wool-and-silk blends, and there were the suiting materials, soft-as-silk navy pinstripes in Super 130 blends. "If you go to Brioni or Saks Fifth Avenue," claimed Mr. Oliver, "you'll pay $2,500 to have a suit made for you."

And how much here? A lot less. All year round, a Super 130 (very fine) gray pinstripe might set you back $1,095. A sport jacket might run $625.

For those of you who have never had a suit made for you, this is how it works: You pick a bolt of fabric. Then you try on a suit from the models hanging along the walls. Saint Laurie offers three different looks: Conservative (like Brooks Brothers), Traditional (like Ralph Lauren), and Fashionable (like Ermenegildo Zegna). It's not so much for fit—you are measured for that—but for the style of shoulders, vents, and lapels. You discuss things such as whether you want a ticket pocket: that extra front right-hand pocket, put there so the conductor always knew where to find the tickets of English commuters snoring their train ride away, now a stylistic affectation. Then you're taken to the back, where you are measured for a pattern. Do you want your suit to be roomy or shapely? "It's actually cheaper for us to make these 'alterations' now, rather than after the suit is put together," said the salesman. This takes at least twenty minutes. A file is made and kept for the future. Delivery time is about four weeks.

In the winter and summer, Saint Laurie has a sale, which includes a table of heavily discounted suit and jacket material, and believe me, these are not what you'd expect: orange-and-mauve plaids or cheap-looking grays. The suitings on this table are chosen from the regular tables, either because the company finds they are running short on the material or the opposite, that they ordered too much. A superb navy pinstripe—a 9-ounce English flannel—is now $699, for a handmade suit! A Super 100 Italian gray suit is on sale for $799 "because we have a ton of gray."

At all times, there is a rack of custom-made 40 Regular men's jackets—models—on sale for prices like $299. Saint Laurie says they will also make suits in the identical materials and jacket styles for women, for the same price, with either a skirt or trousers. They do it rarely, they conceded, but it might be fun to give it a try. I like very long jackets and seldom find them, so this might be a real opportunity. I'll let you know how it turns out.

From the Sublime to the Not-So-Ridiculous:
Moe Ginsburg and the Boys Downtown

As the cheapskate millionaire weaves his way downtown, the rents become lower—and, not surprisingly, so do the prices. But there's a lot of junk downtown, and a lot of the so-called bargain men's clothing outlets clustered around 19th and 20th Streets and Fifth Avenue really don't offer much value. There are, however, exceptions.

Moe Ginsburg is a kind of famous name in New York, and Moe's banner still hangs out over Fifth Avenue and 19th Street. I've never thought the men's clothes at Moe's were a great bargain, and especially now, with the discount outlet malls offering much the same value, I saw no reason to change my mind. That said, Moe's offers an eighth floor "discount outlet" of its own—and that is an entirely different proposition.

On the regular racks of men's sport coats, you can buy a tasteful but thinly woven wool sport jacket by Bill Blass for $220 and a far better Burberrys sport jacket for $420. So far, not too exciting, right? But on the eighth floor, I saw almost the identical sport jacket by Bill Blass, along with jackets by Cerutti and Ralph Lauren University Club (his cheaper line) for—get ready—two for $100, or $59 apiece. That's right. Although there were lots of losers mixed in—there were downstairs too—these were some seriously tasteful, well-made sport jackets. One was a Bill Blass small-check wool and 5 percent cashmere; other brands were Joseph Abboud, Henry Grethel, and Yves St. Laurent. (No Burberrys, alas, but I didn't check each one, either.)

Trousers were $15. Ugly shoes were $10. And topcoats were two for $150; I saw a particularly well-made Cerruti wool-and-angora balmacaan (I hate to say this, but it did resemble the one in Cenci's shop) that had been priced at $280 in Moe's—now in the bargain rack. But I'm saving the best deal for last: Men's summer suits were . . . four for $100.

Four suits for $100? Right. And some of them were the great-looking J. Press–Yalie kind of tan-and-olive chino suits that will be all over the Brooks stores come May. Again, the quality varied, but there were some totally wearable numbers here and also some handsome brown-and-white seersuckers (much preferable to the blue-and-whites, which they also had). They also had some wool suits in these racks but not particularly distinguished ones—and they also had some suits that were two for $100.

If you're still in the mood for shopping after your adventure at Moe's, I recommend one more stop: **Gilcrest Clothes** at 900 Broadway at 20th Street. There Maurice (also known as Moshe) Halevi will help you find a bargain. This is an interesting place, but if your method of shopping is roaming around and looking at the prices, then this place is not for you. There are no prices marked.

But once you get over this somewhat disconcerting method of doing business, the quality and the cost of the jackets, suits, and coats will floor you. The main thing is the quality; it's a lot higher than the run-of-the-mill Bill Blass or University Club outfits, no matter where you find them. The brands here are Perry Ellis Portfolio—not his omnipresent secondary line—Louis Feraud, Ungaro, Jhane Barnes, and Baumler, a German designer whose suits combine a European styling with a very high degree of workmanship. All year round, these finely detailed suits—comparable to the $950 to $1,200 off-the-rack suits in many of the Madison Avenue boutiques—are generally priced between $550 and $600. And at sale times, they are $200 less. Truly luxurious coats run between $249 and $369; sport jackets are around $250 for top quality.

SHOPPING THE SAMPLE SALES: MEN AND WOMEN

As a general rule, I don't bother with sample sales. First of all, a lot of these are frauds. Somebody rents a second floor space for a week, buys a lot of cheap shoes from some bad Brazilian manufacturer, and tries to unload them for $69 or $89. (A shill stands down in the street, distributing flyers shouting "All Shoes—$89!" True, but who cares? The shoes practically crack when you pick them up.)

But I do swear by a handful of sample sales. Schedules of these sales vary, but all have some sort of sale just before Christmas. Two are absolute musts: the sale at **Echo Scarves** over on East 40th Street (only at Christmastime) and the sale at **Portolano** gloves (and cashmere) on West 39th Street (several times a year).

At Echo, the best buys are in their regular-brand silk scarves, although many come because the company also manufactures Ralph Lauren's silk-and-cashmere scarves and mufflers, which are offered at substantial savings. But a $299 cashmere scarf, no matter what the "regular" price is, doesn't interest me for a Christmas gift.

Instead, I head right for the big cardboard boxes in the back room, where scarves of all types are tagged with colored cardboard: red for $5, green for $10, and yellow for $15. While there are a lot of garish scarves in the bins, this year I managed to find a pile of exquisite presents that my friends raved about—all with the Echo label, proclaiming them to be 100 percent silk. I found two-foot-square scarves of heavy silk, in a shadowy gray-on-gray William Morris–type design, with a burgundy border—for $5. And because it's a one-of-a-kind sale (that's what "sample" means), I found its sister, a blue-on-blue with a yellow border, at the same price. (These scarves look like about $65.) I also found a delicious long Isadora Duncan–type wrap in undulating shades of purple, and another one in shades of asparagus green. One was $5; the other, inexplicably marked $15, was soon adjusted. I also got a sumptuous cornflower blue square—two feet across—for $10.

Echo also has absolutely divine men's ties, made in Italy, and looking every inch around $90 or $100—for $15 apiece or four for $50. These ties are really special; they come in mouth-watering colored paisleys and conservative thick silk weaves in tasteful color combinations. For one of my wildest friends, a preservationist and tie collector, I found a distinctive tie I knew he didn't have. It was ivory silk, with finely drawn architectural monuments in black: not a tie for everyone, but he adored it—and he's a very tough person to find a gift for!

Portolano is on the fifth floor of a nondescript office building in the garment district. They have a great sale featuring leather gloves, cashmere shawls and sweaters, and Italian pantyhose, among other accessories. The company makes gloves for Fendi and Moschino, and besides the gloves, they also sell the attractive glove boxes—rich orange for Fendi, a stunning gold for Moshino—for only $1 apiece.

While the Fendi gloves were distinctive, with their little heart appliqués and tassels and whatever, I preferred the fine longer gloves in the finest leather, lined in cashmere and offered in a rainbow of shades, for only $39. I bought a pair of Chinese red-orange and a pair of deep chocolate brown for myself, and a wonderful pair of yellow ones for my friend Ellen, on the theory that the best presents are those that are so impractical you'd never buy them for yourself. And I was right. She loved them! They also had a full range of color in shearling gloves—$120 at Paul Stuart, $35 and $40 here.

My friend Regina bought her daughter a cozy, extra-ample V-neck cardigan sweater in lilac cashmere, with deep blue cashmere trim on the pockets and at the bottom of the sleeves (maybe a man's), for an unheard-of $80. Portolano also had black cashmere shawls with ruffled edges for $80 and $120, and double-faced cashmere shawls for $280—a friend who bought one said they were $1,200 on Madison Avenue, and she would know!

Surprisingly, both Portolano and Echo take charge cards, and the help at both was pleasant and eager to please. At both, bags were checked at the door—apparently a normal precaution by the merchants, although who would bother stealing with prices like these?

At **Makins Hats,** a winner I just discovered while doing research for this book, the sales are scattered throughout the year—the company supplies men's hats to Barneys and Saks; women's hats to Bendel and Saks—but the owner does not take credit cards or checks. (However, there's a cash machine right around the corner!)

At Makins, the owner is testy—just try to get her to crack a smile. But she will—if you're polite and serious about her hats, which you will be because they're splendid. Bring a friend because the policy here is two-for-the-price-of-one. The pairing can be completely dissimilar: I first chose a fine Panama planter's hat like the one Clark Gable wore when he played Rhett Butler, coupled with a velvety black felt homburg. The price: $70 for both. But I finally settled on a black cock-feather creation like something Audrey Hepburn would wear in *Breakfast at Tiffany's*: a breathtaking (but foolhardy) piece of millinery. My friend Regina bought one in brown feathers. Since we took both, they were $100 apiece. They have created a sensation wherever we wear them.

For more sample sale information, subscribe to the *S&W Report*. Or buy *Time Out New York;* each week, they have a section just on sample sales, so you can keep your juices flowing all year long!

THE BIG WAREHOUSE SALE AT BARNEYS

Then there is the well-advertised **Barneys** sale, near their old original, now-defunct store on Seventh Avenue and 17th Street (Barneys ran into some financial problems a while back, but their newer Madison Avenue shop is going strong, or so it appears). This sale is a madhouse, with policemen shepherding bargain hunters with a certain gleam in their eye past ropes and through back doors. Come on, is this really *you*, dear? Then, when you arrive, it's like *Supermarket Sweep*: big plywood tables with hundreds of out-of-fashion, too-small silk-knit tops, soiled and shopworn and maybe ripped, reduced to *only* $279.50. Racks of none-too-appealing clothes. The problem with Barneys sales like this is that Barneys is so cutting edge that the old stuff looks . . . well . . . old. (Much better to go to the Madison Avenue shop after Christmas when the good stuff is marked down.) Another problem with these "warehouse" sales is that, with the advent and tremendous growth of the discount outlets, the designers really don't need to hold them anymore. Last year's cleaner, better-looking stuff, and even some samples, get shipped out to the Barneys and Donna Karan discount outlets.

DISCOUNT OUTLETS: THE NEWS IS NOT ALL BAD

Okay, this doesn't need to be spelled out. By now, everybody's read the stories about how the big discount outlet malls—especially the so-called premium outlets—aren't all they're cracked up to be. Everybody knows a lot of stuff is made for the outlets and never sees the light of a real **Brooks Brothers** or **Ralph Lauren** store, that it's often inferior merchandise.

All that is true: the oxford shirts at Brooks Brothers are less beefy and cost almost as much; the polo shirts at Polo are a thinner mesh. (Major tips: At Brooks Brothers, only the tags with "Brooks Brothers" *in script* are the real thing; at Ralph Lauren, look for things that do *not* say "Ralph Lauren Factory Store" on the tags.) It's true that you can often do just as well at a sale at one of their real Main Street or Fifth Avenue–type shops.

But—that said—there are still lots of genuine killer bargains at the premium outlets in places like **Clinton Crossing** in Clinton, Connecticut, and **Woodbury Common** in Central Valley, New York. (Don't even bother with anything other than "premium," unless you need Carter's baby clothes or Nike sneakers or some of the useful but boring things in the regular outlet stores.)

Here's the key: You must visit them only on holiday weekends. It's bizarre but true. You must go at exactly the times when you usually would avoid such a pilgrimage like the plague. The reason is simple: the holidays are when the shops reduce their standard 20 percent off to as much as 50, even 75, percent off! Which, of course, is the only kind of bargain a real dyed-in-the-wool cheapskate millionaire will leave her pied-à-terre for.

Go for the sidewalk racks. At Brooks Brothers, which is normally one of the biggest rip-offs in discount shopping, there are racks out on the sidewalks with sport jackets for $39.99. I bought six, one July Fourth weekend: three for my brother-in-law Joe, who is, at six foot four and 160 pounds, impossible to fit. Imagine my surprise when I found three 42 Extra Longs. And not in some terrible loud check with outdated lapels. These were gorgeous Harris Tweeds and silk-

and-linen tweeds for summer. And I bought myself a cashmere jacket in 39 Regular in auburn with almost invisible taupe windowpane. Plus, I found two more excellent sturdy and beautifully tailored tweeds for my ex-husband, who wears a more normal 42 Regular. The usual price would have been about $450, with my cashmere probably going for more.

On another rack, I got a wrongly sized turtleneck (regularly $35) for $5. A sidewalk bin had a raft of button-down shirts, striped polo shirts, and plaid flannel shirts for $5 apiece. And, if you get carried away, the stuff is actually returnable—although if something doesn't fit the person you thought it might, you can always bring it to work, hold it up, and shout the price you paid. It'll be gone in seconds—and you won't lose a dime.

Ralph Lauren is another discount outlet where you never know what you'll find. Some days, even holidays, the shop has nothing except a bunch of high-priced polo shirts in orange and fuchsia. I leave, vowing never to return.

Then, on a recent weekend, I ventured in and learned why you can't count this place out.

In the Polo shop at Clinton Crossing in Clinton, Connecticut, about a two-hour ride from Times Square, things didn't look promising. The usual $29.99 tray of men's polo shirts, the usual $39.99 men's shorts. I strolled to the women's department and yawned. The circular racks—my favorite hunting ground—looked the same as ever.

But, look, a fluke (I thought): a pair of exquisite white-wool pants, size 10, for $19.99. These pants really did cost $149.99 at the outlet. Then there was a great black wool blazer—size 12 but it looks great a little big—reduced to $39.99. (According to the ticket, it was marked down from $299.99.) Then a pair of glen plaid heavy-cotton shorts, almost knee length and cuffed, so you can wear them to work, for another $19.99 (from $59.99).

Then on to the back room to look at sheets and towels. I have to admit something: I had *never* gotten even one towel deal here. But checking out the bargain bin, I found some Nantucket-sailing-pants-red all-cotton sheets. No, they really *can't* be $5.99 for both fitted and flat double sheets, I think, but they are. Then there is this exquisite wide-black-and-narrow-white-striped heavy cotton sateen duvet cover (regularly $299.00, now $19.99) and a matching dust ruffle (regularly $119.99, now $12.99). I start making a pile. Then there are some Breton red towels—a discontinued color called "Ruby"—for $3.99 and the matching face cloths for $1.99. I throw them into the pile. Some finely woven gray pinpoint oxford sheets for $7.99 apiece? I grabbed them.

The total for all the clothes, sheets, and towels: $152.99, including tax—the price of a scarf at Ralph's on 72nd Street!

As I'm leaving, I see a new rack of stunning Ralph Lauren Collection Edwardian knee-length jackets in navy blue pinstripe. They are $350 apiece, certainly not cheap, but well worth it. The ticket says they are listed at $1,075, and judging from a recent run-through of the Madison Avenue mansion headquarters, I know that retail price may even be a little low. And the style is certainly right up to season. (There is, of course, one problem. There are no slacks to match. But this is not an insuperable problem. I think: Deep navy slacks would look fine, or maybe even better, cream-colored wool; or maybe you will find the matching slacks some other time. Nevertheless, I passed up the jackets.)

Laura Ashley is another outlet where, on a good day, you can find interesting stuff. Last summer, I found a charming straw hat with a turned-up brim that had been marked down from $29 to $3 at their branch at Hilton Head, South Carolina. I bought four of them, and a navy crepe scarf for another $4 to tie around the brim. At the Laura Ashley branch in Secaucus, New Jersey, I found a divine navy blue velvet party dress with a tiny waist, puffed sleeves, and a can-do price tag: $19.99. I bought two: one for me, one for my sister, just like in the old days when our mother dressed us in matching outfits!

I've bought a lot of Donna Karan stuff, too—again, most of it from a rack on the sidewalk. The prices are not as cheap as the rare, but worthwhile, steals at Ralph Lauren, but if you like Karan's understated elegance and fit, you're stuck. I bought a magnificent wool-crepe navy-black suit here for around $200—a fitted double-breasted jacket and a very long skirt with a slight flare, truly a triple-duty outfit: The jacket looks great with white pants (summer and winter), and the skirt looks swell with my ivory-leather short jacket from Soha's.

Here are a couple of discount outlet stores I always peek into, but from whom I seldom buy:

Barneys. The discount prices are good, I guess, relative to Barney's stratospheric regular ones, but to me, they're still a little high. Also, they seem to have more tiny sizes, like 2 and 4, than she-woman sizes like 8, 10, and, God forbid, 12.

Tahari. Their clothes always seem out of sync: last year's colors, hem lengths, and shapes. But if you're a **Tahari** junkie, and plenty are, the prices are good: suits are often less than $200, and sometimes they sell for as little as $100.

The Only Way to Get There

The only way to get to these discount malls is by limousine. Oh, I know that sounds preposterous, but think about it. If you have friends—and I'm sure you do—you know you're dying to take them along and they're dying to go. So avoid those disgusting bus and train trips by all means. (What if someone were to see you hopping on a Trailways?)

For $200 round-trip, **Carmel Limousine** (212-666-6666) will take you and up to three other people to Woodbury Common. (It's $306 to Clinton Crossing.) That's only $50 apiece, and think of all the fun you'll have. Door-to-door (at least to yours; your friends will have to pay extra to get to theirs) service. And by the way, if you have so many friends, maybe one of them has a car . . .

Discount Shopping in the City—All Year Round

Now a few words about my two favorite discount stores: **Syms** and **T. J. Maxx.** Now a lot of my friends don't go into either of them; they tell me they've never found anything good. Some swear by **Century 21,** a downtown discount emporium that brings thousands of tourists to the Wall Street area on weekends, which is a blessing—because there's almost no one else down there then. But I find Century 21 too crowded and I feel about it as they do about T. J.'s and Syms—so take your pick. Century 21 does have wonderful lingerie and good shoes from time to time. I bought a stunning navy-and-ivory-striped silk jacket there for $99—but it bunched up the first time I had it cleaned.

Daffy's is another possibility—I once found a spectacular Indian silk-paisley dress in grays and golds, very distinctive, for under $100, so it's good to peek in. Another place that's worth dropping into is

Dollar Bill's, across the street from Grand Central Terminal. I'm loyal to it even though I found only one great thing. It's my favorite article of clothing: a one-piece Ferre trouser suit (calling it a jumpsuit is demeaning) in a dark navy wool crepe. Words can't describe it. After five years, people are still coming up to me in the street and asking me where I got it. I paid $200—I think the suit was there because it takes a contortionist to get into and out of it, but believe me, it's worth it!

But here's the thing: You can always depend on T. J. Maxx to have *something,* for either women or men. The same is true of Syms, if you know how to look. First of all, the best bargains are (1) incorrectly sized, (2) "different" in style (I don't mean they're loud, although that may be the case) or (3) part of some special "clear-out" sale. So when you're looking through the racks, make sure you quickly scan the sizes on either side of yours. Pull out anything you like the looks of, and gauge the size. A lot of great stuff lands here because it is wrongly sized. If that size 8 looks like a 12, it probably is! Second, I recently found a terrific Armani silk skirt in the Syms in Berlin, Connecticut, marked down about fifty times to $16. Why? Because it was black with brightly colored roosters and turkeys all over it! Obviously, not to everyone's taste—but it looks divine with a tight black silk T-shirt.

Here are some examples of stuff I found at Syms during a summer sale, from a rack of designer clothes they couldn't sell. For between $5 and $15, I bought some Italian light-blue wool trousers for $10; a delicious, very thick silk-twill fitted jacket by Armani in dreamy pastel colors (including light blue, an instant outfit with the slacks) for $25; and a pair of Calvin Klein summer-weight, ivory-wool trousers for $15. And I've found bargains even in their regular racks, correctly sized and traditional in style. I found a marvelous French "officer's" coat with a high neck and silver buttons for $99; some Sperry Topsiders for $29 (versus the $69 I had just paid in Nantucket); some adorable Babar baby outfits for $9.99; and an old-fashioned Burberrys trench coat with the wool liner for $399 (versus $770 in the Burberrys 57th Street shop). Syms is also particularly good on fancy evening wear. I've bought 1940s–style silk suits for $49 and a plaid, silk taffeta evening skirt for only $29—marked down from $399!

T. J. Maxx is definitely a step down (or two or three) in quality overall, but you can still find deals here. I once found a size 10, navy cashmere polo coat here by Ralph Lauren for $300, but that might have been a fluke. The things you can find here are the basics, often because they're incorrectly sized or in the wrong department. I recently found a hand-knit men's sweater in stunning shades of grays and whites. It looked like about $200, but was priced at $29.99. Why? Maybe because it was marked "Medium" and it was really an ample large. Another time I found two DKNY stretch women's turtlenecks—one black and one white—hanging in the men's department! Because no one wanted them (naturally), they had been marked down to $9.99.

T. J. Maxx is also a great place to find things like great-looking, thick, all-white terry cloth robes—only $25—and Ralph Lauren towels for $5.99. And Donna Karan pantyhose for $2.99. You can also find fancy gift-wrap and greeting cards here for a fraction of the price on Madison Avenue. Also check out the glassware—I found six husky amber goblets from Mexico for $3.99 apiece here.

Don't linger at T. J.'s. You might get depressed. Just run in; dash along the racks, picking out anything good, no matter what size; try it on if you must (or take it home and return what you don't want—it's very easy to do here); and *get outta there!*

Thrift Shops You Might Get Away with Being Seen In

Generally speaking, thrift shops don't yield great buys. However, if you happen to be strolling by, and feel charitable, it might be pleasant to stop in. From time to time, all of them have something interesting; for $25, I once bought a never-been-worn pale-blue wool suit, made by hand by a lady in Mallorca. It's all trimmed in tiny black beads—very Spanish, very unusual. I wear the jacket, which is really terrific, with tight, black velvet pants when I want to look like a mysterious contessa.

There's a list of the more promising places at the end of the chapter, along with the causes they benefit—but I can't guarantee you'll run into a blue Spanish outfit. And you probably won't run into a count (or a countess), more's the pity! The ones with stars are consistently good. Call ahead to find out when the special sales—like "Everything in the shop, 75 percent off"—take place.

● SOURCES

THE UPTOWN SHOPS

Ann Taylor
645 Madison Avenue (at 60th Street),
212-832-2010
Monday to Friday, 10 A.M.–8 P.M.;
Saturday, 10 A.M.–7 P.M.; Sunday,
noon–6 P.M.
The Ann Taylor stores are definitely a step up from Talbot's, with its too-short polyester silk dresses (with belts, long after belts were dead), its tartan plaid shorts, and its knockoff Ferragamo pumps. No. Ann Taylor has simpler stuff, made about as well (*mezzo-mezzo*): pale apricot, short, sleeveless linen dresses; sharp silk jackets, and even a bustier or two! The best time to go is when they're having a sale, which is almost all the time. Their shoes are particularly good deals: they're made in Italy; some are knockoffs of harder-wearing (but more austere or extreme) styles, and when they go on sale, they sell for $59 or $69—hard to beat.

OTHER LOCATIONS

2380 Broadway (at 87th Street),
212-721-3130
Monday to Saturday, 10 A.M.–8 P.M.;
Sunday, noon–7 P.M.

2017 Broadway (at 69th Street),
212-873-7344
Monday to Saturday, 10 A.M.–8 P.M.;
Sunday, noon–6 P.M.

1055 Madison Avenue (at 80th Street),
212-988-8930
Monday to Friday, 10 A.M.–8 P.M.;
Saturday, 10 A.M.–6 P.M.; Sunday,
noon–6 P.M.

World Financial Center, 212-945-1991
Monday, Tuesday, and Thursday,
9 A.M.–7 P.M.; Wednesday and Friday,
9 A.M.–8 P.M.; Saturday, 10 A.M.–6 P.M.;
Sunday, noon–5 P.M.

803 Third Avenue (at 52nd Street),
212-308-5333

Monday to Friday, 10 A.M.–8 P.M.;
Saturday, 10 A.M.–6 P.M.; Sunday,
noon–5 P.M.

1320 Third Avenue (at 75th Street),
212-861-3392
Monday to Wednesday, Friday,
10 A.M.–7 P.M.; Thursday,
10 A.M.–8 P.M.; Saturday,
10 A.M.–6 P.M.; Sunday, noon–5 P.M.

575 Fifth Avenue (at 47th Street),
212-922-3621
Monday to Friday, 10 A.M.–8 P.M.;
Saturday, 10 A.M.–7 P.M.; Sunday,
11 A.M.–6 P.M.

Aquascutum
714 Madison Avenue (at 64th Street),
212-753-8305
Monday to Wednesday, Friday, and
Saturday, 10 A.M.–7 P.M.; Sunday, 12
P.M.–5 P.M.

Barneys New York
Madison Avenue (at 61st Street),
212-826-8900
Monday to Friday, 10 A.M.–8 P.M.;
Saturday, 10 A.M.–7 P.M.; Sunday,
noon–7 P.M.
Nod to the doorman; then check out the scene and men's and women's designers you've never heard of—unless, of course, you're super-hip, which, come to think of it, you must be. Great selection of pocketbooks on the first floor. Fun to browse and maybe get a leeetle more serious about buying during sale times. Forget the Barneys warehouse sale. It's a zoo.

OTHER LOCATION

World Financial Center, 225 Liberty
Street, 212-945-1600
Monday to Friday, 10 A.M.–7 P.M.;
Saturday, 11 A.M.–5 P.M.; Sunday,
noon–5 P.M.

Bergdorf Goodman

754 Fifth Avenue (at 58th Street)
753-7300
Monday to Friday, 10 A.M.–7 P.M.;
Saturday, 10 A.M.–6 P.M.; closed
Sundays
The quintessential New York City department store: two beauty salons and a spa—and the Plaza Hotel right out the door! The sales are fun; the stuff is luxe; the stationery department is a must.

Bloomingdale's

100 Third Avenue (at 59th Street),
212-705-2000
Monday to Saturday, 9 A.M.–10 P.M.;
Sunday, 10 A.M.–9 P.M.

Bonpoint

811 Madison Avenue (at 68th Street),
212-879-0900
1269 Madison Avenue (at 91st Street),
212-722-7720
Monday to Saturday, 10 A.M.–6 P.M.;
closed Sundays (both stores)
This place is grandparents' heaven. . . . But bring lots of greenbacks for the dreamiest smocked frocks and sailor suits.

Brooks Brothers

346 Madison Avenue (at 44th Street),
212-682-8800
Monday to Wednesday, Friday to
Saturday, 9 A.M.–7 P.M.; Thursday,
9 A.M.–8 P.M.; Sunday, 12 P.M.–6 P.M.

Burberrys

9 East 57th Street (between Madison
and Fifth Avenues), 212-371-5010
Monday to Friday, 9:30 A.M.–7 P.M.;
Saturday, 9:30 A.M.–6 P.M.; Sunday,
noon–6 P.M.
Designer dog coats—no self-respecting corgi would be without one. It's all about *that* plaid, so if you have to have it, for heaven's sake, wait for the sales. The markdowns are substantial—20 to 30 percent and sometimes more—and the cheapest stuff is sometimes the best: i.e., the stuff without the *plaid!* They actually have cashmere mufflers, silk scarves, luggage, and even those raincoats, without it. (You might have to really search, though.)

Celine

51 East 57th Street (between Park and
Madison Avenues), 212-486-9700
Monday to Saturday, 10 A.M.–6 P.M.;
closed Sundays

Etro USA

720 Madison Avenue (at 63rd Street),
212-317-9096
Monday to Saturday, 10 A.M.–6 P.M.;
closed Sundays

Fratelli Rossetti

675 Madison Avenue (at 62nd Street),
212-838-4166
Monday to Wednesday, Friday,
10 A.M.–6:30 P.M.; Thursday, 10 A.M.–
7 P.M.; Saturday, 10 A.M.–6 P.M.;
Sunday, noon–5 P.M.
Absolutely fabulous men's shoes—and some nice women's shoes, too—but the men's are the best. And when they go on sale, they're marked down to under $300. This sounds expensive, but the shoes can last forever. And they look so divine!

Gucci

10 West 57th Street (between Fifth and
Sixth Avenues), 212-826-2600
Monday to Wednesday, Friday,
10 A.M.–6:30 P.M.; Thursday, Saturday,
10 A.M.–7 P.M.; Sunday, noon–6 P.M.

Henri Bendel

12 Fifth Avenue (at 55th Street),
212-247-1100
Monday to Wednesday, Saturday,
10 A.M.–7 P.M.; Thursday, 10 A.M.–
8 P.M.; Sunday, noon–6 P.M.
A small but exquisite selection of the finest designer collections of clothing and accessories. The café is inviting, even if a pot of coffee is $5. What the heck. During the sales, their pale wheat-colored merino wool turtlenecks are marked down to $49—and you get those neat chocolate-and-white striped bags. If for nothing else, go here for makeup.

Hermès Boutique Store

11 East 57th Street (between Madison
and Fifth Avenues), 212-751-3181
Monday to Friday, 10 A.M.–8 P.M.;
Saturday, 10 A.M.–7 P.M.; Sunday,
noon–6 P.M.

For the man in your life, a $660 pair of John
Lobb shoes. Or *pour madame*, a $3,000
handbag. A must-see—if only so you can see
how bad the knockoffs are. (Don't buy them—
everyone can tell the difference.)

J. Press Clothers

16 East 44th Street (between Madison
and Fifth Avenues), 212-687-7642
Monday to Saturday, 9 A.M.–6 P.M.;
Sunday, noon–5 P.M.

Men's suits, slacks, and sport jackets start at
$500 but are marked down significantly on
sale. The home of Shaggy Dog sweaters.
Great preppiness. Boola, boola. Go Bulldogs!
(It's a Yale institution.)

Louis Vuitton

19 East 57th Street (between Park and
Madison Avenues), 212-371-6111
Monday to Wednesday, Saturday,
10 A.M.–6 P.M.; Thursday,
10 A.M.–6 P.M.; Sunday, noon–5 P.M.
Not as much fun as Hermès.

Paul Stuart Clothiers

Madison Avenue (at 45th Street),
212-682-0320
Monday to Friday, 8 A.M.–7 P.M.;
Saturday, 9 A.M.–6 P.M.; Sunday,
noon–5 P.M.

Superb stuff. Take a look. Their suits are great
and, during the sales, are almost affordable.
Splurge if you see something you have to
have; they have their stuff made in Canada
especially for them. (*Note:* Paul Stuart clothes
used to be found at Decker's, a now-defunct
outlet store headquartered in Norwalk, Connecticut. I bought a terrific beige-and-white,
double-breasted, linen trouser suit there for
less than $200—it was at least $600 in the
store.)

Prada New York

45 East 57th Street (between Park and
Madison Avenues), 212-308-2332
28 East 70th Street (between Fifth and
Madison Avenues), 212-327-4200
Monday to Wednesday,
Saturday, 10 A.M.–6 P.M.;
Thursday, 10 A.M.–7 P.M.

Ralph Lauren

Ralph Lauren, 867 Madison Avenue
(at 72nd Street), 212-606-2100
Monday to Friday, 10 A.M.–8 P.M.;
Saturday, 10 A.M.–7 P.M.;
Sunday, noon–5 P.M.

Polo Sport, 888 Madison Avenue
(at 72nd Street), 212-434-8000
Monday to Saturday, 10 A.M.–8 P.M.;
Saturday, noon–5 P.M.

A turn-of-the-century mansion is just what
you'd expect, but the sumptuous interior design is worth a trip. Go in some smashing outfit of your own, and out-snob the snobby help.
After you've done that, go downstairs and survey what a store's bathroom is *supposed* to
look like. Now you're ready to go out and find
equally smashing clothes—or the same clothes
—somewhere else for a lot less money.
Monday to Friday, 10 A.M.–7 P.M.; Sunday,
10 A.M.–6:30 P.M.; Sunday, noon–6 P.M.

Saks Fifth Avenue

611 Fifth Avenue (between 49th and
50th Streets), 212-753-4000
Monday to Wednesday, Friday,
10 A.M.–7 P.M.; Thursday, 10 A.M.–8
P.M.; Saturday, 10 A.M.–6:30 P.M.;
closed Sundays

Searle

862 Madison Avenue (at 70th Street),
212-772-2225
Monday to Saturday, 10 A.M.–6 P.M.;
Sunday, noon–5 P.M.

1051 Third Avenue (at 62nd Street),
212-838-5990
Monday to Saturday, 10 A.M.–6 P.M.;
Sunday, noon–6 P.M.

Some claim they've seen the Searle label at
Loehmann's, but regardless, the company
makes great shearling coats and hats and

some nice woolens. Wait for the sale. Maybe the salespeople won't trail after you so much.

Tanino Crisci

795 Madison Avenue (at 67th Street),
212-535-1014
Monday to Saturday, 10 A.M.–6 P.M.;
closed Sundays

Talk about aloof! These people wrote the book—especially if they get a whiff that you're hunting a (sniff, sniff) bargain. But hold fast: It doesn't get any worse than the first disappointed sigh and the faint moue of distaste when you ask for the sale shoes. The shoes on sale are still as dear as a sailor's valentine—but these are probably the best off-the-rack (boy, would they hate that term!) shoes in the whole big city and you should at least see them. On sale (which occurs at least once a year, the first week in January, although they won't tell you if you ask any other time), the shoes drop down to $284, or thereabouts. And I'd buy fifty pairs tomorrow if I had the money . . . attitude and all!

Turnbull & Asser

42 East 57th Street (between Madison and Park Avenues), 212-752-5700
Monday to Friday, 9:30 A.M.–8 P.M.;
Saturday, 9:30 A.M.–6 P.M.; open
Sundays in December only

They make custom shirts here, and the materials are lush, reminding one of the scene in *The Great Gatsby* when Daisy takes out all of Gatsby's beautiful shirts from his drawers and starts to cry. (You can see shirting of close to this quality down on Orchard Street. But then you'd need a tailor. People like to use it for shower curtains and stuff.)

FOR MEN

Davide Cenci

801 Madison Avenue at 68th Street,
212-628-5910
Monday to Wednesday, Friday,
Saturday, 10 A.M.–6:30 P.M.; Thursday,
10 A.M.–7:30 P.M.; closed Sundays

Also Rome and Milan. See if Mr. Cenci will give you his personal tour of the merchandise. He's charming and will tell you all about the various exotic suedes and cashmeres and vicuñas. The clothing here—mostly men's but some fine women's too—is expensive but a very good value, especially during the twice-yearly sales.

Gilcrest Clothes Company

900 Broadway (at 20th Street),
212-254-8933
Monday to Friday, 7:30 A.M.–5:30 P.M.;
Saturday, 8:30 A.M.–5 P.M.; Sunday,
9:30–4:30 P.M.

Great men's clothes—no prices marked—at terrific savings. Ask for Maurice, also known as Moshe.

Moe Ginsburg

162 Fifth Avenue (at 19th Street),
212-982-5254
Monday to Friday, 9:30 A.M.–7 P.M.;
Saturday and Sunday, 9:30 A.M.–6 P.M.

Long live Moe's! And may they always have their eighth floor "outlet" shop operating—featuring four suits for $100! (Yes, really!)

Saint Laurie Merchant Tailors

350 Park Avenue (at 51st Street),
212-317-8700
Monday to Friday, 9:30 A.M.–6:30 P.M.;
Thursday, 9:30 A.M.–8 P.M.; Saturday,
9:30 A.M.–6 P.M.

Custom-made jackets and suits at bargain prices. During sale times, in the winter and late spring, dozens of different materials for suits are marked down; an exquisite gray pinstripe, made for your particular body, can cost you only $699.

THE ORCHARD STREET SHOPS

Arivel Fashions

150 Orchard (between Rivington and Stanton) 212-673-8992
11 A.M.–6 P.M., seven days a week

Forget the furs—or not—but this place has good suede trouser suits in luscious auburn and lots of Dr. Zhivago shearlings downstairs. Bargain. Hard.

Beckenstein

133 Orchard (between Rivington and Delancey) 212-475-6666
9 A.M.–5:30 P.M., seven days a week
For men only, more or less. Beckenstein's offers a delicious collection on cotton shirt fabrics and wool and flannel materials for jackets and pants—and the front room is all bargain remnants. They do not have a tailor in-house, but can recommend someone.

Ben Freedman

137 Orchard (between Rivington and Delancey), 212-674-0854
9 A.M.–6 P.M., seven days a week
This place is super-cheap: men's belts for $4, ties for $5, pants for $6. Racks outside. You get the idea.

Rita's Leather Fair

176 Orchard Street (between Houston and Stanton), 212-533-2756
10 A.M.–6 P.M., seven days a week

Soha's Leather

132 Orchard Street (between Delancey and Rivington), 212-674-8868
10 A.M.–7 P.M., seven days a week
A solid selection of leather jackets for adults and children crammed into an alleyway. The prices marked are about triple what you can get them for if you haggle. (Okay, maybe only double . . .)

THE DISCOUNT STORES

Century 21

22 Cortland Street (between Broadway and Church), 212-227-9092
Monday to Wednesday, 7:45 A.M.–8:30 P.M.; Thursday, 7:45 A.M.–8 P.M.; Saturday, 10 A.M.–7:30 P.M.; Sunday, 11 A.M.–6 P.M.

Daffy's

111 Fifth Avenue, 212-529-4477
335 Madison Avenue, 212-557-4422
125 East 57th Street, 212-346-4477
1311 Broadway, 212-736-4477
All have different hours; call the one you want to visit.

Dollar Bill's

32 East 42nd Street, 212-867-0212
Monday to Friday, 8 A.M.–7 P.M.;
Saturday, 10–6; Sunday, noon–5 P.M.

Filene's Basement

620 Avenue of the Americas (at 18th Street), 212-620-3100
Monday to Saturday, 10 A.M.–9 P.M.;
Sunday, 11 A.M.–7 P.M.
2220-26 Broadway (at 79th Street) 212-873-8000
Monday to Saturday, 10 A.M.–9 P.M.;
Sunday, 11 A.M.–6 P.M.

Loehmann's

101 Seventh Avenue (at 16th Street) 212-352-0856
Monday to Saturday, 9 A.M.–9 P.M.;
Sunday, 11 A.M.–7 P.M.

Syms Clothing

400 Park Avenue (at 54th Street) 212-317-8200
Monday to Friday, 9 A.M.–7:30 P.M.;
Saturday, 10 A.M.–6:30 P.M.; Sunday, noon–5:30 P.M.

T. J. Maxx

620 Avenue of the Americas (at 18th Street), 212-229-0875
Monday–Saturday, 9:30 A.M.–9 P.M.;
Sunday 11 A.M.–7 P.M.
The Manhattan store is great for sheets, towels, gift-wrap, stockings, underwear, and men's clothing. There are more bargains in women's clothing out in the suburban malls, but maybe that's because the city stuff gets picked so quickly.

THE GREATEST SAMPLE SALES

Echo Scarves

10 East 40th Street, 212-686-8771
Great scarves, including those made by Echo for Ralph Lauren. Call for sale information.

Gabrielle Carlson

251 East 10th Street, No. 4
212-995-8063

A press-time discovery. Fabulous filmy silks, taffetas, and wools in the latest, most flattering styles. Things cost a small percentage of what you'd pay in a blue-chip boutique. Call for information.

Portolano
32 West 39th Street, 5th floor
(between Fifth and Sixth Avenues),
212-719-4403
Sample sales for three days every month.

OTHER SAMPLE SALES WITH BARGAINS

Burberrys Collection
512 Seventh Avenue, 7th floor
(at 37th Street), 212-221-0988
Sample sale in spring.

Carolina Herrera
48 West 38th Street, 3rd floor (between Fifth and Sixth Avenues),
212-575-0557
By appointment only; contact Patty Rose at extension 4014 for an appointment.
A series of sale dates in December, January, and February.

Donna Karan/DKNY
550 Seventh Avenue (at 39th Street)
212-789-1500
Sample sale runs several times a year at the Parsons School of Design (40th Street and Seventh Avenue).

Fernando Sanchez
5 West 19th Street, 7th floor (between Fifth and Sixth Avenues),
212-929-5060
Sample sales in December and April; fax your address to 212-633-1289.

Givenchy Couture
21 East 75th Street (between Madison and Fifth Avenues), 212-772-1322
By invitation only, in December. Call and speak politely; you'll get invited.

Malo Cashmere
745 Fifth Avenue, No. 1225 (at 58th Street), 212-753-7015
Sample sale in May at the Parsons School of Design (40th Street and Seventh Avenue).

Makins Hats, Ltd.
212 West 35th Street, 12th floor
(between Seventh and Eight Avenues)
212-594-6666
Sample sales in late November and in the spring.

Metropolitan Design Group
80 West 40th Street, 8th floor (between Fifth and Sixth Avenues),
212-944-6110
Sample sales for several days in early December and in the spring. Handbags and accessories on the eighth floor and clothing on the second floor.

Oscar de la Renta at Le Firme
37 West 57th Street, 4th floor (between Fifth and Sixth Avenues),
212-755-6900
Sample sale in December.

Patricia Underwood
498 Seventh Avenue, 24th floor
(at 36th Street), 212-268-3774
Sample sale in May.

Rafael Sanchez Designs, Ltd.
35 West 36th Street (between Fifth and Sixth Avenues), 212-967-8214
Sample sales in December and in the spring.

Sulka
111 Eighth Avenue, 5th Floor
(near 15th Street)
Sample sale in March.

Tahari
1114 Sixth Avenue, 48th floor
(at 38th Street), 212-921-3600
Several sample sales a year, at undetermined times. Try calling—maybe you'll hit one.

TSE Cashmere
745 Fifth Avenue (at 58th Street)
212-319-5118
Sample sales in December and in the spring.

PERMANENT SALES OF SAMPLE MERCHANDISE

Alberene Scottish Cashmeres
435 Fifth Avenue, 3rd floor
(at 38th Street), 212-689-0151
Monday to Friday, 9:30 A.M.–7 P.M.;
Saturday, 10 A.M.–7 P.M.;
Sunday, 1 P.M.–5P.M.
Savings—50 percent every day.

Subito
West 36th Street, 9th floor
(at Fifth Avenue), 212-290-2646
Monday to Friday by appointment only,
9 A.M.–4 P.M.
Sells samples only—all year round.

THE OUTLET MALLS

Clinton Crossing Premium Outlets
Route 81 off I-95, Exit 63, Clinton,
Conn., 860-664-0700
Monday to Saturday, 10 A.M.–9 P.M.;
Sunday, 10 A.M.–8 P.M.
Polo, Donna Karan, Brooks Brothers, Emanuel
Ungaro, Tommy Hilfiger, Tahari, Kenneth Cole,
Mikasa, Calvin Klein, Barneys, Coach, and
about sixty more. Especially good on holiday
weekends.

Woodbury Common Premium Outlets
Exit 16 on the New York State Thruway
I-87, Central Valley, N.Y.
914-928-4000
Monday to Saturday, 10 A.M.–9 P.M.;
Sunday, 10 A.M.–8 P.M.
The Big One. More than 220 stores carrying
discounted merchandise by Polo Ralph Lau-
ren, Williams Sonoma, Neiman Marcus,
Gucci, BCBG, Max Azaria, Eileen Fisher, A/X
Armani Exchange.

THRIFT SHOPS
The best ones are marked with a star.

Arthritis Foundation Gift Shop
121 East 77th Street (between Lexington
and Park Avenues), 212-772-8816
Monday to Saturday,
10 A.M.–5:45 P.M.; closed Sundays
Benefits those suffering from arthritis and re-
lated diseases.

*City Opera Thrift Shop
220 East 23rd Street (between Second
and Third Avenues), 212-684-5344
Monday to Wednesday and Saturday,
10–6; Thursday, 10–7; Sunday, noon–5
For the opera, of course.

Good Old Lower East Side Thrift Shop
169 Avenue B (at 10th Street)
212-358-1231
Monday to Saturday, 10 A.M.–6 P.M.;
Sunday, noon–5 P.M.

514 East 13th Street (between Avenues
A and B), 212-358-1242
Monday to Saturday, 11 A.M.–5 P.M.;
closed Sundays
Dedicated to tenant advocacy, housing preser-
vation, literacy, and job creation.

*Housing Works Thrift Shop
143 West 17th Street (between Sixth
and Seventh Avenues), 212-366-0820
Monday to Saturday, 10 A.M.–6 P.M.;
Sunday, noon–5 P.M.
202 East 77th Street (between Second
and Third Avenues), 212-772-8461
Monday, Wednesday, Friday,
10 A.M.–6 P.M.; Thursday, 10 A.M.–
8 P.M.; Saturday, 10–6; Sunday, noon–
5 P.M.

306 Columbus Avenue (at 74th Street)
212-579-7566
Monday to Friday, 11 A.M.–7 P.M.;
Saturday, 10 A.M.–6 P.M.; Sunday,
noon–5 P.M.
Provides housing, support services, and advo-
cacy for homeless people living with AIDS and
HIV.

Irvington Institute Thrift Shop
1534 Second Avenue (at 80th Street)
212-879-4555
Monday, Tuesday, Friday, 10 A.M.–
6 P.M.; Wednesday and Thursday,
10 A.M.–8 P.M.; Sunday, noon–5 P.M.;
closed Saturdays
Supports research in immunology relating to
the treatment and prevention of diseases.

Memorial Sloan-Kettering Thrift Shop
1440 Third Avenue (at 82nd Street)
212-535-1250
Monday to Wednesday, Friday,
10 A.M.–5:25 P.M., Thursday, 10 A.M.–
7 P.M., Saturday, 10 A.M.–5 P.M.;
closed Sundays
Supports patient care, education, and research programs at the hospital.

*Spence-Chapin
1850 Second Avenue (at 96th Street)
212-426-7643
Tuesday to Friday 10 A.M.–6 P.M.;
Saturday, 9 A.M.–5 P.M.; Sunday,
11:30 A.M.–5 P.M.; closed Mondays

1473 Third Avenue (at 83rd Street)
212-737-8448

Monday to Friday, 10 A.M.–7 P.M.,
Thursday, 10 A.M.–8 P.M.; Saturday,
10 A.M.–5 P.M.; Sunday, noon–5 P.M.
Benefits adoption and family services.

Thrifts and Things
1871 Second Avenue (at 96th Street)
212-876-7223
Monday to Thursday, 10 A.M.–6 P.M.;
Friday, 9 A.M.–4 P.M.; closed Saturdays
and Sundays
Supports the child care agency for Hale
House, which benefits children born addicted
to drugs and alcohol or with HIV.

CAR SERVICES

Allstate Limousine Service
163 Eighth Avenue, 800-453-4099 or
212-333-3333

Carmel Limousine Service
2642 Broadway, 800-227-7378 or
212-666-6666

EAT WHILE YOU SHOP

Dean & Deluca
560 Broadway (corner of Prince Street)
212-226-6800
Monday to Saturday, 10 A.M.–8 P.M.;
Sunday, 10 A.M.–7 P.M.

Diamonds and Other Baubles—We Go Bargain Hunting and Learn How Not to Be Ripped Off

If you're new to the city, you may not know Manhattan's Diamond District, the wild array of jewelry shops along 47th Street between Fifth and Sixth Avenues. Besides individual shops, whose windows are packed with as many plush-lined boxes as their owners can jam in, there are flea markets of a sort: bigger emporiums with dozens of merchants' stalls. The signs are loud, and there are a few barkers who are even louder: men (they are almost always male, because this area is full of Orthodox Jews who run all-male businesses) are out on the pavement shouting out encouraging news. "Bargains inside!" "Ladies, come inside!" "Hello! We just got a new shipment." There are also some shops that specialize in antique and estate jewelry at ferocious prices.

So how does anyone except a total expert know how to shop here? If you find something you like, how can you make sure it's real? How can you tell if you're paying too much? What are the trickiest stones to buy? And what do all those letters mean—*VS, VS2, VS3*—when they're applied to diamonds?

The good news is that, yes, cheapskate millionaires can save hundreds and even thousands of dollars by buying rings and things here, some of them every bit as rare and valuable as those at Tiffany's. I proved that in just one day's outing with a wholesale jewelry merchant acting as a friend I had along on my shopping trip. (See the results later in this chapter.) But the shopper has to beware—to demand certain things in writing when making a purchase—and to become as educated as possible. There are several ways to do that.

The first is to get a recommendation from a friend, according to the expert known on 47th Street as GemoloJoe. "That's your first lead," said Joe, who doesn't use his last name. "If your friend bought a stone from one of the dealers here, had it checked out, and is satisfied, that's a good place to start." Failing that, or in addition to that, he said, get the jeweler to certify it. New York's **Gemological Institute of America** (GIA) is the standard. "The jeweler doesn't have to say anything," he explained. "The papers say it all."

But many jewelers on 47th Street will balk at that—not necessarily because the stone is being offered fraudulently, but because it takes several weeks and costs several hundred dollars, which, not surprisingly, he will ask you to pay. But it may be a good investment, and certainly will help your peace of mind. Still, judging from my own cursory investigation and the opinions of trusted dealers interviewed for this chapter, out and out barefaced fraud is rare.

"Chances are, you're not going to walk out with what you think is a one-carat diamond and it isn't even a diamond," said GemoloJoe. What's more likely, according to the experts, is that you might get shorted: on weight, color, or clarity. But according to Fred Cuellar, a jeweler and diamond importer who has written an invaluable book called, appropriately, *How to Buy a Diamond: Insider Secrets for Getting Your Money's Worth* (Casablanca Press, 1998), you can prevent being taken for a total sucker—on 47th Street or anywhere else. (Mr. Cuellar and GemoloJoe agree: the *worst* place to buy a gem is in a mall.)

DIAMONDS

The first thing is to familiarize yourself with the terms and classifications below. If the dealer realizes you know something about buying stones, he will be more likely to deal with you in a civilized way. Some people complain about the diamond dealers being rude, but you must remember, they are used to dealing with other jewelers and antique dealers. Most are happy to deal with you—no matter how smart you are, they will make more money with you than with another diamond dealer. But that's okay. You'll still save a bundle.

Now remember how I suggested in Chapter 1 that you go to the most prestigious clothiers before you go discount shopping? The same idea applies here. So go to Tiffany's or Cartier's, and pick out the style or type of ring or earrings or whatever it is you want. And note more than just the carat size. Have the sales agent note the color and quality grading (with diamonds) and the point of origin, if it is known. And make sure you really examine that stone for both color and proportion. Hold it up to the light. Ask to borrow a jeweler's loupe—or even better, bring your own, with 10X magnification, the standard. Also, make your own drawing of the setting: Was it a 3-carat oval sapphire with two half-carat triangular diamonds on either side, set in platinum? (Don't forget to jot down the quality of the surrounding diamonds, too.) So you might have a sketch like this:

Or the ring might be an oval ruby circled by diamonds—the so-called Diana setting:

When you get to 47th Street, you don't have to actually produce the sketch; just describe the ring you want. In his book, Mr. Cuellar insists that buyers should see the stones without the setting. If you buy a stone here without the rest of the ring to go with it, almost any jeweler—probably even your neighborhood jewelry shop—can supply the gold or platinum band and set the stone the way you like it.

Now try to remember the color of the stones you saw at Tiffany's: the richness of the rubies, the deep timeless green of the emeralds, the sparkly white of the very best diamonds. To get the attention of the dealer, describe what you want accurately and succinctly, whether it is a 1-carat VS1 round diamond or a 3-carat cushion-cut sapphire. To help you, here are the clarity grades for diamonds, according to the GIA. This is what you should see—or not see—under 10X magnification in your loupe:

Flawless. Free from inclusions.

Internally flawless. Free from inclusions; may have slight blemishes.

VVS1 and VVS2. Minute inclusions or blemishes the size of a pinpoint.

VS1 and VS2. Inclusions or blemishes smaller than a grain of sand. No dark spots (carbon), fractures, or breaks.

SI1. Inclusions or blemishes larger than a grain of sand—and they can be carbon or fractures. Nevertheless, these flaws cannot be seen with the naked eye.

SI2: Borderline quality. Now the flaws become visible to the naked eye: pinpoints, feathers, carbon, clouds, crystals.

I1, I2, and I3: poor quality. If these diamonds are in an antique ring you love at an auction, buy it for what you think the setting is worth.

Color Grades for Diamonds

Diamonds are color-graded D (colorless) to Z (fancy colors.) Unless you get into the very expensive, deeply colored diamonds (the famous canary diamonds, for example, which are *deep* yellow, not the sickly yellow of a poorly colored stone), the rule is, the whiter the diamond the better. Mr. Cuellar recommends taking a white business card and holding the stone against it as a test. If you can see *any* yellow, it's no better than a K—and, in fact, he says, most stones are really M and N. The GIA rates colorless diamonds D, E, and F, getting more yellow as they go down the scale. The experts recommend you go for a grade H or I: nearly colorless—only an expert can tell the difference between those stones and whiter ones.

Near 47th Street

Not far from the Diamond District, scattered around Art Deco office buildings lining Fifth Avenue, the *serious* jewel merchants—the wholesale ones—have their businesses. One of these wholesalers is a charming woman named Babette Goodman Cohen. Mrs. Cohen graciously offered to show me—and you—the ins and outs of buying gems in New York City, a process that can, and should, scare even the most inveterate shopper.

We decided to test three kinds of retail jewelry shops: a random sampling of Diamond District shops and then several other kinds of retailers as well. Mrs. Cohen chose **H. Stern,** a well-known retail chain headquartered in Rio de Janeiro with branches all over the world; **Fortunoff,** known as a "value" retailer; and—what survey could be without it?—**Tiffany & Company,** which Mrs. Cohen initially said she thought actually had very good value. (After our visit, she said she was starting to feel differently . . .) To better compare prices and quality, we decided beforehand that, in every store, we would ask to see the same two types of jewelry: a large sapphire ring surrounded by diamonds and a pair of diamond stud earrings, totaling about 1 carat. Mrs. Cohen was introduced—not by name—as my friend, who was helping me shop.

The results amazed even me, accustomed as I am to widely varying prices in just about everything.

But before we went on our merchants' tour, Mrs. Cohen sat me down in her office at I. B. Goodman, her family business, and gave me a brief lesson that would help me understand the types of stones I was going to see during the day. It was a fascinating lecture. Some of the information I would pretend I didn't know, but would use it to pose intelligent questions. Other stuff proved vital to know and to use on the merchants if they seemed either vague or uncommunicative.

Some General Rules for Diamond Buying

Here are some general tips, gathered from Mrs. Cohen and other experts.

ON WEIGHT

In earrings especially, carats are usually "total weight," that is, the weight for both earrings together. Thus, if you want two half-carat studs, you'll ask for one carat, total weight.

Often, you'll get a price break—"Let's see if anyone offers us one," Mrs. Cohen said before starting—if you buy a weight just *below* a standard size. And, she said, this works all the way up the scale, from just below one-half carat up to just below 6, 7, or 8 carats. In other words, if you are looking for 1-carat total-weight earrings, you

might ask to see .88 carat or .94 carat. "If they don't ask you if you're flexible in this regard," the expert advised, "you might ask if you buy total weight .88, can you get a major deal?"

ON QUALITY

Buyers should check out the four Cs: color, cut, clarity, and carats. "Now trust me," said Mrs. Cohen. "Cut is the most important because it defines prettiness. I can see the difference in every diamond. The average customer doesn't recognize it for what it is, but you'll inherently realize some stones are prettier than others."

Besides the different cuts for the face of the stone, certain stones are cut deeper or shallower. This is very difficult to see if the stone is set into a ring, because the settings can be designed to obscure this, especially if the stone is cut shallow to appear bigger. (The only reason someone would cut a stone too deep—which makes it looks smaller—is that the stone's flaws demand such a cut or the stone will break.) If the stone is cut too deep or too shallow, it won't be as pretty, it won't sparkle as much, and won't look deep enough. But, as Mrs. Cohen pointed out, "bigger is better to a lot of people—especially people who don't know what they're looking at." So if a stone, especially a colored stone, looks watery and dull—and seems large for the money—it may be a shallow cut.

If you're looking for an engagement ring—or any piece of jewelry—Mrs. Cohen advises shoppers to settle on a budget first. "If you have $1,000 to spend, you may then decide the size. Within that budget, if you prefer a bigger stone, then you know you'll have to give up some clarity, which may or may not be noticeable to the naked eye." Diamonds, she said, "are a commodity, like rice or tobacco: Price is based on quality and size." And if you buy the diamond or emerald or sapphire at the right price—no matter how flawed or perfect—it should hold its value, she said.

Generally speaking, you shouldn't buy as good a stone for earrings. They get dirty, Mrs. Cohen said, and they're just not looked at with the same care. Thus, an SI2 might be good enough for earrings, but your dream might be a VS1 engagement ring.

SAPPHIRES

Okay, I admit it—I picked a sapphire ring as my test case because, hey, why not dream? I've always wanted one. And I was delighted when Mrs. Cohen said they were her favorite colored stone—I noticed she stressed "colored." (I won't describe the diamond ring she wore; just trust me that it was magnificent!)

With sapphires, rubies, and emeralds, unlike diamonds, color is key, with brilliance, often translated as "life" or "sparkle," coming in second. With sapphires, I thought I knew that the so-called cornflower blue was the one to pick, but Mrs. Cohen informed me that the description is a misnomer. In real life, cornflowers are a lighter blue than the most valuable sapphires, so it might be best to put that word out of your mind. Instead, think rich, very, very rich cobalt— not the navy stones that look almost black—the velvety blue stones that are still recognizably blue in daylight, even in a ring on your finger.

To show me, Mrs. Cohen had her assistant find a plain manila envelope, tucked in among many other manila envelopes in a plain metal drawer. She took out a GIA certificate, like those described above. When she unfolded the certificate, a much smaller manila envelope fell out. She shook out the stone, which was wrapped in tissue paper.

It was not what you'd call a rock, but it was plenty big enough for the biggest ring finger. It glittered in a way I'd never seen a sapphire glitter. Its color was pure, fascinating. I wanted it.

Too bad.

The loose stone was a Kashmir sapphire, untouched by any "enhancements," a big word in the world of colored gems. As such, it is rare on two counts. First, because Kashmir long ago banned sapphire mining, it must be at least forty years old, Mrs. Cohen explained. Then, because it is untreated, it is placed in a category shared by only an estimated 5 percent of all sapphires. Third, it is cut (close to flawlessly) in a cushion shape, a very rare and difficult cut to make—and very beautiful. The 4-carat stone, she said, is worth about $60,000.

Back into the manila envelope.

"If you're going to pay so much, the stone must be untreated," the jewelry experts say—and you should make sure you get a certificate to prove it. Not only sapphires, but also rubies and emeralds are heated to enhance them. Take sapphires. When they are mined, they may be a light, light blue. Or they may have color fading, or stripes of varying colors, within the same stone.

The stones are heated right at the mines—in Bangkok or Burma or Australia—which brings out the blue everyone loves. There are also sapphires in yellow, pink, and white. These are obviously specialty stones. We did see a necklace that combined all of them, and Mrs. Cohen reported that in the 1980s, Italian jewelers combined the yellow and light blue sapphires in rings and bracelets, but it's an acquired taste.

Ethically, a retail merchant must tell you if a stone has been treated—but only if you ask.

Tip

If a merchant says a colored stone is untreated—and one did on our tour—he must be willing to write this on an invoice and guarantee it. Usually, jewelers will only give you a certificate from an impartial gem appraisal firm if the stone is expensive because the certificates cost between $150 and $350 each. (Don't forget, you can always offer to pay for it and see what he says, as just another gauge of his reliability.) But, as investments, stones with certificates are generally worth the extra you pay now.

Here are the major sapphire-producing countries, and a quick primer on how to recognize each of them.

Kashmir. The best: the dark (but not too dark) velvety cobalt blue. These are rare because the country stopped producing sapphires forty years ago. Retail price key: $10,000 to $50,000 a carat.

Burmese. Very close to Kashmir stones in quality. There are some Burmese sapphires that are untreated. Price key: $2,000 to $20,000 per carat.

Ceylonese. From Sri Lanka (formerly Ceylon). Wildly variant. Some can be exquisite, and 99 percent of them have been treated. The very best ones look very close to the Kashmir stones and are priced accordingly. Mrs. Cohen shook out of a manila envelope about a dozen stones; each one was a different shade of blue and each was striped or somehow irregular in color. They also come in off sizes. "There's nothing wrong with them; it's a natural fact," said Mrs. Cohen, "but these irregularly colored stones *are* cheaper." Price key: $800 to $20,000 per carat.

Australian. The least valuable, generally. Untreated, these stones are often gray or black, and even after they have been enhanced, they are deep, deep blue, almost black. Some people prefer them, perhaps because they have been told that the darker stones are more valuable than the lighter ones. (Yes, but not *this* dark!) Price key: several hundred dollars per carat, at the most. (The wholesale on these stones is $50 or $60 a carat, according to the dealers.)

If you are looking for rubies or emeralds, the experts give the following advice:

Emeralds. Emeralds may have the biggest potential of all the stones for fakery and dishonest dealings. In nature, emeralds are extremely rare and are naturally the most flawed of all the stones. Because they would look cracked and imperfect without treatment, almost all emeralds are doctored—filled with some kind of oil which renders the flaws invisible to the naked eye. Jewel merchants have refined these additions to a science, and even the best gemologists can sometimes be fooled. An honest retailer will tell you if you ask—make sure you try to find out the extent of the coloring and the infill. But don't buy emeralds unless you know what you're doing or have an expert along. Get a watertight guarantee that what you are buying is exactly what it's purported to be, and try to obtain some kind of appraisal so you know you're in the ballpark as far as value. And, of course, always deal with a well-known and responsible shopkeeper—one who has been in business for a significant amount of time.

Rubies. While not quite as fragile as emeralds, rubies, besides being enhanced by heat, are often filled with what the Fortunoff brochure calls "a glass-like byproduct of the heating process." These stones are called "fissure-filled" rubies, and even Fortunoff wrote that "this enhancement technique may wear over time if treated harshly or exposed to strong solvents or abrasive." So don't have your emeralds or rubies steam-cleaned by some sidewalk jewelry cleaner—they really do have these while-you-wait cleaners at many of the lesser-grade "antique" flea markets!

Other stones that are usually enhanced. Aquamarine (mined as greenish stones; some people prefer them that way); tanzanite (when mined at the foot of Mt. Kilimanjaro, it's orange-brown, but it becomes a mouth-watering deep shade of purple-blue when heated) and blue topaz (when a dull-looking clear or brownish topaz is heated, it becomes sky-blue).

By the way, diamonds, too, can be enhanced in different ways, including a technique that focuses tiny laser beams at the imperfections and "vaporizes" them, according to Fortunoff. Resins then fill the holes left by the lasers. They can also be heated, although this happens less often than with colored stones.

So let's see what we found when we went, incognito, to the Diamond District and beyond.

WE GO SAPPHIRE AND DIAMOND HUNTING

Our first stop was a random one: **Peach Tree Jewelers, Ltd.,** at 580 Fifth Avenue. There, a clerk named Victor showed us several sapphire rings encircled with small diamonds, the ring that has been called the Diana setting since the Prince of Wales gave her one for their engagement. The two rings we zeroed in on were terrific looking: They looked a bit like the cushion setting, but were called "oval"—the cushion cut is a squarer stone. The larger one was a little over 2.5 carats and was handsome, with a gold band; the smaller one (I use the term loosely; these were *very* ample) was 2.2 carats, with a good-looking white gold band. Both rings were marked around $16,000—he said he would give either to us for $6,000. (He offered this price without even telling us the marked price; we noticed it ourselves on the tab.) After much deliberation, we decided we preferred the smaller stone. The 2.5-carat stone had a purple tone and didn't seem as sparkly. Not surprisingly, Victor complimented us on our good taste; the smaller, more blue stone, he said, was untreated. Hmmm . . .

Next we asked about diamond earrings for my sister. (I really do have one, but I'm not in the practice of giving her diamond earrings.) I started out by asking to see earrings of total weight 2 carats. Victor showed me some nice big studs; they were $2,000. "Whooh!" I said. "I love her, but not that much." At this point, Victor made a suggestion: Why not buy her one-half carat stones (total weight: 1 carat) with a "bezel" setting for $1,000? What is a bezel? It's a mounting in which the stones are surrounded by a small gold ring. And as Victor pointed out, with the bezels around them, the half-carat earrings looked as big as those double the size—and, of course, at half the price! (We liked his initiative.)

We politely told Victor the truth: this was our first stop and we wanted to tour a lot more shops. He gave us his card, and before we left, offered to take $500 off the total price (the new price: $6,500 for both) if we took both the sapphire ring and the earrings. We thanked him and left.

THE EXPERT WEIGHS IN: "It's hard to believe the stone is untreated," Mrs. Cohen said, "but I suppose if he puts it on the invoice, it's okay. He said the store had been there twenty-five years. That's a good sign. But the sapphire definitely had zoning [the irregularity of tone, which, in this stone, I hadn't noticed]. That's why I think it was treated." On prices: "Six thousand dollars is expensive for that ring; the earrings aren't bad for $1,000. That's okay, he said he only sold white goods [whiter stones]. He told you he'd give them to you for $500? That's very good for the earrings. But I think you should be able to find a ring like that for $4,000—I'd offer him $4,000 for both and see what he says." On Victor: "He was very good—very good selling. I like it that he took you to a different price point [the $1,000 bezel studs]. He handled that very well."

We walked around the corner and down 47th Street itself. We stopped briefly at **Peter J. Germano,** wholesale jewelers at a stall inside 50 West 47th Street, which we had chosen only because there was an enormous "sapphire" in the window that Mrs. Cohen said wasn't a sapphire at all, but was tanzanite. We stopped in just to see whether the salesclerk—who declined to give us his name—would tell us what it was. "Could I see that enormous sapphire?" I asked. He said (bored now) that it was not a sapphire but a tanzanite, which made Mrs. Cohen, as a member of the jewelry fraternity, very happy. "See, he told you right away!" she said delightedly because 47th Street doesn't always have the best reputation for honesty—especially for amateurs like me. The tanzanite ring, by the way, weighed 6.5 carats. The price? $6,300. A sapphire in this shop, very nearly the same size, was $8,000. "It's not a great stone," said the clerk, making Mrs. Cohen happy again at his honesty.

> **THE EXPERT WEIGHS IN:** We didn't stay long. Either the clerk knew we weren't serious or was just bored; he wasn't very encouraging. "As he said, it wasn't a great sapphire," said Mrs. Cohen.

One more shop on 47th Street: We were both bowled over by an exquisite antique sapphire ring in the window of another collective. The 12.9-carat (I *told* you we had good taste) stone was not, as we thought, a Kashmir sapphire, but hailed from Ceylon, according to Afshin Shaddaie, a partner at **M. Khordipour Enterprises.** Like most of the jewelry in Booth 41, this was an estate piece. It was set in an antique (and dated-looking) setting which I liked but Mrs. Cohen did not. The price of the ring was $78,000. I gasped, and Mr. Shaddaie said he had another excellent, smaller stone (sigh—only 9 carats) that was out on approval and might be back the next week. (Out on approval? Good idea: Wear it to a big party, but that would be more than tacky. . . . Pause . . . Wouldn't it?) I should add that there was an absolutely exquisite and finely crafted Victorian gold necklace that knocked my socks off: a half-inch thick band of the finest mesh imaginable with dozens of little gold daisies dropping from it. Unfortunately, it was $8,500. Too expensive, I suppose, but certainly hard to find another one. This is definitely a place for serious shoppers with deep pockets. Killer stuff.

> **THE EXPERT WEIGHS IN:** "He could have said it was Kashmir, but he didn't. Twelve point nine carats for $78,000—that's $6,000 per carat. It's not expensive. It was a beautiful stone. If I were buy-

ing sapphires, I'd try to buy it. If I were buying, I'd offer him half as much. He'd say, 'Oh, my God, you're crazy.' You have to have nerve. You have to be willing to get kicked out. Sure, it's a lot of money. You could buy a house. But everything is relative: You can't run with a house on your finger! You can't take a house to work with you . . . or to a cocktail party!"

We left 47th Street and headed uptown to **H. Stern,** at 645 Fifth Avenue, a store we thought would be about halfway in price between Fortunoff's and Tiffany's. But we ended up being shocked. The saleswoman, Melina El-Ani, showed us some diamond studs with a total weight of 1.45 carats. "Fifteen thousand dollars?" said Mrs. Cohen, who generally had not uttered a word in these shops. "I can't believe it!" Ms. El-Ani explained that the stones H. Stern used were better than the ones Victor at Peach Tree showed us. Hers were VS1 and very white. Studs with a total weight of 1 carat and a G color were priced at $8,000. We asked about the bezel settings, and she fetched us some very, very small studs (even with the visually enlarging 18-carat gold setting they looked small) with a total weight of about .62 carats. The price: $2,800. H. Stern offers an unusual guarantee: You can bring your gemstone purchase back for a full refund for a year.

THE EXPERT WEIGHS IN: "That's interesting about the year return policy, but I'm shocked—let's go to Fortunoff's."

At **Fortunoff,** the well-known Manhattan "value" merchandiser, Claude Keldany showed us several sapphire rings. We chose one that was about the same size as the one Victor showed us—a fine-looking oval stone surrounded by diamonds and set in platinum. The clerk said she had no idea where the stone came from and implied it was unimportant. The price was a surprise: $4,700. But no bargaining here, Ms. Keldany told us when we asked. The service was excellent: There was only one pair of diamond studs left, she told us without checking. We asked to see them, and they were tiny but the price was right: $995. Fortunoff offers several free brochures: One is on enhancements and is a must. The other is their catalogue, which shows another very nice-looking 2-carat sapphire ring surrounded by diamonds—for $1,400. I bet it was sold out.

THE EXPERT WEIGHS IN: "See! I told you Fortunoff's was good. We sell to them, and I know they don't mark up as much as some of the others. But even the saleswoman said these weren't great stones."

Now for the crème de la crème: **Tiffany's.** Mrs. Cohen explained that the Tiffany imprint itself adds value; the jewelry world is full of Tiffany collectors. But at Tiffany's, we were destined to be disappointed again. Karen Rieloff Oteiza, the saleswoman, was charming. (During our chat, she took a telephone call from a woman who had decided the ring her husband had just given her was too big. "Don't worry about it," said Ms. Oteiza, with that Tiffany cool. "Return it after the baby is born, and if you need another one, we'll exchange it!" After the call, she explained: "She's going to have a baby in three weeks; she shouldn't worry about the ring now!") Our favorite ring was a 4.21-carat cushion-cut sapphire. The style was different from the other ones we'd seen: no Diana ring of diamonds. Just two triangular diamonds on either side of a beautiful blue stone. How much do you guess it was? Because this is Tiffany's, maybe, uh, $14,000? Heck no, Tiffany's wanted a cool $26,010. (Where *did* they get that $10—should one offer $26,000?) The total weight of the diamonds was .47, and let the truth be known, they looked a little flimsy, as if they were not quite set in there properly. And they weren't exactly glittering, but that could have been the lighting. They were highly ranked—E and F; VVS1 and VS1. But the stone? Where was it from? "We don't know," said Ms. Oteiza.

THE EXPERT WEIGHS IN: "What were they asking? $26,000? I have to say I'm shocked. I know I told you Tiffany's was actually good value, but after today I changed my mind." She also found the bright-red velvet that lines every case distracting. "I can't even see the stones," she said, holding the $26,000 sapphire up toward the ceiling lights. "It's a lovely stone, but in terms of the whole *ring,* including the setting, I actually prefer the $6,000 ring in the first shop we went into." Also, Tiffany's is mobbed with tourists. "You can come in some other day by yourself, and look at diamond earrings."

SHOULD YOU BUY JEWELRY AT AUCTION?

Over lunch, Mrs. Cohen was discouraging about buying jewels at auction. "There are no bargains at auction," she said flatly. "Nowadays, the auction houses are retail stores. The trade puts in a lot of merchandise, in order to make a quick sale. They have a captive audience, and you can end up paying twice or even three times the estimate." Not only that, but if a bargain slips by, the dealers are there, ready to grab it. "Yes, maybe you'll be able to buy a string of used pearls," she said, "but they'll have somebody else's perfume on them, somebody else's perspiration."

She knew from personal experience. "The times I have gone to auction with a list of items, I've never gotten anything. The retail customer's always going to pay more."

I asked Mrs. Cohen about traveling to Brazil to buy emeralds the way some people do. "I see a lot of people making mistakes," she said. "My opinion is you'd better buy from a retailer you know in a town you live in. If something goes wrong, you can always go back. A lot of things can go wrong with emeralds. They can be treated with oiling techniques, and if they haven't been done right, the oil can dry up and the fillings become visible. And don't even think of taking them to be steam-cleaned. They are the most fragile of stones."

Mrs. Cohen was very pleased with the tour and she found it interesting that whereas in the past, shopkeepers boasted of where the stones, especially the sapphires, originally were mined, now "they seem to sell away from that point."

"They can't really know, you see," she said. "I've been to the actual mines, and even then, you know, they could bring the stones in from somewhere else." Without an electron microscope—and even sometimes with one—it's almost impossible to tell. "Too many exposés have tripped them up," she said wryly.

A WORD ABOUT PEARLS

A whole book could be written about pearls—and several have been. But Tiffany's puts out a wonderful little pamphlet that tells all about them.

While diamonds are rated by the four Cs—cut, clarity, color, and carats—pearls are rated by luster, clarity, nacre (surface transparency), roundness, and size. Again, the colors are a matter of taste. According to Mrs. Cohen, Americans like a rosy glow; the Japanese, a silver tone, and in South America, they like their pearls a creamy color. "That only makes them more valuable in those countries," she said. Sometimes, pearls are dyed to make them blacker or grayish-blue or pink or golden.

While people might spend hours rolling individual pearls to test their roundness, there is only one real fear: that they aren't pearls at all. To see if they are glass, Mrs. Cohen said, look at where the hole is, to see if you can detect peeling. But with real pearls, she added, you have to be careful. Don't even think of using nail polish or nail polish remover around them.

🍎 SOURCES

DIAMOND CERTIFICATION

Gemological Institute of America (GIA)
580 Fifth Avenue (between 47th and 48th Streets), 212-221-5858
Monday to Friday 8 A.M.–3 P.M.
This organization is nationwide and is known as highly reputable. The company will grade your diamond (VS, VS1, etc.) and weigh it. Customers are advised to come in the morning; the afternoons get fairly hectic.

JEWELERS

Let's be clear. These are the jewelers visited by Babette Goodman Cohen and myself. Neither of us recommends any of them; what we discovered, along with Mrs. Cohen's on-the-spot comments, is reported in the chapter. In general, when you are buying loose jewels or jewelry, it's always best to have an expert along! But whatever you do, don't pass up a trip to 47th Street—it's one of the most fun places for sightseeing, at the very least.

Fortunoff
681 Fifth Avenue (at 54th Street)
212-758-6660
Monday to Wednesday, Friday, Saturday, 10 A.M.–6 P.M.; Thursday, 10 A.M.–7 P.M.; closed Sundays

H. Stern
645 Fifth Avenue (at 52nd Street)
212-688-0300
Monday to Saturday, 10 A.M.–6 P.M.; closed Sundays

M. Khordipour Enterprises, Antique and Period Jewelry
10 West 47th Street, Booth 41 (between Fifth and Sixth Avenues),
212-869-2198
Monday to Thursday, 10 A.M.–5:30 P.M.; Friday, 10 A.M.–3 P.M.; closed Saturdays and Sundays

Peach Tree Jewelers, Ltd.
580 Fifth Avenue (at 47th Street)
212-398-1758
Monday to Saturday, 10 A.M.–6 P.M.; Sunday, 10 A.M.–5 P.M.

Peter J. Germano
50 West 47th Street (between Fifth and Sixth Avenues), 212-719-2160
Monday to Friday, 10 A.M.–5 P.M.; Saturday, 10 A.M.–4 P.M.; closed Sundays

Tiffany & Company
727 Fifth Avenue (at 57th Street)
212-605-4363
Monday to Wednesday, Friday, Saturday, 10 A.M.–6 P.M.; Thursday, 10 A.M.–7 P.M.: closed Sundays

Gourmet Food Fit for a Millionaire—It's Party Time! (Don't Read This Chapter If You're Hungry . . . or Thirsty)

SAVE MONEY AND TIME: HEAD TO NINTH AVENUE (IT'S THE ONLY PLACE YOU HAVE TO GO)

By far the absolute number one place to find food for a party—food that looks like a million and costs pennies—is on Ninth Avenue, under the shadow of the Lincoln Tunnel, just below West 42nd Street. Everything's here, from loin lamb chops to exotic black olives to couscous to dried peaches to Chilean sea bass. You can pull up to the curb in your chauffeur-driven Jag and not seem out of place. Or you can take the subway from anywhere to Times Square, stroll over, and feel right at home. It's a very democratic place.

The only thing you'll need, if you don't bring Raoul and the Jag, is strong arms: Should you start with the produce and lug the baby potatoes and cantaloupe ($1 apiece) or start with the super-cheap leg of lamb (fresh at $1.89 a pound)? Maybe start at the **Cupcake Café,** where you can nibble the best apple and walnut muffin—really more like a fruitcake—and sip a cup of decaf, all for $2. Wouldn't it be nice if all of life consisted of such choices?

Okay, let's start at **Stiles Farmers Market,** which, even in winter, is chock full of produce piled up like, well, a farm market, but one without the cachet of the Hamptons. Grab those baby potatoes. They're only 33 cents a pound. Then how about the asparagus for $1.50 a pound? (No, not a misprint, as they say inside the matchbooks.) You know those yellow bell peppers? Usually $3.99 a pound, right, even in the suburbs? Try 75 cents a pound. What year is this? 1933? Bosc and d'Anjou pears are 75 cents a pound, too. Mesclun, everybody's favorite salad greenery, is $3.99 a pound (at the **Gourmet Garage,** $8.99). Six ounces of Portabella mushrooms: $1.75. This place is amazing. Fresh (some months fresher than others) corn, Chilean apricots, and great atmosphere.

Next door is the **Big Apple Meat Market,** and it's picturesque, if picturesque means three or four butchers in bloodied white coats chopping away at sides of beef right there on a big table next to the front door, where you walk in. There's something really gross about this place—until you see the prices. It's weird: You walk down these high racks full of cello packs of raw meat encased in blood. The whole place has sawdust on the floor. Is this sanitary?

Hey, what the heck? It all looks very fresh, obviously a little *too* fresh for some more timid souls. But whole legs of lamb are $1.98 a pound, and beef loins are $4.98 a pound. Shell steaks are $2.98 a pound (yes, that's right), and loin lamb chops go for $4.98 a pound. If you're a vegetarian, you won't go near this place. And if you're a meat eater . . . it might be best to send your cook. The sight—but not, thank goodness, the smell (there isn't any)—lingers in your memory for a while.

There are a couple of more standard butcher shops here: men standing behind a glass-fronted case full of meat that's already cut up and not drenched in blood. But guess what? They're more expensive. There's still some interesting stuff. **Esposito and Sons,** at 500 Ninth Avenue, has the look of a neighborhood institution and is selling pig's feet, honeycomb tripe, filet mignon, and some tasty pork chops for $3.79 a pound. Nearby, **Michaels and Sons Meat Market** has a wonderful sign out front, under the big front window, advertising RABBITS, DUCKS, QUALES, TURKEYS, HAM, PORK CHOPS AND SUCKLING PIGS. Boy, it's been a while since I had a suckling pig and saw a Spanish chef in Baltimore cut it with a porcelain plate. After the last cut, the chef ceremonially threw the plate into the fireplace and the guests applauded. But I digress. The cost of the pig at Michaels? $2.89 a pound, and they usually weigh between 16 and 20 pounds. Now all you need is the Spanish chef . . .

If meat offends you, what about fish? The **Central Fish Market** has Chilean sea bass, fresh salmon, monster shrimp, and fresh tuna for what must be a record low: $3.99 a pound. Oysters in the shell are $4.99 a dozen, and mussels are 69 cents a pound.

So what do you need to cook all these delicious roasts and crustaceans and things? Spices! Go to the **Ninth Avenue Deli Grocery,** and choose from crushed red pepper and imported curry, cumin, and paprika—a small bagful, more than you'll probably ever need, for 75 cents. Do you like risotto? Arborio rice is $1.89 a pound. Couscous is $1.49; dried peaches, $4.50; whole almonds, $5; fresh halvah, $3; and corn nuts, $2.69—all by the pound. Looking for a house present? The store has these gutsy-looking bars of olive oil soap, covered with lots of Greek lettering, for $1.25.

Not to be outdone, the **International Grocery and Meat Market,** at 529 Ninth Avenue, offers the basic parsley and paprika, but also features sorrel flowers, French chicory, star anise, St. John's bread (big, shriveled carob pods), chamomile, and mint, for the same kinds of giveaway prices. **Aphrodisia,** a wonderful spices and scents emporium on Bleecker Street, is great. But it's hard to beat 75 cents for a quarter of a pound of spice.

Two wonderful stage-set kinds of places can be found here on Ninth Avenue: Peek into **Manganaro's,** a great-looking Italian groceria with prices that contrast with the rest of the markets along the street. Prosciutto di Parma is $19.99 a pound—certainly not a bargain. And the salesclerk who addresses me is so angry she must be a member of the family. Some poor guy was trying to get a sandwich in the back, and she practically bit his head off! Ah, Old World charm. Next, stop into **Supreme Macaroni Company**—you might decide to stay for lunch. Hot and sweet sausage on rigatoni with peppers, onions, and mushrooms, or chicken penne with sundried tomatoes? But the best thing is that in the front of the store is a macaroni store, selling briliantly colored little cookable jewels from glass-fronted metal bins. The pasta is $2.75 a pound.

Aspiring cheapskate millionaires can create a whole dinner party shopping on Ninth Avenue alone. I recently put together a rather grand spread for twenty people for about $100. This was the menu:

Roast leg of lamb, rolled in fresh rosemary and thyme
Mesclun salad with baby artichoke hearts
Ratatouille

Basmati rice with currants and Middle Eastern spices
Apple pie with cheddar cheese

Another party for forty-five cost less than $150 and featured honey-cured ham and turkey stuffed with oysters. And I got all the food right here!

WE TEAR OURSELVES AWAY FROM
THE SMELL OF CUMIN . . .

If you're shopping on Orchard Street (Chapter 1), walk north to Houston Street and turn left. There you'll find **Russ & Daughters Appetizers,** with its most tantalizing window. You'll see some of the most divine dried fruits, all for bargain prices: jumbo pears, Turkish apricots, nectarines, papaya spears, mango slices, and more, all for $3.99 to $5.99 a pound. I have absolutely no idea what to do with these delicacies, but they look so terrific. Couldn't you serve them piled up on glass compote dishes, edged with sugar or graced with white-lace paper doilies? Couldn't you serve them for appetizers with sweet punch at a holiday party? Couldn't you put them on the bottom of a pan and bake an upside-down cake?

Then there are the different types of olives—also fun in fancy little dishes at cocktail parties (see where to get cheap liquor at the end of this chapter): Casablanca olives that make you think of Ingrid Bergman, pistou olives that make you think of Adolf Menjou. Then there are Arbequina olives and Picholine olives—all for $2.99 a half pound. It's a fantastic shop, with its old-fashioned display cases and gold lettering trumpeting Nova Scotia salmon and smoked eel (ugh!) and pickles and divine breads.

A few blocks north at **East Village Cheese,** you could find the ingredients for a whole cocktail party here—except for the booze. The people who work here don't go out of their way, but they don't have to. The news is all in the window: dozens of signs proclaiming the day's bargains. Unlike some stores with only one cheese on special (as a loss leader), this place has about a dozen cheeses for $2.99 a pound, including a delicious Italian fontina, a Danish blue, and a low-fat mozzarella. Raclette is $4.99 a pound; St. Andre—usually upward of $9 a pound—is a little over $7 here. Italian Reggiano

Parmesan is $9.99 a pound, and Greek feta with green olives is $2.99 for a 12-ounce jar. Walnut torte from Germany is $3.49. A stick of Cabot's Vermont cheddar is $1.49, and a big wheel of brie is $24.

But there's a lot more than cheese. Caribbean salad is $4.99 a pound; a quarter-pound of Nova is $4; corned beef and pastrami are $3.99 a pound; and rare roast beef is $6.99. Fire-roasted sweet peppers are $1.50 for a half pound (why bother to roast them yourself?), cornichons are $2 for half a pound, and sundried tomatoes are $5.99 a pound. Italian (versus American) prosciutto is $12.99 a pound (remember, it was $19.99 at Manganaro's?), and Alaska row caviar ("sushi quality") is $5 a quarter pound. Fresh pesto is $7 a pound, and a twenty-five-ounce bottle of French apple-and-black-currant drink is $2.79. That gives you some idea. Plus shelves of a fantastic assortment of fresh breads.

And as you're leaving, your shopping bags full, grab an overstuffed sandwich—smoked turkey and roasted peppers with honey mustard is only $3.

FOR SMOKED SALMON AND CAVIAR

Okay, what's the point of being a millionaire-to-be if you can't break down every so often and scarf up some smoked salmon on tiny toast points? That's very doable, if you just buy the salmon from the cheapest, best places in town, listed below. But what about caviar? Well, that's a slightly different ballgame, especially if you really *can* tell the difference between beluga, ossetra, and sevruga. (As one wag might say: about $1,000 a pound!)

The fanciest name in town for both caviar and smoked salmon is **Petrossian,** at 182 West 58th Street. Although the per-ounce prices of caviar are high here, it's probably a good place to start—and their $22 prix fixe lunch may just put you in the mood for caviar shopping. The lunch itself is a great deal: Begin with assorted hors d'oeuvres of smoked cod and trout, with some salmon roe and foie gras thrown in. Then choose among seared marinated salmon, a foie gras club sandwich with Portabella mushrooms, and other entrées—and a glass of wine or champagne to boot. For $39, you can have a plate of selected caviars, different entrées, and dessert, but no wine. (There is also a three-course prix fixe dinner for $35 offered at any time in the evening.)

At Petrossian, 3.5 ounces of beluga caviar—the finest and an amount just sufficient for three or four dainty caviar eaters—costs $250. At **Caviarteria,** its closest competitor, this amount normally costs $203, but recently the store had a sale and was offering it for $175. (Beware—these are prices for buying in the shop. If you purchase by mail, the prices soar, partly because of the fragility of the caviar, which needs to be specially packed in ice.) When you compare the two shops' prices for, say, smoked Scottish salmon tenderloin—the so-called czar cut (unsliced and superior quality)— Caviarteria again comes out cheaper: 1 pound for $45 at Caviarteria; 1 pound for $60 at Petrossian.

But there are better places to buy both caviar and salmon.

Some cheapskates swear by **Murray's Sturgeon Shop,** an Upper West Side landmark since 1946. This small shop is known for its smoked fish: sturgeon, Nova Scotia salmon, whitefish, and so forth, and for its pickled herring. It is the quintessential New York experience, and if you want a cup of homemade soup (borscht, perhaps?) it's a swell place. And their beluga caviar is fractionally cheaper than that of both Petrossian and Caviarteria: $54.95 an ounce. Their Scottish salmon is cheaper, too, although not offered in the czar cut: it costs $7 a quarter of a pound.

But for both caviar and Scottish salmon, the *real* cheapskate millionaires have their chauffeurs head to the West 70s and Broadway, where they take their pick between **Zabar's, Citarella,** and **Fairway.**

All three are neighborhood standbys whose success has turned them into zoos on the weekends. (Don't even think of going there on a Sunday afternoon.) Both stores have excellent values on cheeses, and Fairway, particularly, has lovely crunchy lettuces and delectable peppers in rosy reds and luminescent yellows. The prices are excellent on everything at Fairway, and, especially when they have a sale, at Zabar's too. People travel from all over the city to go to these stores, with a side trip to **H & H Bagels** down the block.

Perhaps because they are so close together, prices at all three stores are almost identical for both caviar and Scottish salmon. For the finest beluga, Zabar's charges $49 for 2 ounces and Fairway charges $44 for 1.75 ounces; Citarella charges $45 for 1.75 ounces. Compare these prices with Murray's—$54.95 for one ounce—and you see what a deal this is: less than half the price!

Looking at the salmon prices, all three markets charge about $24 a pound for their hand-sliced Scottish salmon, the richest-tasting, really smoky stuff, redolent with the aroma of the North Sea, but without the excessively salty taste found in cheaper smoked fish. Compare the prices here to Petrossian's for the same hand-sliced salmon: $54 a pound. Fairway offers what I think is a great bargain if you like the lighter-flavored salmon that tastes more like sushi: their own smoked, hand-cut Eastern salmon, similar to the Eastern salmon Murray's sells for $36 a pound—Murray's likes it better than the drier Scottish salmon and, in fact, charges $8 a pound more. At Fairway, the Eastern salmon goes for $16 a pound—and a pound of this scrumptious stuff can make canapés for at least a dozen hungry guests.

COFFEES

Check out the coffee specials at **Porto Rico Importing Company.** The everyday prices are about the same as "gourmet" coffee in the Stop and Shop, maybe a little less—$5.99 and $6.29 per pound—but the selections are sumptuous: Nairobi blend (half French Colombian, half Kenya AA), Budapest blend (half French Colombian, half Colombian supremo), Turkish blend (half Vienna Colombian, quarter Costa Rican, quarter Ethiopian). Plus the real Jamaican Blue Mountain from the Wellingford Estate (so there!) at $40 a pound, and dozens more. But every Thursday afternoon, they choose one of their regular varieties to sell for the next week at significantly less: $3.99 or $4.99 a pound. They also have water-process decaf in sixty-seven—yes, that's right—different roasts and flavors, including really unappealing ones like Pumpkin Spice and Egg Nog. They also ship: Give them a call at 800-453-5908, and they'll fax you a list of all their coffees and prices.

LIQUOR AND WINE SHOPS

The real cheapskate millionaires forsake **Sherry-Lehmann,** and seem to gravitate toward **Garnet Liquors** at 929 Lexington. I knew this even before I asked Paul Zimmerman, who writes about football for *Sports Illustrated* and in his spare time is a well-educated oenophile, for the best place for would-be cheapskate millionaires to shop. "Garnet," he said immediately, and **Grand Liquors** in Astoria, Queens. "They all have the same wines," he said dismissively, "but the same wines are cheaper there. And the sparkling wines are particularly good."

Perhaps the wines may look the same to him, but to me they're pretty advanced. Garnet often runs a half-page ad in the Wednesday *New York Times* Dining Out section, listing what looks like about one hundred wines, ports, and champagnes and their vastly varying prices. How to know if the '96 Revillon St. Armour for $9.99 is really twice as good as the Georges Duboeuf Beaujolais? And what's the difference between the Pul-Mont Folatière for $47 and the plain old Pul-Mont for $25.99? And would I look like the piker I am if I served imported "champagne alternative" Grandin Brut for $5.99? Or should I splurge and pop for the Mumm's Cordon Rouge at $22.99?

Ask the experts.

Mary Mulligan, America's only woman Master of Wine—and one of only eighteen in America—wrote *Wine for Dummies* in the popular series of books. She is blunt: "A lot of wine out there is just crap." If you don't know what you're doing, she adds, stay away from California wines and concentrate on the French and Italian "second growth" labels. Stay away from the "hot properties"—famous estates like Mouton Rothschild—which can run a bottle up to $100 and more. Go for "Le Petit Mouton" instead. These secondary vineyards still won't be cheap, she explained. They might cost $30 or $35, but that's a lot less than $90 or $100. "A way *not* to be wise is to buy wines that are highly rated by Robert Parker and the *Wine Spectator*," she said. "I have no problem with these critics, but if they rate a wine 92 or above, the wine quickly sells out, the price goes up, and the price for the next vintage goes up."

Not only are secondary vineyards cheaper, but then there's another category to look for—"wines with a story" that give the party giver something to chat about with his or her friends. If these friends are millionaires, they're not going to be impressed with a mere Rothschild anyway. Ask the wine merchant what has a fascinating story, suggests Ms. Mulligan. "Was it made by the first black-owned winery in South Africa? Was it made exclusively by women? Was it made from some grape that was extinct but the producers revived it?" she continued. "If there's a story, you'll never be embarrassed by the wine."

Ms. Mulligan gave the following guarded recommendations to

cheapskate wine shoppers: Garnet Liquors and its sister store, **Gotham Wines and Liquors.** ("At Garnet, there's no service—try to go in the middle of the day—but at least you know you're getting the lowest prices," she said.) For low-low-end wines, even boxed wines, super-cheap, she suggested **Pop's,** in Island Park, New York. The store delivers to Manhattan twice a week and offers volume discounts. Not only that, but the staff is knowledgeable, she said, and will help you choose. She also mentioned **Astor Wine and Spirits** as being "great for help and advice"; **Nancy's** for consulting about which wine to serve with which food; **Crossroads Liquors** for German, Spanish, and Italian wines, and the fairly new **Chelsea Wine Vault** at the Chelsea Market.

Joshua Wesson, who with his partner Richard Marmet started **Best Cellars,** a new concept in cheap wines, agrees in principle with Ms. Mulligan: Don't overextend yourself trying to grab a big-name label. Buyers who are looking to serve an inexpensive wine and not make fools of themselves had better stay away from the fancy names, he said. And generally, they should eschew what he called "the kings of wines": the French Bordeaux and Burgundies. "Bordeaux at the low end are iffy," he says, "and Burgundies are the most iffy." Without "going around and tasting hundreds of wines—you'd have to taste so many—just wandering into the neighborhood Safeway or asking the clerk at the corner liquor shop and grabbing a $7 Bordeaux is a low-odds proposition," he continues.

Besides the Bordeaux and Burgundies, Mr. Wesson advises you to stay away from:

California Cabernets ("CalCabs" to the cognoscenti)
Pinot Noir from anywhere
Barrel-fermented Chardonnays
Wines made from viogniers, "the hot white grape."

These wines take a fair amount of care to produce well, and therefore, the good ones tend to be a lot more than $10 a bottle.

Instead, you'd be safer sticking to these wines:

Shiraz and shiraz blends from Australia. Most reliable makers:
    Rosemont and Lindeman's
Merlots from Chile. Montes and Veramonte

Malbecs from Argentina. Trumpeter and Trapiche

Sauvignon Blanc from California and Washington State. Buena Vista from California; Hoge from Washington

Semillon-Chardonnay blends ("Sem-Chards") from anywhere. Penfold's from Australia; Columbia Crest from Washington State

Sparking wines: Cavas from Spain. "As good a methode champagnoise as you're going to get"; Cristallino and Marques de Gelida

Dessert wines: Moscato d'Astis, as long as it is no more than two years old. "Less fizzy, less sweet, and a higher-quality grape than Asti Spumante. A whole different ballgame, much more refined—a grown-up version." Two makers are Bera and Icardi from Italy. Tasting a Moscato d'Asti for the first time, Mr. Wesson says, "is almost always a revelatory experience: It tastes like fresh peaches or apricots."

Tawny Ports from Australia. Yalumbo and Penfold's

Voicing an opinion that is contrary to popular belief, Mr. Wesson counsels value-fixated consumers to look for more recent vintages. Only 10 percent of the wine bottles in the world get better as they age, he says—the ones you don't want to (I won't say "can't") afford. "That means that 90 percent don't get better," he chuckles, "and many get worse." These lower-priced wines—the ones listed as the Young Reliables—should be drunk fresh and juicy. "We've been caught up in the English notion that old and faded is better than young and juicy," he says. The cheaper wines, like the ones he sells, are "everyday wines meant to be consumed every day; they are vivacious, energetic—and that only depreciates with time."

Buy Shirazes, Merlots, Malbecs, Sauvignons Blancs when they are no more than three years old. In fact, Mr. Wesson says, if you have a choice between a two-year-old and a three-year-old . . . pick the two-year-old.

His advice will help you when you're in the discount wine shops all over the city, the best of which are listed at the end of this chapter. There, the sales staff is busy ringing up bottles at the cash register and taking down delivery orders over the telephone. Take Mr. Wesson's list with you.

Or you can just go to **Best Cellars,** near the corner of 86th Street and Lexington Avenue, where Mr. Wesson and Mr. Marmet have set up a wine shop with a shtick—every wine is under $10—and read the signs. Written by Mr. Wesson himself, they read as if the guy who writes J. Peterman's catalogue has taken to composing odes to the grape. The prose verges on parody, but is extremely entertaining and may even be educational.

Here are a few examples. Of one $6.99 Chianti, he writes: "Crafted by the small Tuscan town of Conte Dante Santoni, the wine is a guileless palate pleaser made to flatter just about any tomato dish it's paired with. Great with red-sauced pasta, pizza, baked ziti, calzone . . . even ketchupped burgers. F.Y.I. A Sun-Dried's Best Friend." Of a French Côtes du Rhone that costs $8.99, he writes: "A superhero of a black cherry–flavored gamay-fed red. Under the right circumstances, say, in a glass, next to some roast duck—Domaine du Pavillon Côte Roannaise just might convince you it cost double the price—Now that's our kind of wine!" (Amen!) The signs are full of bad puns ("Call out the Reservas," says one) but the advice is sound. For a Domaine St. Luc 1996, the owner proclaims: "The southern Rhone is chock full of neat little nooks and crannies where great, but relatively unknown wines—like this Coteaux du Tricastin—are made." Yet he warns the unwary that the wine may taste "a tad spicy on the glass (and we mean cracked black pepper spicy)." All this education, and a bottle of wine too, for $8.99.

Best Cellars also has whites: a "silky" Australian Chardonnay (tasting of "perfectly ripe fruit—melon, pineapple, pear, mango, mixed with a deft touch of sweet vanilla oak"), some petit Chablis (which smacks of "green apples, pears, and a hint of grapefruit"), a Jaffelin Rully, a tawny port in a cool-looking bottle for $8.99. The store also offers a few champagnes, cognacs, and special spirits—none of them for under $10—along with glasses and corkscrews.

Although neither of the owners is there very often, the young staff seems both affable and knowledgeable. The handsome shop is arranged by taste and style, rather than type or country: Fizzy, Fresh ("Clean, Lipsmacking, Thirst Quenching"), Soft, Luscious, Juicy, Smooth, Big, and Sweet.

It's a perfect atmosphere for the last stop before your party!

🍎 Sources

FOOD SHOPS

Aphrodisia
264 Bleecker (between Sixth and
Seventh Avenues), 212-989-6440
Monday to Saturday, 11:30 A.M.–
7 P.M.; Sunday, noon–5:30 P.M.

Big Apple Meat Market
575 Ninth Avenue (at 42nd Street)
212-563-2555
Monday to Saturday, 7:30 A.M.–7 P.M.;
Sunday, 8 A.M.–5 P.M.

Central Fish Market
527 Ninth Avenue (at 39th Street)
212-279-2317
Monday to Friday, 8 A.M.–7:30 P.M.;
Saturday, 8 A.M.–5 P.M.

Cupcake Café
522 Ninth Avenue (at 39th Street)
212-465-1530
Monday to Friday, 7 A.M.–6 P.M.;
Saturday, 8 A.M.–6 P.M.;
Sunday 9 A.M.–5 P.M.

East Village Cheese
40 Third Avenue (at 10th Street)
212-477-2601
Monday to Friday, 8:30 A.M.–6:30 P.M.;
Saturday, Sunday, 8 A.M.–6 P.M.

Esposito and Sons
500 Ninth Avenue (at 38th Street)
212-279-3298
Monday to Saturday, 8 A.M.–7:30 P.M.;
closed Sundays

Gourmet Garage
453 Broome Street (at Mercer Street)
212-941-5850
7 A.M.–9 P.M., seven days a week
Check the telephone book for other
locations.

H & H Bagels
2239 Broadway (at 80th Street)
212-595-8003
Open 24 hours, seven days a week

**International Grocery and
Meat Market**
529 Ninth Avenue (at 39th Street)
212-279-5514
Monday to Saturday, 8 A.M.–6 P.M.;
closed Sundays

Manganaro's
488 Ninth Avenue (at 38th Street)
212-563-5331
Monday to Friday, 8 A.M.–7 P.M.;
Saturday, 9 A.M.–7 P.M.; Saturday,
11 A.M.–5 P.M. (winter only)

Michaels and Sons Meat Market
516 Ninth Avenue (between 38th and
39th Streets), 212-279-2324
Closed Sundays and Wednesdays;
other days, 10 A.M.–6:30 P.M.

Ninth Avenue Deli Grocery
609 Ninth Avenue (at 43rd Street)
212-582-1747
Open 24 hours, seven days a week

Porto Rico Importing Company
201 Bleecker Street (between Sixth
Avenue and MacDougal Street)
212-477-5421 or 800-453-5908
Monday to Saturday, 9 A.M.–9 P.M.;
Sundays, noon–7 P.M.

Russ & Daughters Appetizers
179 East Houston (at First Avenue)
212-475-4880
Monday to Saturday, 9 A.M.–7 P.M.;
Sunday 8 A.M.–5:30 P.M.

Stiles Farmers Market
569 Ninth Avenue (at 41st Street)
212-695-6213
9 A.M.–6:30 P.M., seven days a week

Supreme Macaroni Company
511 Ninth Avenue (at 39th Street)
212-564-8074
Monday to Friday, 12:30–3 P.M. and
5–10:30 P.M.; Saturday, 5–10:30 P.M.;
closed Sundays

FOR CAVIAR AND SALMON

Caviarteria
502 Park Avenue (at 59th Street)
212-759-7410
Monday to Thursday 9 A.M.–7 P.M.;
Friday, Saturday 9 A.M.–8 P.M.;
Sunday 11 A.M.–4 P.M.

Citarella
2135 Broadway (at West 75th Street)
212-874-0383
1313 Third Avenue (at East 75th Street)
212-874-0383
Monday to Saturday, 7 A.M.–9 P.M.;
Sunday, 9 A.M.–7 P.M.

Fairway Fruits and Vegetables
2127 Broadway (at 74th Street)
212-595-1888
Opens Monday at 7 A.M.; then open
24 hours a day until Sunday midnight

Murray's Sturgeon Shop
2429 Broadway (between 89th and
90th Streets), 212-724-2650
Sunday to Friday, 8 A.M.–7 P.M.;
Saturday, 8 A.M.–8 P.M.

Petrossian
182 West 58th Street, 212-245-2217
Monday to Saturday, 10 A.M.–9 P.M.;
Sunday, 10 A.M.–6 P.M.

Zabar's Deli and Gourmet Foods
2245 Broadway (at 80th Street)
212-787-2000
Monday to Friday, 8 A.M.–7:30 P.M.;
Saturday, 8 A.M.–8 P.M.;
Sunday, 9 A.M.–6 P.M.

WINE AND LIQUOR STORES

This list includes the wine shops named in the
chapter, plus a few other recommended neighborhood wine and spirit shops.

Acker Merrall & Condit
160 West 72nd Street, 212-787-1700
Monday to Saturday, 9 A.M.–10 P.M.
This shop bills itself as "America's oldest and
finest wine shop"—and the help has the attitude to back it up. But if you persevere in your
quest for the cheapest, most marvelous wines,
you may end up with a deal. At any time of
the year, Acker Merrall, as it is most often
called, has sale bins marked by red stickers.
Recently, the store offered a Canyon Road
Chardonnay ("with hints of pineapple") that
received an 85 from *Wine Spectator*. The bin
was empty—alas—probably because the wine
was only $7.99 a bottle. Everything is sort of
thrown in together, which makes it fun to
browse: a $16.99 bottle of 1997 Paolo Scav-
ino was next to a $599 bottle of 1982 St.
Emillion.

Astor Wine and Spirits
12 Astor Place (south of 8th Street and
Broadway), 212-674-7500
Monday to Saturday, 9 A.M.–9 P.M.;
closed Sundays

Best Cellars
1291 Lexington Avenue (at 87th Street)
212-426-4200
Monday to Thursday 10 A.M.–9 P.M.;
Friday, Saturday, 10 A.M.–10 P.M.
Every bottle of wine under $10, plus a few
more expensive cognacs and things. Free delivery in Manhattan on orders of twelve bottles
or more.

Chelsea Wine Vault
In the Chelsea Market (on Ninth Avenue
between 15th and 16th Streets)
212-462-4244 or 888-309-9463
Monday to Wednesday, Friday,
Saturday, 10 A.M.–8 P.M.; Thursday,
10 A.M.–10 P.M.; closed Sundays

Crossroads Liquors
55 West 14th Street (at Sixth Avenue)
212-924-3060
Monday to Saturday, 9 A.M.–9 P.M.;
closed Sundays
When I lived on Jane Street in the Village, this
was my neighborhood wine shop, and it's a
pretty special one. The shop mails out
"insider's" deals every so often. But it pays to
stop in; even the newspaper ads don't tell the
whole story, or give the best deals.

Garnet Liquors

929 Lexington Avenue (at 69th Street)
212-772-3211
Monday to Saturday, 9 A.M.–9 P.M.;
closed Sundays

This is where the wine cognoscenti like to buy. The ordinary stuff is ordered at a discount, but there are enough fancy bottles around to make sure they don't feel like they're slumming. The staff here is very helpful and will help you select something in your budget; there are plenty of wines here for under $10—and out of six bottles I tried here, four of them were good enough to order cases!

Gotham Wines and Liquors

2519 Broadway, 212-932-0990
Monday to Saturday, 9 A.M.–8:50 P.M.;
closed Sundays

Grand Liquors

30-05 31st Street, Astoria, Queens
718-728-2520
Monday to Thursday, 9 A.M.–9 P.M.;
Friday, Saturday, 9 A.M.–10 P.M.;
closed Sundays

K and D Fine Wines and Spirits

1366 Madison Avenue (at 96th Street)
212-289-1818
Monday to Saturday, 9 A.M.–9 P.M.;
closed Sundays

Home of the $3.99 bottle of La Francesca Pinot Grigio—I've served it at many a large party. And you get a 10 percent discount if you order a case!

Nancy's Wines

313 Columbus Avenue, 212-877-4040
Monday to Thursday, 10 A.M.–9 P.M.;
Friday, Saturday, 10 A.M.–10 P.M.;
closed Sundays

As their wine buyer, Nancy's has Willie Gluckstern, who wrote the book *Wine Avenger* and helped compile wine lists for more than two hundred restaurants. The store features what the manager called the largest selection of German wines, including Rieslings, in the world. Also check out the shop's more than 180 wines under $10, which are in stock all year round. Or browse the champagne collection, specializing in the smaller growers; for between $30 and $40, you can buy the prod-uct of a single small family—versus that of giant champagne factories like Moët. Deliveries are free in the neighborhood, with a sliding scale for the rest of the city. Ask for one of the Spingarn brothers, Evan or Jason, the co-managers. (Or ask for Nancy, the sole proprietor.) If you're interested in the harder stuff, Nancy's has a nonpareil collection of both saki and single-malt scotch.

Pop's Wines & Spirits

256 Long Beach Road, Island Park,
N.Y., 516-431-0025
Monday to Thursday, 8 A.M.–8 P.M.;
Friday, Saturday, 8 A.M.–9 P.M.;
closed Sundays

Ask for Victor. Deliveries to Manhattan twice a week.

Sherry-Lehmann

679 Madison Avenue (at 62nd Street)
212-838-7500
Monday to Saturday, 9 A.M.–7 P.M.;
closed Sundays

The most beautiful Toulouse-Lautrec tins for large orders and, despite their rather snobby image, some real bargains. Check out the Wednesday *New York Times* Dining Out section.

On the Town: Stepping Out to the Bars and Clubs

While fancy restaurants charge an astronomical amount for a full-scale dinner—often a disappointing affair presided over by some haughty potentate with a pad—New York City is packed with places for cheapskate millionaires to spend an evening surrounded by luxe, charm, and other well-dressed denizens of the metropolis. Just amble in, order a drink, and soak up that million-dollar atmosphere, for a (relative) pittance.

Bobby Short illuminates the Carlyle Hotel for a good chunk of the year, but it's hard to see him on the cheap. After the $50-per-person cover charge, it's all downhill—pocketbookwise—after that. But just across the hall, in one of the most charming bars in the city, great entertainers like Barbara Carroll and Peter Mintun sing or play their hearts out in **Bemelmans Bar**—for only a $10 cover.

The walls of Bemelmans are covered with charming murals by M. Bemelman himself, and there are little bowls on each table filled to the brim with whole macadamia nuts and other delicacies. The drinks cost $10, sure, but a bowl of those nuts could easily run to that much. And the atmosphere is delightful—and if you don't stay past 9:30 P.M., when the live entertainment begins, there is no cover charge.

But perhaps my favorite hangout at the Carlyle is the space called the **Gallery.** The walls are papered with some exotic Italian wallcovering, which in turn has been hand painted in a sprightly, vaguely Moorish motif. Now here is a place to come and watch the world pass by; as the waiter said, "You can sit here and watch them all: celebrities, politicians, presidents, and prime ministers." Last time I was there, a young woman in a large black velvet hat hailed me as I passed through. "Didn't I just see you in Palm Beach?" she asked. (All my life, I've wanted to be asked that question.) We chatted—although I never really found out who she thought I was.

Nevertheless, she had the right approach. She came in at about 6 P.M. and staked out the best corner table. She made friends with the aforementioned waiter. She ordered a $10 glass of wine. And she stuck around for hours, watching the crowd, hailing anyone she felt like. On a recent Friday night, the Gallery wasn't at all crowded, and there is seldom any pressure to move along.

Another thing I like about the Gallery is that it is open anytime you might want to go there, from ten in the morning to one in the morning, through breakfast, a delightful afternoon tea, and into the evening hours.

If you're looking for something a little jazzier, try **Patria** at 250 Park Avenue South in the Gramercy Park–Flatiron District. This bar and restaurant is hopping, with a surging, lively group around the elevated bar. The décor and food is Nuevo Latino, but even the biggest cheapskate can fit in here. Unlike **Life,** the current club-of-the-moment, Patria is not youth-snobbish or rude. Patria is welcoming, and the fact that the patrons are mostly young and dressed in black is not inhibiting to the smattering of an older hip crowd. This is a wonderful, happy, elegant place! The monster margaritas and Mojitos are $8 but well worth it, and you dawdle. Perhaps the best things here are the appetizers: They are served piled up in wrought-iron holders—and you can easily organize a meal. For $5, you can choose between the large platter of salsa with plantain chips, black beans and rice, coconut crunch rice, or the tostones with smoked chili mojo. If you're in the mood for a splurge, definitely try the oysters Rodriguez ($16—ouch!). Just about anything here is heavenly and scenic, especially the people.

If you're feeling jaded and you're looking for an entirely different experience, try the upstairs parlor at the **Firebird,** an amazing new restaurant in the Theater District that is patterned after prerevolutionary Russia. The downstairs is sumptuous—and highly touristic.

"We have Fabergé artifacts—no eggs—but we don't tell you which they are, for security reasons," says Oleg Orebchuk, who is decked out in the full-dress uniform of a Kuban Cossack officer and who will give anybody—even you—a free tour. He says he gives thirty or forty a day. And it's a hoot! The restaurant, decorated with original paintings by Leon Bakst and with Nijinksy's costume from *Firebird*, is definitely worth visiting. You might want to skip the dinner and head for the parlor upstairs, which allegedly has furniture from the czar's apartment. "Maybe not the *best* furniture from the czar's apartment," conceded Mr. Orebchuk in his thick accent. "But where else can you go and sit in real czar's furniture?"

Where else, indeed. The small parlor, with its bay window and its overstuffed charm, is a find, and although the four formal dining rooms were alive with activity downstairs, the parlor seemed calm—and the kind of place you could come with friends and sip decadent vodka to your heart's delight. A glass of Absolut vodka is just $6.50. But the best thing may be the caviar prices: An ounce of beluga is only $66—about half the price of most restaurants; sevruga is $29.50. The list of appetizers that can be served in the parlor is delightful, including fruitwood-smoked salmon for $13 and potato blini with marinated herring with crème fraiche and salmon roe for $12. If you want to feel like a cheapskate millionaire—pre-1917—check in here, and don't forget to ask Oleg for the tour! (But keep a straight face; he really takes it all quite seriously—or appears to.)

Oh, I forgot to mention there is usually a harpist or a classical guitarist playing, with no extra fee.

New York City is getting more and more exotic. Another new favorite of mine is the bar called **Fez** in the Time Café on Lafayette Street and its sister **Fez North** at Broadway and 84th Street. This is a soothing Moroccan-style lounge where you can sip your thick black coffee or drink your wine to your heart's content, sitting at carpet-covered banquettes, leaning on big brass cocktail tables. I've been to Casablanca, and this is definitely the closest you're going to get to it in the Big Apple. But like the other places I like, this is a place where you can come in the evening to be romantic—or just to read—and you won't be hassled by either waiters or patrons. (The opposite is true down in the basement, where the scene is chaotic and there is a $20 cover charge to listen to entertainers not yet on the cognoscenti's radar screen.) But this place has one of the cheapest

Diet Cokes in town—$1.75—as well as a martini for $6.25. The bar also features the Fez: Absolut Citron, Chambord, and fresh-squeezed lime juice, for $7. The Flying Carpet combines Stoli Razberi, Midori, and lime juice, with a cherry. When you're feeling blah, you can drop by and feel rich and romantic—what could be better?

If you're one of those millionaires who must be where the scene is, investigate **Moomba,** at 133 Seventh Avenue South, where the fashion crowd hangs out; even when they're not in residence, two beefy guys guard the velvet ropes at the front. They looked expectantly at me. "I'd like to come in," I said bravely. They were taken aback. "Oh, okay," said one, after a pause. (What is one *supposed* to say to gain entrance to these portals?) Inside, the place is perfectly normal, with the big item being the Moombapolitan, a drink modeled after the Cosmopolitan, that goes for $7. Why the guys at the door? I asked and was told they were needed for later—the *"fashionistas,"* said one of the owners, come in about half past eleven.

If you're the type whose idea of a great time is spotting Johnny Depp and Puff Daddy, head straight for the V.I.P. lounge at Life, a club on Bleecker Street. If the velvet ropes and the bouncers don't turn you off, the attitude of the staff will. And don't even think of showing up before midnight, or you'll *really* see some attitude. But if you pass muster, you can hang over a drink for $8, and you will have the satisfaction of knowing you are in the vortex of totally hip New York City.

When you've done the fashion scene and are ready for the neighborhood scene, try the **Rio Mar,** which is reminiscent of the old Greenwich Village low rent scene. But the place has what the scribblers of yore called "raffish charm": any millionaire could slum here with perfect aplomb. Rio Mar, at the Montmartresque corner of Ninth Avenue and Little West 12th Street, beckons, and its loud and happy chattiness spills out into the street. If you come between noon and 3 P.M., there are some interesting and cheap specials—cazuela de mariscos, a seafood platter including fries or rice and a salad, for $7. But it is at night that the place really hums. There are platters of peanuts in their shells on the bars and tapas such as mussels or warm octopus with paprika and olive oil for $4.75. Order a martini for $5.50 and a platter of octopus—or just nibble the peanuts—and see a lot more of the real New York than you would at the V.I.P. Lounge.

🍎 Sources

New York City is packed with places for cheapskate millionaires and their friends. Here are some of their favorites—from the homey neighborhood joint to the chic (but chilly) nightclub. Just because you might want to know, I added the price of an Absolut martini—and a Diet Coke.

BARS, CLUBS, AND NIGHT SPOTS

Astor Bar

316 Bowery (at Bleecker Street), 212-253-8644
Monday to Friday, 6 P.M.–2 A.M.; Saturday, Sunday, 6 P.M.–4 A.M.
Diet Coke, $1.75; martini, $7.50.

Bayamo

704 Broadway (between 4th Street and Washington Place), 212-475-5151
Monday to Thursday, Sunday, noon–midnight; Friday, Saturday, noon–1 A.M.
Live music on Tuesdays, and Thursdays; $12 minimum on band nights. Happy hour every day, 4 P.M.–7 P.M., with half-price margaritas, draft beer, and house wine.
Diet Coke, $1.75; margarita, $5 (not really a martini place).

Bemelmans Bar in the Carlyle Hotel

36 East 76th Street (between Madison and Park Avenues), 212-744-1600
Monday to Saturday, 11 A.M.–2 A.M.; closed Sundays
$10 cover per person after 9:30 P.M.
Diet Coke, $5; martini, $12.50.

Birdland

315 West 44th Street (between Eighth and Ninth Avenues), 212-581-3080
Monday to Thursday, 5 P.M.–midnight; Friday to Saturday, 5 P.M.–1 A.M.; closed Sundays
Happy hour with a big band orchestra playing 5 P.M. to 8 P.M. ($7 cover; $3 wine and beer). Southern cuisine and live music every night, usually jazz.
Diet Coke, $1.75; martini, $7.

Bleecker Street Bar

56 Bleecker Street (between Lafayette and Crosby Streets), 212-334-0244
Noon–4 A.M, seven days a week
Special on beer: 24 ounces is only $1 more than a pint (16 ounces).
Diet Coke, $1.75; martini, $6.50 for premium.

Café des Artistes

1 West 67th Street (between Columbus Avenue and Central Park West) 212-877-3500
Monday to Saturday, 5:30 P.M.–midnight; Sunday, 5:30–11 P.M.
Parlor room open for drinks only (not dinner); there's a wonderful tiny bar with dishes piled high with hard-boiled eggs and a great bartender.
Diet Coke, $4.50; martini, $8.

Cibar

56 Irving Place, 212-460-5656
Monday to Thursday, 5 P.M.–2 A.M.; Friday, 5 P.M.–3 A.M.; Saturday, 6 P.M.–3 A.M.; Sunday, 6 P.M.–2 A.M.
Known for their chocolate martini. Diet Coke, $5; martini, $10.

The Evelyn Lounge
380 Columbus Avenue, 212-724-5145
Monday to Friday, 4 P.M.–1 or 2 A.M.;
Saturday, Sunday, 6 P.M.–4 A.M.
Swanky, dark, sexy underground bar.
Diet Coke, $2; martini, $8.

Fez
380 Lafayette Street (between 4th Street
and Great Jones), 212-533-3000
Sunday to Thursday, 6 P.M.–2 A.M.;
Friday, Saturday, 6 P.M.–4 A.M.
Moroccan cocktail lounge plus live
music in the basement. Cover for
entrance into basement varies with the
featured musical attraction.
Diet Coke, $1.75; martini, $6.25.

Fez North
2330 Broadway (between 84th and
85th Streets), 212-579-5100
Sunday to Thursday, 6 P.M.–2 A.M.;
Friday, Saturday, 6 P.M.–4 A.M.
No entertainment. Prices same
as for Fez.

Firebird
365 West 46th Street (between Eighth
and Ninth Avenues), 212-586-0244
Sunday to Thursday, 5 P.M.–10 P.M.;
Friday, Saturday, 5 P.M.–11:30 P.M.
Amazing re-creation of pre-Revolution-
ary Russia—plus free tours by Oleg.
Diet Coke, $3.75; martini, $6.50.

Florent
69 Gansevoort Street (between
Washington and Green),
212-989-5779
Monday to Thursday, 9 A.M.–5 P.M.;
Friday, Sunday, open 24 hours
French diner; check it out at 3 A.M.
Diet Coke, $1.25; martini, $6.50.

The Gallery in the Carlyle Hotel
36 East 76th Street (between Madison
and Park Avenues)
Noon to midnight, seven days a week
Prices same as for Bemelmans.

Global 33
93 Second Avenue (at 5th Street),
212-477-8427
Sunday to Thursday, 5:30 P.M.–2 A.M.;
Friday, Saturday, 5:30 P.M.–3 A.M.
Opens at 5:30 P.M. for happy hour.
Tapas restaurant with a DJ.
Diet Coke, $1; martini, $7.50.

Knickerbocker Bar & Grill
33 University Place (between 9th and
10th Streets), 212-228-8490
Tuesday to Thursday, 11:45 A.M.–
1 A.M.; Friday, Saturday, 11:45 A.M.–
2 A.M.; Sunday, 11:45 A.M.–12 A.M.
Live music, Wednesday to Saturday at
9:45 P.M. Cover varies by musical
attraction; not always a cover.
Diet Coke, $2.50; martini, $6.25.

The Knitting Factory
74 Leonard Street (between Broadway
and Church), 212-219-3055
5 P.M.–2 A.M., seven days a week
Live music every night; show times
usually at 8 P.M., 9 P.M., and 11 P.M.,
seven days a week. Admission ranges
from $8 to $20 depending on the show.
Happy hour: 5 P.M.–6 P.M.—$2 off
drinks; 6 P.M.–7 P.M.—$1 off drinks.
Diet Coke, $3; martini, $7.

Lansky Lounge
104 Norfolk Street, 212-677-9489
Saturday to Thursday, 8 P.M.–4 A.M.;
closed Fridays
Cocktail bar from the Al Capone era;
weeknights feature different special
events like a swing dance night or a
wine-tasting night. This nightspot caters
to Orthodox Jews and is, therefore,
closed Friday nights.
Diet Coke, $3; martini, $8.

Life
158 Bleecker Street, 212-420-1999
All week long, "mostly 10 P.M.–5 A.M."
Diet Coke, $4; martini, $8.

Match

160 Mercer Street (between Prince and Houston), 212-343-0020
Restaurant: Monday to Thursday, Saturday, 11:30 A.M.–2 A.M.; Friday, Saturday, 11:30 A.M.–4 A.M.
Downstairs bar: Wednesday to Thursday, 6 P.M.–2 A.M.; Friday, Saturday, 6 P.M.–4 A.M.; closed Sundays and Mondays
Downstairs level of the restaurant is a bar area with a DJ on weekends and sometimes live entertainment.
Diet Coke, $3.50; martini, $8.

Moomba

133 Seventh Avenue South (between 10th and 11th Streets), 212-989-1414
6 P.M.–2 A.M., seven nights a week
Diet Coke, $3; martini, $12.

Morgan's Bar

237 Madison Avenue (at 37th Street) 212-726-7600
Monday, Tuesday, 5 P.M.–2 A.M.; Wednesday to Saturday, 5 P.M.–4 A.M.; Sunday, 6 P.M.–1 A.M.
Another of Ian Schrager's totally decorated hangouts. This one is preferred by the anti-chic and has a slightly calmer scene.
Diet Coke, $4; martini, $10.

Patria

250 Park Avenue South (at 20th Street) 212-777-6211
Monday to Thursday, 6 P.M.–11 P.M.; Friday, Saturday, 5:30 P.M.–midnight; Sunday, 5:30 P.M.–10:30 P.M.
Nuevo Latino.
Diet Coke $3.50; martini, $9 (but better for inventive cocktails and monster margaritas).

Pommes Frites

123 Second Avenue (between 7th and 8th Streets), 212-674-1234
11:30 A.M.–midnight, seven days a week

Serves only French fries and nonalcoholic drinks; limited seating.
Diet Coke, $1; French fries, $3, $4.25, and $5.50.

Pravda

281 Lafayette Street (between Prince and Houston), 212-226-4944
Monday to Thursday, 5 P.M.–3 A.M.; Friday, Saturday, 5 P.M.–4 A.M.; Sunday, 6 P.M.–3 A.M.
Swanky. Large and exotic drinks. They pride themselves on their house brands of vodka.
Diet Coke $2; vodkas, $6–$9.50; martini, $8.50.

Prohibition

503 Columbus Avenue (at 84th Street) 212-579-3100
Open at 5:30 P.M. every day; no set closing time
Diet Coke, $2; martini, $7.

Rio Mar

7 Ninth Avenue (at Little West 12th Street), 212-242-1623
Neighborhood Spanish restaurant; an occasional strolling guitarist.
Food and drink specials from noon to 3 P.M. daily.
Monday to Thursday, Sunday, noon–1 A.M.; Friday, Saturday, noon–2 A.M.
Diet Coke, $1.75; martini, $5.50.

The Room

144 Sullivan (between Prince and Houston), 212-477-2102
5 P.M.–4 A.M., seven days a week
Mostly undiscovered; no hard liquor.
Diet Coke, $2; pint of beer, $5; glass of wine, $6–$8.

Sweet & Vicious

5 Spring Street (between Elizabeth and Bowery), 212-334-7915
5 P.M.–4 A.M., seven days a week
Diet Coke, $2; martini, $7.

BEER BARS

Heartland Brewery

35 Union Square West (at 16th Street)
212-645-3400
Monday to Friday, noon–1 A.M.;
Saturday, noon–2 A.M.; Sunday,
11:30 A.M.–2 A.M.
Only serves their own signature brews,
along with buffalo burgers, chicken
wings, and things.
Diet Coke, $2.50 (refillable);
microbrews, $4.75–$5.35.

Swift

34 East 4th Street (between Lafayette
and Bowery), 212-227-9438
Noon–4 A.M., seven days a week
Irish pub, lots on tap; great any night of
the week but best Thursday, Friday, and
Saturday; DJ in the back room, which
has picnic-style tables good for big
groups.
Diet Coke, $2; microbrews, $4–$5.

DJ/DANCING

Orchard

200 Orchard Street, 212-673-5350
Tuesday to Saturday, 6 P.M.–4 A.M.;
Sunday, Monday, 6 P.M.–3 A.M.
In the newly hip Lower East Side. Go on
Friday or Saturday to see their funky DJ.
Diet Coke, $2; martini, $6.

Where Are the Chocolates on My Pillow? Hunting for Hotels and Other Cheap Places to Hang One's Hat

You've just arrived in New York City, and you don't want to impose on your friends. Stay here a little longer, and that instinct will vanish, but until it does, you want to find a cheap little place to stay. You just open the paper and figure you'll start calling and select the one that sounds nicest. Guess what? There aren't any. In New York City, there is no tourist center exactly like the one in London's Victoria Station, where visitors can show up and be offered a place for the night at a bargain price. This is New York, after all; this is no place for babies, for people who don't know their way around. There are no streets known for their bed and breakfast inns, where a weary traveler can be sure to find something. Nah! No way.

We make it tougher, even for the wealthy and would-be wealthy. But, my dear, there are ways. . . . Luckily for you, a number of smaller "boutique" hotels—with a wide variation in services, from fancy-neighborhood-bathroom-down-the-hall to seriously chic—are starting to open, at still bargain prices.

Then there is the strategy outlined below, in which a well-to-do retired hotelier explains exactly how to bargain for a room for $100 a night—at the Plaza or some other ritzy palace. And then, hidden away, there are hundreds of bed and breakfast rooms, many of them in private houses. I list the services where you can find them. And lastly, there are "informal" (read: "illegal") sublets all over the place.

Then there are tenants in big apartments, who are probably paying next to nothing in rent because their apartments are rent-regulated, who will give you a room for a fee. These exist—I know of several—but they will not be listed in this book, because if the managing agent of the building found out, these people would be booted out unceremoniously. But I'm just letting you know: These "arrangements" do exist. You find them by asking around at work or among your friends and relations.

First of all, you can try to get a deal at a big-name hotel.

TO STAY AT A LANDMARK HOTEL, YOU GOTTA HAVE CHUTZPAH

Almost all the city's hotels have the same types of specials, which usually include room amenities like minibars and terry cloth robes, complimentary use of the health club, special weekend rates, shuttle service to the Theater District and Wall Street, and no charge for kids under a certain age to stay in their parents' room.

The trick is to get a *real* deal from a great hotel, and in New York City, this isn't easy. To find out how to get such a deal, I went to Bernard Goldberg, the king of the boutique hotels. In Manhattan, there is an increasing number of small, elegant hotels, often in posh residential neighborhoods, that are priced below the famous landmarks like the Plaza. Some of them are great deals, especially if they're still new on the scene. But I wanted Mr. Goldberg to give us all the benefit of his expertise on how to get deals from even the big boys: the Plaza, the St. Moritz, and the Pierre.

Here's how he'd do it if he didn't already have one of the most stupendous apartments in the city: an aerie overlooking Central Park, with a grand piano in his living room.

"First," he said, "you gotta be adventurous—if you don't have nerve, it won't work. You wait until the afternoon of the day you want to check in. Let's say it's a $300 room, chic and wonderful. If you call the day before, you'll pay $300. No, you call the hotel at four that afternoon—they always have cancellations. Offer them one-third."

Wouldn't it be better to go there in person? "Yes. Go there. Ask 'Do you have any cancellations?' Ask for a single room. Say 'This is my limit: $100.' "

An unsold room is unsold forever (for that night), he explained. "They will never recoup." The hotels can't afford to advertise that they will do this, Mr. Goldberg continued. "That will make them look like a cheap hotel." He paused. "You will get the room for $100."

Now there are naturally some caveats, which we worked out. You have to look very presentable: Neat and clean are the operative words. And you have to be charming without being a phony or too glib. Don't even think of being sexy. Just be friendly and direct. This all depends on you. "You'll talk to the desk clerk," said Mr. Goldberg. "You tell them right up front you don't have the money. Remember—you're not dealing with the owner, and you don't want to deal with the owner. The desk clerks have the authority, believe me, and you've got to remember they don't have much money, either. And if you handle yourself correctly, they'll be sympathetic. Make sure you tell them you don't need a fancy room—even a back room would do. The way you should start is by saying 'I'll take your worst room, but here's what I've got: $100.'

"I would say it's a rare instance when you're not accommodated by a desk clerk—they'll come up with something. Just be nice. Say 'I've always loved (or read about) this hotel,'" he said. "You know how to do it."

If you time it right, you can wangle staying for a week or maybe whatever time you need. Sunday night is the best night to arrive, Mr. Goldberg said. "You know they'll be busy Thursday, Friday, and Saturday nights. So come Sunday and once you've nailed down one night, offer to pay a little more per night—say, $125—for the whole week."

So try that at your dream hotel. I dare you!

CHEAP BOUTIQUE HOTELS FIT FOR A (CHEAPSKATE) MILLIONAIRE

Here's the great news: For under $100, you can get a terrific hotel room in almost any quadrant of the city: the Upper East Side, the Upper West Side, the Theater District, and Greenwich Village. You can even stay in a wonderful hotel at 111th Street and Broadway, right near Columbia University.

Ian Schrager really began the concept of the inexpensive boutique hotel in New York City with his Paramount Hotel. At one time, youngish aspiring musicians, photographers, and models would check in for about $125. No more! The Paramount is now $220. The same with the Wales, Mr. Goldberg's former hotel. When he had it, it was $150; now it, too, is $220.

But don't worry. I've unearthed a series of new cheap but elegant small hotels, scattered through New York.

Let's start on the Upper West Side.

On the peaceful block of West 88th Street between West End Avenue and Riverside Drive is the **Hotel Riverside.** With its spanking-new emerald green canopy and its freshly gilded door surround, this small hotel is the quintessential tourist hotel. Some of the rooms are tiny with a double bed and not much else, but there are plenty that hold two double beds and a simple refinished pine desk and chair. The hotel has just been renovated, and there is new beige carpeting and boringly attractive wallpaper everywhere, including the gleaming, well-maintained corridors. Each room has a luxurious bath—more luxurious than the room, in fact, with its deep red granite counter, almond fixtures, and tiled-to-the-ceiling walls. There is also a modern TV hooked up to cable, and each room has its own thermostat. Basically, all of the rooms are the same price: $100 to $130, depending on the season. This is a good deal. However, check the Internet at www.hoteldiscounts.com for a slightly better deal. In the winter, when the retail price is $100, the Web offers the room for $95.95—not an enormous discount, but it gets one thinking. What about trying Mr. Goldberg's strategy: Offer the deskman, Barry, $75 a night for a week's stay. (Barry said he might negotiate a longer-term stay but that something like a month "isn't encouraged." Although Barry didn't mention it, the Riverside also has rooms with a shared bath, for $69.95. Once you find your own apartment, this might be a great place to stash the in-laws!

Before we go over to the East Side and visit the best deal of all, let's work our way downtown on the West Side.

In the Theater District, there are four small hotels I can recommend. The first is **The Mayfair,** where you can eat at a very pleasant restaurant—and get a very attractive double room with vaguely Biedermeier touches for $130, with bath, of course. This place, although a bit more expensive, more than one-ups the Riverside. First, it has a better location, on West 49th Street a few blocks from the

TKTS booth, which sells Broadway and off-Broadway show tickets for that night at half price. And second, it has a much better lobby, full of glass-topped round tables and comfortable tapestry-covered tufted easy chairs. Besides fresh lilies in a Canton blue china vase, the lobby features completely paneled refinished walls, recessed lights, and marble floors—you could ask a Rockefeller to pick you up here. The bathrooms in the rooms are also a step up: green marble from head to foot, with your own hair dryer.

Then, it's down to one of the prettiest blocks in Greenwich Village: 11th Street between Fifth and Sixth Avenues, where you will find the **Larchmont Hotel.** There, what had been an SRO (single-room occupancy) hotel has now been transformed to a "European style" inn: read "no private bathrooms." But again, the lobby is luscious, done over with a brownstone feel: tufted leather couches and Edwardian chairs and a classy "concierge" behind the attractive desk. Alas! When you get off the elevator at your floor, it still has a little of the old SRO flavor. They went for the cheap paint job; just slap it on over the old landlord-favored "orange peel finish" (too large a nap on the paint roller) and lots of doors opening off a narrow hallway. Hey, but who cares? There's a continental breakfast served in the downstairs café—open only to hotel guests—and a double room costs only $85 or $90. And the rooms are handsome: They've got a touch of the Raj look, with reproductions of antique prints of tigers and other beasts, flower-printed quilted bedspreads, and bamboo-rattan headboards and chests of drawers. Some of the rooms are pretty good-sized, too. The bathrooms are similar to those in a London bed and breakfast; clean but not particularly inviting. The best thing is the neighborhood: It's really quite posh.

But the best of the cheap hotels is **The Bentley,** although not everyone wants to be on East 62nd Street and York Avenue. (The 62nd part is great; the York is a teensy bit east for easy tromping and shopping.) But the hotel itself—and the magnificent rooms—are more than worth a $5 cab ride to get to the subway, or to Bloomingdale's. For a ridiculously low price, you can stay in a three-and-a-half-star hotel. And this hotel is super-chic. Okay, so maybe it's an Ian Schrager knockoff; it still has its own look—and the rooms are far better than those at any of Schrager's once-cheap city hotels.

Take Room 1004, for instance. Wow! This room is vast, with views of the East River and York Avenue from four enormous picture windows, with great beige Roman shades. You could have a party in here, and according to the hip African American bellhop, Sam (get him if you can), many have. "When they check in, they say they're one person," said Sam. "But when they leave, you see five or six of them." Ah, well. Sam showed me a suite, too, which wasn't anywhere near as appealing. But if you have a couple of kids, or friends, it might work better. The couch in the "living room" folds out to a double bed. But as Sam says: Ask for a room with 04 on the end. That's the corner, but any of the rooms ending in 01, 02, or 03 have river views.

A few years ago, The Bentley was an office building, built in the 1960s to house the National Urban League. I don't know what it was like as offices, but it sure rocks as a hostelry. The lobby is splendid, with a three-inch white-marble counter, mica hanging lamps, and marble floors inset with Deco rugs, with the hotel's signature nickel circles stuck in. The circles appear on the elevator walls and on some of the furniture; the powder room off the lobby has a nifty zebra-wood sink vanity, with a dozen of those circles the size of 50-cent pieces glued to the front of it. There are tall vases of flowers every-where, and outside each room, a burnished steel vase is hung next to the door, and filled with orchids.

Okay, okay, you say, what's the price for all this luxe? That's the best thing. This hotel currently costs $105 a night (even for room 1004) and $170 for the suite. And you may be able to get it for less: The hotel discounts site on the Web (mentioned below) is offering rooms here for $99.95. Grab it while you can! The Bentley is part of a chain with five other boutique hotels scattered about town—addresses and names below—and right now, they're all offering rooms for less than $100. This is a rave.

DEALS OVER THE NET

Every day, there is a new Web site devoted to cheap travel. And most of them are just advertiser-driven baloney. However, there are two sites I've found that are updated fairly often and are worth a search. The first one, mentioned above, is www.hoteldiscounts.com. This site gives the navigator dozens of choices in the low- to moderate-priced category. The descriptions of the hotels are little more than blandly written ads, but the maps of the neighborhoods surrounding these hotels are pretty useful, especially if you have some grasp of the city. The real advantage of this site is that the prices seem to be *current!* You supply the dates you want, and they will actually book the hotel at those prices immediately.

Another interesting site—just because the descriptions of the places are so much better—is Fodor's hotel site: www.fodors.com. You won't learn much about the prices—vague descriptions like "Under $135" turned out in some cases to be totally wrong. One such description was disproved by a telephone call. The hotel was actually $265 a night, according to the reservations clerk. But no matter—the descriptions are fun. Read them. Lobbies are "bland," staffs are "harried," and rooms are "little more than dormitory-style cells." After you check this site out and decide which ones to try, go to the discount hotels site and see if you can make a match. Although I detected no errors with the latter site, it might be wise to first call the hotel yourself and see what the retail rate is—and proceed accordingly.

THE BED AND BREAKFAST SERVICES

In New York City, the cheapskate millionaire in the city for a short respite from endless croquet matches might like to stay at a short-term rental apartment in a fancy neighborhood—or, if he or she wants to recreate a European experience, to stay in a bed and breakfast.

Abode Ltd. offers "furnished apartments for short-term stays." Shelli Leifer, who runs the service, says out-of-towners can stay a minimum of four nights all the way up to a couple of months. The firm usually has thirty to thirty-five apartments available all over town. Asked to give a few examples, she said she had apartments on West 77th Street, East 93rd Street just off Fifth Avenue, 31st Street between Park and Lexington, and throughout the West Village.

Sometimes the apartments are in brownstone apartments that had previously been rented out on a yearly basis. But the tenants move out, Ms. Leifer explained, and the landlord decides to completely renovate with a fully equipped new kitchen and bath—and to offer the apartment on a much shorter-term basis. Do the landlords do it because they can make more money? "Whatever their reason is, I don't get into it," she said primly.

Adobe also has apartments in twenty-four-hour-doormen buildings: anything from a studio to a three-bedroom with a brace of baths. All are no smoking allowed. Prices for the studios begin at $135 a night and range to about $400 a night for the three-bedroom, two-bath units.

At the **Bed & Breakfast Network of New York,** Leslie Goldberg said he could find accommodations for someone who wants to stay a night or a couple of months. "Somebody might be coming into town for a movie project, or maybe a couple from the suburbs might be coming in for the weekend to see a Broadway show." There is a choice of two hundred locations, and there are two different categories: hosted and unhosted.

Mr. Goldberg wants to make it perfectly clear. "We don't help everybody," he said. "Those who want something very, very inexpensive should go to the YWCA or the YMCA."

If you can make it past the initial interrogation, the single rooms rent for $70 to $90 a night and range from $1,350 to $1,800 a month. (For $1,350, you'll get "spartan" quarters, he said, and will probably share a bath.) Although the Network features rooms scattered around Manhattan, there aren't any above 103rd Street. But Mr. Goldberg does offer some in historic Brooklyn brownstones no more than a fifteen-minute subway ride to Wall Street.

Both services offer some apartments or rooms in co-op buildings, which raises an interesting question: Don't some co-op boards object to renting out rooms on a nightly or monthly basis?

"That's between the host and the buildings," Mr. Goldberg said. "There have been eight or ten instances over the years—we've been in business since 1986—where the situation became uncomfortable, and the host felt the arrangement threatened his status in the co-op. If someone feels threatened, I would recommend they not do it."

Ms. Leifer had another approach. In buildings where there is a doorman—who might presumably tell the board—"We tell our guests there is a doorman," she said, "and that it's customary to tip him."

The doormen have not been a problem, she concluded.

CHANGING YOUR ROOM ONCE YOU FIND ONE

Say you've just gotten a great deal at The Bentley or one of the wonderful new small hotels. You've just seen your room, and it doesn't quite measure up: It's dark and overlooks an airshaft. You, of course, want—and deserve—a large room with the best views the place has to offer. Well, unless the whole hotel is booked up, you've got to have another one! Don't worry, this isn't as hard as getting a $100 deal at the Plaza.

Just tell the bellman you're not happy with the room. Whatever you do, don't unpack. He probably won't be surprised. These things happen all the time. The best thing to do is to immediately head back down to the front desk, bellman in tow. When both of you come up to the desk, you'll stick out. All the incoming guests will be watching to see how you're treated.

The key thing here is to be friendly, but firm: "I'm terribly sorry, but I'm not happy with my room and I'd like to look at another one." Circumstances permitting, the clerk will just hand the bellman another key. But these front desk clerks seem to be getting tougher. The clerk may say, without looking up, something like: "That's the best we can give you tonight; check back tomorrow." That may or may not be an option. Just politely, with a smile, ask to speak to the manager. To avoid that kind of conference, the clerk may give you a different key or you may have to talk to the manager. If the manager appears, be as charming as you can. "My best friend loves this hotel, and she (or he) always stays here whenever she's in town. She says the rooms are just lovely, but I've been just given . . . well, kind of an unattractive one. Surely you have something better?" Look earnest. At this point, you'll almost certainly get a better room, or the manager will explain why you can't change. If at this point, he promises you a better one the next day, accept his promise graciously—and then hold him to it. I've never known a manager not to keep his word on something like this.

☙ SOURCES

THE PICK OF THE SMALL HOTELS

The Bentley
500 East 62nd Street, 212-644-6000
One of the greatest deals of all: a superb Art Deco–influenced, brand new hotel—with huge rooms that start at $105. Ask for Room 1004, but if you can't get it, there are plenty of other nice ones. If this hotel is full, try its sister hotels: Ameritania Hotel (230 West 54th Street, 247-5000), Amsterdam Court (226 West 50th Street, 459-1000), The Moderne (243 West 55th Street, 397-6767), the East Side Inn (201 East 24th Street, 696-3800), or Hotel Ellington (610 West 111th Street, 864-7500).

Broadway Inn Bed & Breakfast
264 West 46th Street (between Broadway and Eighth Avenue)
212-997-9200 or 800-826-6300

If you want an inexpensive B & B in the heart of the Theater District, check out this simple forty-room hotel, where a double room with a private bath goes for $115; a suite with a fold-out sofa and kitchenette is $195.

Chelsea Inn
46 West 17th Street (between Fifth and Sixth Avenues), 212-645-8989
This smallish inn in the heart of historic Chelsea is headquartered in an old brownstone, and the rooms look like something you'd find in a shingled cottage on Cape Cod. Room with shared bath, $109–$119; studio with bath, $139–$149; suite with bath, $169–$179.

Hotel Riverside
350 West 88th Street (near Riverside Drive), 212-724-6100
Double rooms usually cost $110; at press time, the special rate was $75 a night.

Larchmont Hotel
27 West 11th Street (between Fifth and Sixth Avenues), 212-989-9333
Double rooms range from $90 to $109.

Malibu Studios
2688 Broadway (at 103rd Street) 212-222-2954 or 800-647-2227
This neighborhood is changing fast; it's close to Columbia University with its student scene, and there are ethnic restaurants galore. The Malibu is also one of the cheapest hotels in the city: $89 for a double room from January through March, and $99 for the rest of the year. The rooms come with a private bath, and feature a TV and a desk.

The Mayfair
242 West 49th Street (between Eighth Avenue and Broadway), 212-586-0300 or 800-556-2932
Rooms start at $110 per night in the winter and go up to $200.

The Milburn
242 West 76th Street, 212-362-1006 or 800-833-9622
If you're an opera buff, this fifty-room, fifty-suite hotel might be up your alley; it's near Lincoln Center. This is a fun place: The lobby is a Bavarian fantasy, and the hotel offers suites with kitchenettes, complete with microwave and coffeemaker. In February, the double rooms are $129 and suites and one-bedrooms are $149. The rates jump March 1st through June: Double rooms are then $155; one-bedroom suites are bumped to $175. The suites come with queen-sized sofa beds.

Washington Square Hotel
103 Waverly Place (between Sixth Avenue and MacDougal) 212-777-9515 or 800-222-0418
You'll feel as if you just stepped into a Henry James novella. This hotel, at the northwest corner of Washington Square Park, has that beeswax-and-turpentine smell of highly polished antique furniture. The staff is attentive, but alas, the rooms are small. And some don't even have windows! But the location couldn't be better—especially if you love Greenwich Village—and there's a good restaurant downstairs, a rarity in small hotels. Rates are reasonable: Double rooms are $129. They come with a private bath, phone, TV, and, for your diamonds, your own safe.

BED-AND-BREAKFAST AND APARTMENT SERVICES

Abode Ltd.
212-472-2000; outside the New York–Connecticut–New Jersey–Pennsylvania area: 800-835-8880
Mailing address: P. O. Box 20022, New York, NY 10021
Web site: www.abodenyc.com
Specializes in furnished apartments. Information available by phone weekdays between 9 A.M. and 5 P.M., and the answering machine is left on 24 hours a day.

Bed & Breakfast Network of New York

130 Barrow Street, 212-645-8134
Mailing address: 134 West 32nd Street,
Room 602, New York, NY 10001
Information available by phone Monday
through Sunday from 8:30 A.M. to 11 A.M.
and 1:30 P.M. to 5 P.M.

City Lights Bed and Breakfast Ltd.

212-737-7049
Mailing address: P. O. Box 20355,
New York, NY 10021
Information available by phone Monday
through Friday from 9 A.M. to 5 P.M., and Saturday from 9 A.M. to noon.

Location, Location, Location: How to Find Your Dream Bargain Apartment in a Market As Hot As a Street Vendor's Grill

In New York City, the number one recreational activity is not sex or ice hockey or going to the movies. It's *talking about real estate.* You can't avoid it: passing people on the street ("It's a walk-up, but I told the agent . . ."); crushed against people on the subway ("The bathroom's okaaaay, but I told the landlord he'd have to . . ."); in the elevator ("So if I buy the one-bedroom next door, I can break through . . ."); and most treacherously, at cocktail parties ("Say, is it really true you write about real estate?"). You'd think the population, which, as far as I know, has been nattering about real estate since the market's last high, at the end of the 1980s, would get sick of it.

So how does a millionaire-on-the-move find his or her dream pad without paying out a substantial portion of those coupons so lovingly clipped every month? How does one afford a delicious pied-à-terre without Mummy threatening to disinherit? It's easy—but only if you know how.

The goal is to find an apartment that looks like a lot more money than you're paying, in rent or monthly mortgage checks.

Each person looking for a dream apartment will approach this in a slightly different way, but on Sunday morning, or Saturday night, or whenever you can find it, the first priority activity is reading the *New York Times* real estate classifieds.

Reading these advertisements is an acquired skill, and one couple hunting for a rare condominium two-bedroom once told me they had invented a game. First, he would read *her* the ad, without the price. She would try to guess the price. Then she would read *him* the next ad, and he'd try to guess the price. At the end of six months of looking, they were able to get within $5,000 or $10,000 of the asking price. Not only that, but by the time they actually bought a place, they were able to guess the exact building!

So that *you* won't have to wait that long to find something, here is The Insider's Guide to Reading the Classifieds.

A GLOSSARY OF COMMON PHRASES USED IN REAL ESTATE ADVERTISEMENTS (FOR EITHER RENT OR SALE)

Opening Lines

Cozy. Lilliputian. Don't even think of a double bed—or a three-seater couch. Think hot plate. Be ready to store your clothes back home with Mom.

Charming. See above.

Perfect pied-à-terre. See above.

Great starter apartment. See above.

Feels like a house. If it's cheap, it's probably one of those awful duplexes carved out of a tenement in the 1970s, with tiny sheetrocked rooms and a wobbly circular iron staircase.

Freshly painted. The agent can't find anything else to say.

Hardwood floors. See above.

Nu windows. See above.

Great investment. They've tried and failed to sell it to anyone who would actually *live* in it.

Wreck. Believe it.

Diamond in the rough; create your masterpiece; looking for Prince Charming; Cinderella special. Wreck.

Needs TLC. Probably less than "wreck," but worse than "needs cosmetics."

Garage. Means it's postwar, probably "plain vanilla": white bricks. (Check out how much they'll sock you for the garage rent.)

Owner says sell. This is its fourth year on the market. (Hint: There's a reason why.)

Anxious owner. Same as above. (Call their bluff: Offer half.)

Estate wants offers. In my experience, this means the estate wants *high* offers—like, preferably, above the asking price.

Loc loc loc. Okay, we all know about the value of location. *However,* when they really tout it, it usually means the apartment is a pit—on a nice block.

Garden view. Take your pick. This apartment overlooks (*a*) an airshaft, (*b*) the back of somebody else's building, or (*c*) some dirt and some dying evergreens in a sad, sunless attempt at a courtyard.

Courtyard view. See above.

Quiet. Pitch black.

Nothing else like it. Do I really want to be *this* different?

Must be gone by this weekend. Or what?

Nuts-and-Bolts Terms

WBF. Wood-burning fireplace.

CAC. Central air-conditioning.

FDR. Formal dining room.

ALC STU. Alcove studio. Means it has an L—possible to hang sheets and make a bedroom for your college roommate, infant, or whomever.

FS DM. Full-service (full-time) doorman.

PT DM. Part-time doorman.

EIK. Eat-in kitchen.

WEIK. Windowed eat-in kitchen.

WIC. Walk-in closet.

PH. Penthouse. (Always ask if it has a terrace; Manhattan real estate brokers recently have been labeling top-floor servants' rooms "penthouses.")

W/D. Washer and dryer.

Lo Mt. Low monthly maintenance. (This is a very good sign.)

If it doesn't say it . . . tips for reading between the lines:

If the ad doesn't specify that the monthly maintenance is low, it isn't.

If the ad doesn't say there is a doorman, there isn't.

If the ad doesn't say the building is prewar (erected before the Second World War), it isn't.

If the ad doesn't say "Lite" or "Hi Flr" or "Sunflooded," you'd better have a yen for mushroom farming at noon.

NOW GO OUT AND GET IT

So what else do you need to find a cheap apartment?

A lot of luck, and a lot of chutzpah. But you wouldn't be in New York City unless you had both. And now that you know how to read the ads, you can skim through them relatively quickly, no matter what newspaper they're in.

When you've narrowed down the ads, circled every one that might be worth calling on—and don't confine yourself to any one neighborhood; the market's just too hot right now—you're ready to telephone the agent.

DIFFERENTIATING THE APPROACHES: RENTING

Because there will be dozens of homeless waifs telephoning on every inviting ad for a bargain rental, you want to nail down your telephone approach.

You might want to begin this way: "Hello, my name is Suzie Potzlusni (or whoever) and I need to rent an apartment right away."

Say this even if there is voice mail. This immediately separates you from the merely curious. It also gives a time element: You are a serious person who will go elsewhere unless the agent calls you right back. You might even give a deadline, although allow some flexibility. You might say: "I have to find something by the end of the week, so I hope you can call me right back." But with rentals, especially if they're real, you'd better keep calling and hope to get the agent to pick up the phone.

Once you are speaking to the agent, offer to meet her right away to see something in the same price range, even if he or she says the apartment you called about is gone. A lot of times, the agent deliberately chooses to advertise something because she has a lot of similar ones as backup. This is a smart technique: Instead of renting one apartment, she'll end up renting three or four—on only one ad.

Go with your gut reaction. If the agent says the apartment you called about is gone—and it usually is—but she says she has three others in the same price range,

decide right then whether you like this agent. It sounds funny, but it really works. If you get a bad feeling from her, politely decline and telephone others. But you can tell if the agent is genuine; she'll offer some facts about the other apartments: "One is only three blocks away and the building is better . . ." and so forth. If the agent refuses to tell you any more than that the apartment you called about is gone and suggests you "come in and fill out an application form," forget it. She's probably just trying to get you in there, so she can put pressure on you to move up to a much more expensive apartment.

At the end of the conversation, ask what the agent's fee is for the rental. (For one thing, it's a way to judge how easy the agent will be to work with; the good ones will tell you right away and won't give you any attitude.) The standard rate in Manhattan is 15 percent of a year's rent. This is steep, but they can get it. Remember to figure this into your calculations: If you plan to stay in this place for only a year and then move up, the agent's fee is a bigger factor than if you plan to settle down.

Also wait until the end of the conversation, when, it is hoped, rapport has been achieved. Then ask whether the apartment you'll be seeing is rent-stabilized or is a sublease in a co-op building that will last one or two years at the most. You need to know this so you can make your plans. Co-op subleases are fine; they can be lovely places. But they won't be *yours* the way your very own rent-stabilized rental will be. Because in New York City, unless you become a real millionaire and are paying more than $2,000 a month in rent (in which case you'll be forced to move out or pay market rent) or move up to a better one, you've got your rental apartment *forever* if it's rent-stabilized.

New York City has a weird system through which most of the city's rents are regulated by the state. The rents on these rent-stabilized apartments can rise only a certain percentage each year unless a tenant moves out. Then they can also rise more if the landlord does documented renovations. So if that's what you want, plan to spend a while looking, investigating not only the classified ads but also the stealth methods that follow.

Stealth Methods 101

In Manhattan, there are different ways of beating the odds on ever finding a rent-stabilized apartment (much cheaper than the prevailing market rent). New York City is funny. It has all these fabulously expensive, newly built apartments (like Donald Trump's personal penthouse at the top of Trump International—the one he built for Marla and Tiffany and then put on the market for only $100,000 a month). But it also has all these fabulous older apartments that are occupied by amazingly wealthy people paying next to nothing for them because of the city's rent-control laws. (If you're paying less than $2,000 in monthly rent, your rent is regulated, no matter how many millions you have!) Now, without getting technical, every so often there is a political movement to change the laws, and every so often they nibble away at it with some minor reform, but basically, there are still hundreds of thousands of apartments that are lived in by people paying way, way, way below the market value.

So your goal—a Mission Impossible, as it were—is to try to find one of these rent-stabilized apartments. Here are the best, most reliable ways to find one.

THE NEWSPAPERS

It's tough to find them here, but it certainly has been done—by me, and lots of my friends. Look for odd rental figures: If an apartment is renting for, say, $1,023 a month, that could well be a rent-stabilized apartment. (But it could also be a sham. This is New York, after all. Check it out.) Don't forget: If you call on an advertisement and that apartment is gone, ask the agent what other rent-stabilized apartments she has.

THE LANDLORDS

Canvas the neighborhoods you like. Walk into buildings you like the looks of, and jot down the owner's name. Call. If they don't have any apartments in that building, they may in the dozens of others they own.

THE MOVERS

On a spring day toward the end of the month, walk down almost any side street in Manhattan, and you'll see a couple of moving trucks and vans. Ask the movers—or the former tenants—for the story. It may very well be that the landlord was waiting to make sure the people actually *did* move out before trying to rent out the apartment, which, by law, will probably remain rent-stabilized. It may also be that the landlord wants to do some renovations to the apartment to get the additional percentage he is allowed by law. But if the apartment is rent-stabilized (and most rentals of this type are), he can raise the rent by only a certain percentage no matter how much work he does. Naturally, you'll ask the tenant if you can get a peek at the place. But no matter what, call the landlord or managing agent *immediately!* Do not delay one instant. This could be your way to save thousands of dollars a year.

If the landlord's representative says this apartment is available, say you'll be right over to fill out the paperwork. Make the point that you'll be an ideal tenant, blah, blah, and that you can write a check for the apartment right away. In other words, push as hard as you can.

SELECTED AGENTS

Besides the agents who advertise regularly in the *Times*, there are a few agents who work closely with the landlords and actually do have real rent-stabilized apartments from time to time. Try **Bernard-Charles,** a small company in Greenwich Village. Not only have I gotten several rental apartments from them, but recently a friend of mine found one for her daughter through his agency. It was in a converted power station on Jane Street, a charming street in the West Village, right off Eighth Avenue and only a few blocks from the 14th Street subway station. The apartment is a 400-square-foot studio—large by most standards—with a foyer, an eat-in kitchen, and a wonderful, big picture window overlooking a small neighborhood park. The monthly cost is a little over $1,000; the market value is about 60 percent higher.

The Rent Warriors and a Few Words on Manhattan Rental Prices

In New York City, there are people who have nicknamed themselves Rent Warriors: men and women, many of them young (the old ones have already found their good-to-the-grave last-ditch bargain apartment) who are constantly on the lookout for their Ultimate Cheap Dream, a rental apartment for less than $600 a month. Now I know that perhaps in Oregon or Wyoming or Mississippi, $600 a month is probably a lot for an apartment—any apartment. But in the Big Apple, $600 doesn't even pay for a powder room in Trump Tower.

Right now, the average studio apartment—listed in the classified ads as two rooms but there's really only a living room, a closet for the futon, a closet-sized alcove for the kitchen, and, if you're lucky, a closet with a door to the bathroom—goes for more than $1,300 a month and can easily soar to $1,800 if it's large or has a great view or if there's a doorman. A market-rate one-bedroom can reach $2,500 in the time it takes to say "Line around the block." And apartments with more bedrooms rise in price, marching to some kind of unfathomable geometric progression.

The Rent Warriors call local, small-time agents like Bernard-Charles in Greenwich Village. They might also call **Douglas Hochlerin,** who works for himself on the Upper East Side of Manhattan. Mr. Hochlerin got his fifteen minutes of fame when he was written up after he found a one-bedroom in the East 80s for a young stockbroker for $322 a month. (The article's title? "$322 a Month—And Only One Roach.")

Recently, Mr. Hochlerin took time out of his busy life to give advice to those who wish to find the best deals.

"First," he said, "I would try to find a broker who works with rent-stabilized apartments. I would ask him: 'Do you have any undermarket-value rent-stabilized apartments?' Because most of the ads are only for market-value apartments. They're going to tell you they don't deal with that kind of stuff."

Right. Mr. Hochlerin graciously gave his competitor, **V-W Realty,** as another example of brokers who specialize in these rent-stabilized apartments. "Don't bother calling **Gumley-Haft** or **Corcoran,**" Mr. Hochlerin continued, mentioning two large Upper East Side firms known for apartment sales. "They wouldn't even have those listings."

Mr. Hochlerin explained why. "There's only a few landlords that don't renovate their apartments when somebody moves out. That's the key."

The rental agent just rented out a rent-stabilized two-bedroom apartment on York Avenue and 75th Street for $566. If it had been renovated by the landlord, the rent would have risen to market value, $2,000, he said—and more than that if it hadn't been on the first floor.

Another apartment he just rented out was a large one-bedroom on First Avenue and 68th Street for $940 a month, to two young women fresh from college. The unrenovated apartment still had a bathtub smack in the middle of the kitchen.

"They both were magna cum laude," said Mr. Hochlerin with a streetwise chuckle. "Don't give us that magna cum laude in New York City! Magna cum laude—it's still a bathtub in the kitchen for you, girls! And they were smart all right—smart enough to know they were getting a great deal."

While the apartment has what one might call old-fashioned conveniences, once the lease is signed, these well might be changed. The two young women may now approach the landlord, who, in return for giving them a proper shower and bath space, can bill them one-fortieth the cost of those renovations each month—a pittance. Mr. Hochlerin dismisses the story of the man who rented the two-bedroom for $566 and then proceeded to renovate—at his own expense. "He could've had the landlord pay for it. He shoulda called his broker to check."

Using the Regular Agents

The Rent Warriors also check in with the regular agents from time to time. Pick one you like, and work with him or her. Brokers can find cheap rentals in their computers—if they try. Just for fun, I asked

Claudio Santos, a sales agent with **Citi Habitats,** to look up some dirt-cheap stuff in his office computer. In one day, we found apartments that ranged from two studios with shared bathrooms in a building with a doorman, in the Flower District—the West Side in the twenties—($343 and $453); to a spick-and-span studio in a venerable 1914 building, built by Vincent Astor, on West 45th Street ($704); to a bright three-bedroom walk-up near Mount Sinai Hospital on the upper Upper East Side ($850). And there are obviously more. The problem is first finding them, then landing them.

The newspaper of choice for cheap rentals is still the **Village Voice,** whose advertisements, mostly from real estate agents, appear on the Internet as soon as they are placed, often days ahead of publication. Just remember: If it is an advertisement placed by an agent, you will have to pay a fee unless it says otherwise.

Nancy Packes, who runs **Feathered Nest,** a rental and sales agency, suggested calling developers of glossy luxury rental buildings that are under construction and asking if they have filled their allotment of subsidized units. (Many new buildings are built with tax breaks which require that 20 percent of their apartments be set aside for moderate-income tenants. And nobody in the building—or out of it—knows who are the people with the lower-priced apartments!)

Whatever approach one takes, brokers in the trenches advised carrying a full portfolio of pay stubs and reference letters to every showing—just in case. Because the most important thing, they agreed, is that if you find an apartment you want, jump at it.

More Ways to Find One

If you're a real Rent Warrior, you don't even want to pay a broker's fee. If you haven't had any luck calling the landlords directly, there are other ways to find a cheap rental apartment. For the most part, I would forget apartment-finding services, advertised both on the subway walls and on the Internet. An investigation I did showed many of these places up. Their biggest problem was that they had listings so old they creaked. Here are some better ways.

 Call your friends or, if you're new in town, colleagues from work who live in rent-stabilized buildings. They can introduce you to their building superintendent, commonly called the super. This is the man to know! For a mere tuppence (in New York, this means $20), he can tell you about people who might be moving out. But since such opportunities are rare, you'll need to know a lot of supers, and spend a couple of hundred dollars. (In case you think this sounds expensive, you could save a couple of hundred dollars in the first ten days of living in your new apartment, if you're lucky enough to find an undermarket one.)

Never visit anybody without asking the doorman or super if there are any apartments available. I once found a great studio in a fancy building on lower Fifth Avenue this way.

Look in local shop windows, windows of laundries, dry cleaners, veterinarians, any place at all that might let a landlord post a "For Rent" sign on their bulletin board. Rental ads in the *New York Times* cost close to $100 a week, and a lot of the old-time landlords—especially if they've got a place renting for $400 a month—won't want to spring for them. And often, the downstairs retail tenant *is* the landlord, so be cheerful and act smart and alert.

In New York City, you can't underestimate attitude. New Yorkers can spot a self-defeated, hangdog look from across the street, and nobody's going to take any trouble with somebody who looks like that. And because you never know which little deli hides your great deal, be personable with each deli owner you meet. If you're too tired and crabby, you might as well turn around and go back to your hotel or friend's couch because nobody's going to do you any favors—and you just might blow the chance of a lifetime. (And that doesn't mean putting on some wacky, zany, overzealous pushiness, either. It just means be very friendly, whatever your own personal brand of friendliness is.)

"Yes, there are still bargains," said Doug Hochlerin. "And there always will be—you just gotta reach out and ask somebody. And ask. And ask." And be willing to pay out some money to learn the answer.

THE OTHER ALTERNATIVE: BUYING THE PLACE— LOCK, STOCK, AND BATHROOM

Buying your own apartment does, naturally, have a certain cachet. For one thing, you can be like every other owner: constantly complaining about your co-op board. Of course, if you have a cheap rental, you can just be smug and say obnoxious things like: "Oh, well, I'm glad I don't have to worry about those things—I have a six-room apartment overlooking Central Park and I only pay $1,100 a month rent!" (Of course, if you want to go on *living*, you also might *not* say that!)

But really, there are considerable advantages to owning your own apartment. Buying a cheap apartment in New York City can be a great deal. First, it's easier to find a cheap apartment to buy than it is to find a cheap place to rent. Not only that, but after you find it— even adding in the exorbitant monthly carrying charges, called maintenance—it may actually be cheaper than renting, especially when you consider all the tax deductions you'll get.

Finally, the investment. When you rent, no matter what you pay, you're throwing money out the window. If you buy wisely and inexpensively, you'll actually make money, lots of it if you buy well. (At the moment, I'm fixing up two apartments I bought for $80,000—if I sell them, I expect to get close to $300,000!)

Starting Out

Right now, the Web is a much better place to find apartments for sale than for rent. Brokerage houses do tend to focus more on the expensive co-op and condo apartments on their Web sites, although there are plans to change that. But the newspaper is still better than the Web overall.

I've found lots of interesting apartments in the paper—and bought some of them too. One Sunday about two years ago, I saw an ad for a two-bedroom prewar apartment on West End Avenue at 89th Street for $120,000. Many people would have figured it was too low to be credible. I called on it, and about two weeks later, signed a contract for . . . $104,000. That was about a week after I was told that somebody had bid more. That somebody turned out to be a musician who happened to mention that he wanted to play the drums a lot in the apartment. Before the deal got too far along, the agent asked the board president if that'd be okay and, well, you can guess the rest. I was recalled from my heartbroken state and asked if I'd still go through with the purchase. I did. After redoing the apartment, I sold it about a year ago for $165,000, without paying a broker's commission. That advertisement had come right out of the paper, placed by a broker I'd never met. (And haven't run into since.)

My first loft also came from the newspaper—again, with such a ridiculously low figure that I'm sure most people never bothered: a SoHo loft, about 1,200 square feet, for $70,000. The loft was raw, and I spent a good year living with mice and sawdust. Nevertheless, when it was finished, any millionaire would have been tickled green to live and entertain in it, its three fireplaces crackling away on a winter party night. I sold it for $287,500 to an architect in I. M. Pei's office, who painted it all black, I heard. Anyway, by all means, shop the classifieds. Learn the code.

I should now say a word about neighborhoods. When you're looking for a rental, as Doug Hochlerin says, "Forget about neighborhoods. Just get an apartment, already!" But the choice is greater when you're looking to buy, and the newspaper ads are arranged by neighborhood. Gramercy Park is an example of a neighborhood that just a few years ago, had great cachet and was underpriced, but alas, prices have soared. For one-bedrooms in wonderful prewar doorman buildings, look now towards—you're not going to believe this— the Upper East Side, which still has a posh reputation but, aside from the Park and Fifth Avenues Gold Coast, is underpriced and full of bargains. There is currently a bargain one-bedroom—only $125,000—in a wonderful Gothic Revival building between Madison and Park Avenues in the East 70s, and you can't get much better than that. It suffers from having been converted to a co-op in the 1970s, so the kitchen needs sprucing up, but it has a wrought iron balcony running the full width of the apartment—not big enough to stand on, but lovely filled with tomato red geraniums. Although this apartment will be gone by the time you read this, there are plenty more out there.

Just take a look at the paper. If you're on the Internet, you may be able to enter key words, like "TLC" and "needs work" and "fixer-upper" and "Cinderella." Oh, and occasionally there's an honest ad, so try "Wreck." One Sunday, I found at least two dozen of these ads, and because the classified ads are so expensive, they often don't run the same ad twice so each week is a potential bonanza.

And you can get pretty good at sussing out the real lemons. Ask the following questions, in just this order. Obviously, if you get a "no-way" answer immediately, you politely hang up and try the next.

Here are the questions, in the order of priority, given that there is a low price listed in the paper. (Otherwise, don't even call.) You'll probably have also figured out if it's prewar, although you may want to confirm this and find out if there are any prewar details left, like crown moldings, paneled doors, wainscoting.

What is the monthly maintenance? This is the amount you are charged every month. It includes such things as taxes on the building (versus on your apartment) and salaries for the porters, the doormen, and the superintendent.

How many square feet is the apartment? If they say they don't know, it's probably a dodge—I've used it myself. Defeat it by asking them to describe the layout and to give the approximate room sizes. If they don't want to play, thank them politely and hang up. It's not worth another second of your time.

What kind of light does it have? Don't just settle for "Good." How many hours a day? All rooms? Does the apartment face the street or the "courtyard" (another euphemism for air-shafts and totally bleak)? Does it face north or south?

What shape is it in? Surprisingly, people are usually pretty honest. Nobody wants to waste time showing a do-it-yourself wreck to somebody who wants pristine, "just order the baguettes from Dean and Deluca" condition.

Does the building have a doorman? If this really matters to you, you can ask it sooner.

At the end, you'll want to ask the address. If you ask this first, they'll probably get nervous, so save it until last. After all, if you're going to make an appointment to see it, they'll have to tell you anyway. Again, depending on how finicky you are about the exact block—you'll already know the neighborhood by the ad—you may ask sooner. But if you want to know right away, ask only for the block, for instance, 79th between Park and Lex. They probably will want to talk to you a little longer to make sure you're not a kook and I don't blame them. Please remember that real estate agents have some justification for being suspicious. You could be a thief, trying to learn if an expensive furnished apartment is vacant. Or you could be just a curious neighbor. Or—and this is most likely—they worry that if they give out too much information, you'll go over on your own and try to make your own deal—cutting out the agent!

Co-ops and Condos

In New York City, apartments for sale are of two types: co-operatives, nicknamed "co-ops," and condominiums, not surprisingly nicknamed "condos." Since most of the nonrental apartments in Manhattan are co-ops, and because those that are condos are usually priced sky-high, bargain hunters won't have to worry too much about it. But just so you know: In a co-op, the buyer actually owns shares in the apartment corporation that are assigned to a particular apartment. In a condo, the buyer actually owns the square footage. There has been a lot of talk lately about condo boards getting tougher, but that's really only in the million-dollar-apartment category. If you or your favorite cheapskate millionaire-to-be did in fact stumble on a condominium at a bargain price, here's what it would mean to you: In a co-op, the board scrutinizes you when you buy the apartment—especially where you're getting the money and whether you can afford to maintain the place. (In both types of apartments, there are monthly fees.) A co-op board can prohibit or limit sublets and almost always wants to screen the prospective tenants. A co-op board then repeats the agony—including reference letters and a personal interview—on whomever you try to sell the apartment to when you're ready to leave. Welcome to New York City! In a condo, it's not anywhere near as bad—usually minimal applications, easy subletting, and easy sales. Now, do you *wonder* why condominiums usually sell for more? (And why the city's relatively small number of houses—no boards at all—are breaking all price records right now?)

Working with Your Own Broker

After years and years of crummy brokers who've shown me apartments that are so far removed from anything I've described that they might as well be on Uranus, I've learned know how valuable a good broker can be. So if you hear about someone good from a friend, call the agent up—immediately.

First, set up a meeting for coffee. If she doesn't want to schedule one in the next week, again, hang up. She's either too busy or too uninterested.

Over coffee, tell the agent exactly what you're looking for. Be ruthless. If you really *are* looking for a large one-bedroom under $150,000, say so, and don't apologize for it. If the broker is any good, she'll take you back to her office and start researching things on the office computer. I recently asked my agent to get me a list of all Manhattan two-bedroom apartments for less than $200,000. Impossible, you say? She found eighty-six. I looked at the list and one thing immediately became clear: About one-quarter of them had monthly maintenances that were sky-high, well over the $1 per square foot average I use as a rule of thumb.

But that still left more than sixty two-bedroom apartments for less than $200,000. The second thing I could see from the list was that some of the "bedrooms" were actually dining rooms. These dining rooms are actually great things to have—especially if you don't need the two bedrooms—but they are, generally speaking, not as valuable as the second bedrooms. (Despite what the agent will tell you, a dining room should not become a bedroom unless you're really hard up: They're generally sandwiched between the living room and the kitchen. If, however, the architect's layout christened the room a study, it's better. Studies are usually off the front hall, but they serve beautifully as . . . studies—and guest bedrooms, with a sofa bed.) After I eliminated the four-room apartments with one bedroom, the list still showed dozens of cheap two-bedrooms.

Not that a good agent is going to give that list to a stranger. You could just go off and negotiate for the apartment on your own, as was explained above. But this does show you what the agent can find for you. And how long would it take to find those apartments in the newspapers?

I make no recommendations in this book for real estate companies, although I do list some of the biggest ones—and a few good small firms—at the end of the chapter.

Once you get a really great real estate agent—one who will do just about anything to make a sale, including research—tell her to try checking the "dead" listings in her company computer. Dead listings are one-time listings that were withdrawn for some reason. A really good agent will key into these listings, bring them up on her screen, and scroll through them to see if there's anything worth calling about. Why are these listings so great? First, in a rising market, these listings are old, probably at least a couple of years old. That means they'll have old (lower) prices. Second, they may be wrecks, which is why they didn't sell in the first place. The owners may be grateful to get this place off their hands; they've been paying maintenance all this time. Third, if the owner is not living there, he may have decided to rent it out, and if the listing is a year or two old, he may be getting to the point when he absolutely has to sell. Co-op boards usually allow only one or two years of subletting. That's how I got my two apartments for $80,000: They were both wrecks; one had been rented out, and the co-op board was threatening to take back the apartment unless the owners sold it. That search unearthed at least a dozen properties—and all of them were great deals.

Foreclosures

If you think finding an apartment through a broker sounds complicated, finding a foreclosed one is nearly impossible. My cousin Robin, who's a lawyer, just found a two-bedroom condo (none of those pesky co-op board interrogations) for $237,000 somewhere north of 96th Street on Central Park West. So it's possible, but I'd advise against it. There have been lots of articles about how hard it is—you usually can't even get to see the space and you must bid blindly—so unless you know something or someone I don't, stick with the methods detailed above.

Seeing the Apartment—What to Look For

Once you're ready to view the apartment, you want to be prepared. If the real estate market is as hot in Manhattan as it is right now, you're going to have to be ready to make an offer—if not on the spot, then sometime the same day. So there's no time for repeat visits.

Invest in one of those rolling rulers that can measure dimensions easily. Remember: Advertised square footages are rarely accurate. It isn't anybody's fault; usually, the real estate agents just guess or take the owner's estimate, which is equally likely to be at fault. I've had agents walk into my 625-square-foot apartment and say cheerily: "Well, this is about 1,000 square feet, right?" Alas, no. What does it matter to you? Quite a bit. First, if somewhere down the road you'd like to sell it, you'll undoubtedly be more honest (now won't you?) and many buyers *do* do the math to arrive at a per-square-foot cost. Second, and most important, you'll want to know so you can do your own sketchy floor plans to figure out what furniture you'll be able to fit into it, and where. So besides measuring just the room sizes, if you're really interested, measure the distances between doors and windows so you can figure out if you can fit in your queen-size bed and the Louis Seize bureau you just bought at Tepper's.

Whenever possible, try to determine the apartment's exposures over the telephone and visit during the time of day when the light will be the brightest. (It's somehow easier to visualize the darkest times than it is the lightest.)

While you're looking around, let the agent know you'd like to pretend you're alone in the apartment—in other words, figure out a nice way to stop her incessant talking, which she may be doing on purpose to cover the hellish traffic noise or the children screaming through paper-thin walls. Don't be afraid to ask her to turn off the lovely stereo or to open the venetian blinds, which may be disguising an airshaft. It sounds corny . . . but do flush the toilet and run the shower and the kitchen taps. If there's no water pressure, there could be several fixable reasons, but if it's because it's the penthouse and the water doesn't make it up there, you might have to invest in your own auxiliary water pump and you might want to make that a part of the negotiations. (Or there may be nothing that can be done. Find out now.)

Ask the agent how long the apartment has been on the market and what similar apartments in the building have sold for. Don't accept any vagueness here! If she says she has to look it up, offer to accompany her back to her office and her computer. This is vital information, and will be invaluable in preparing your bid.

Closing the Deal

Now it's time to bid. For me, that's one of the most exciting parts of the real estate game. (And it *is* a game, just like playing the stock market.) For the novice, the most important thing is to stay calm and to always think before you speak. This sounds obvious, but believe me, it is much harder than it sounds. It's just human nature, for instance, to fall for the "phantom bidder," the customer in the wings who, according to the agent, is either just about to bid or just about to bid higher. So be cool, and think out your bid in advance.

As you know, it's best to begin negotiations with as much knowledge as possible, especially information on what comparable apartments in the same building have sold for—recently. And it's also important to gauge the times: If this is a lightning-fast market, there may well be a bidding war. Or the negotiations could take on the form of a sealed-bid auction, in which the bidders place only one "last and best" bid in a sealed envelope.

In New York City, sealed-bid negotiations were once a rare thing, but they have become much more common, especially for the most desirable apartments in all price ranges. Here's how the experts say you can get a fair deal:

First, make sure you understand the rules, and that the rules are fair. There should be a time and a place all the bids are opened. The seller doesn't have to pick the highest bid; especially with a co-op, the winning bid usually combines money and "board worthiness": the people who are chosen are the most likely to pass muster with the co-op's board of directors. Either you or your agent may decide to attend the bid opening.

Second, carefully map out your bid. The experts advise you to always choose an odd number. If the asking price on the apartment is $250,000, "so many people will bid $250,000 or $255,000," said Hall Willkie, head of sales for Brown Harris Stevens in Manhattan. "I tell people to bid $255,013, or whatever," he said. (He explained that many people put in their envelope a bid such as this: "Two percent higher than the highest bid." It doesn't work, he said. Those people are routinely disqualified.) Most important, bid what you feel comfortable with, but do not hold anything back. There are no second chances. "Bid so that if you lose, you won't be kicking yourself," said Betsey Dean, a manager at Stribling Associates, also in Manhattan.

Finally, if you lose, get over it. Don't whine. Don't call the broker—or the seller—and try to get them to reopen the bidding. (Some of the richest people are the poorest sports, the brokers say.) Learn from the experience. But if you *do* win . . .

Finding the Money

It used to be that prospective home buyers found their dream house and then stopped into their friendly local bank and filled out an application for a mortgage. No more! Now the savvy buyers—and you have to be one these days—get prequalified by a mortgage broker. That way, they know exactly how much they can afford before they even telephone for an appointment to look at a Park Avenue pad. If you really have guts, you can submit a much more attractive bid by saying it's an "all-cash" deal. (Most sales are contingent on getting a mortgage; if you don't get it, you get to walk away with your down payment, usually 10 percent of the purchase price.) For the sellers, it makes your bid mouthwatering because they know that if you don't get the mortgage, they get to keep the down payment—and people don't usually make all-cash offers unless they're certain they'll have no problem getting the money.

The city is full of good mortgage brokers. Try to get a reference from someone who's used one. Or check with your attorney.

And after that, you're ready to decorate. . . .

❧ SOURCES

SOME BROKERS WHO HANDLE RENTALS

Bernard-Charles
44 Greenwich Avenue, 212-243-0043
A small but serious old-fashioned company with ties to old-line Greenwich Village landlords. This is a great first telephone call—and if they say they have something in your price range, don't waste a second getting down to see it!

Citi Habitats
50 Madison Avenue, 212-685-7300
340 West 57th Street, 212-957-4100
353 East 78th Street, 212-794-1133
Ask for Claudio or any of their agents who specialize in *cheap* rentals. Be up front with this right away. And give them your true limit.

Douglas Hochlerin
212-628-9404
The king of the cheap rentals. He works for himself and knows a lot of landlords, especially on the Upper East Side. But don't forget, he charges a hefty commission, which, if you get a true deal—like the $322-a-month one-bedroom—is more than worth it, especially if you're going to stay a while.

Feathered Nest
310 Madison Avenue, 212-867-8500
This company handles more top-of-the-line rentals, but check them out if you have a little more money to spend—they often get things that nobody else has.

V-W Realty
956 Fifth Avenue, 212-721-6466
Another cheapie rental agency, recommended by a competitor—so maybe it's good!

NEWSPAPER OF CHOICE FOR RENTALS

The Village Voice
36 Cooper Square, 212-475-5555
Free at Manhattan newstands, restaurants, shops, lobbies. They also have a great Web site: www.villagevoice.com. New ads entered at midnight every night except Sunday and Monday. This is *the* resource for the cheapest advertised rentals.

FOR SALES, ESPECIALLY

Ashforth Warburg Associates
969 Madison Avenue (uptown)
212-439-4500
795 Broadway (downtown)
212-327-9600
This is a well-respected agency with one hundred agents. Ask for Fred Peters, who is the president of the company—but only if you're serious. Strengths: the Upper East Side, Central Park West, and Greenwich Village. Mid-to upper-level stuff, generally—although not so long ago they had a terrific atelier with double-height ceilings near Bloomingdale's, for only $125,000.

Bellmarc Realty
Bellmarc Brokerage (strengths:
Gramercy and Chelsea), 352 Park
Avenue South,
212-252-1900
Bellmarc East, 1015 Madison Avenue,
212-517-9100
Bellmarc Downtown, 16 East 12th
Street, 212-627-3000
Bellmarc West, 452-A Columbus
Avenue, 212-874-0100
Bellmarc Brokerage (strengths: Sutton
and Murray Hill), 681 Lexington
Avenue, 212-688-8530

Despite their attempts to go upscale—their color advertisement features lots of million-dollar apartments—Bellmarc is still known for its cheap apartments. They have zillions of agents, and many of them are the pushy, striving salespeople you love to have on your side! (Don't be put off by agents if they're aggressive; only be put off if they're lazy.) Call Bellmarc for rentals too.

Charles H. Greenthal

488 Madison Avenue (residential sales and appraisals), 212-688-8900
173 West 85th Street (West Side residential sales), 212-769-9700
Greenthal has a big management wing, so they often get apartments from one of the buildings they manage before anybody else.

Coldwell Banker Hunt-Kennedy

238 West 78th Street, 212-877-1300
1200 Lexington Avenue,
212-327-1200
401 Avenue of the Americas,
212-255-4000
Their big asset is that they are one of the few Manhattan brokerages to be tied in with a national chain. Obviously, that's going to help more in selling than in buying. Ask for JoAnne Kennedy or Will Hunt.

The Corcoran Group

645 Madison Avenue, 212-355-3550
200 West 72nd Street, 212-721-4600
25 East 21st Street, 212-979-7700
49 East 10th Street, 212-253-0100
2253 Broadway (gallery),
212-721-7227
37 West 65th Street (rentals only)
212-877-2711
As you can tell from the addresses, this is one of the city's biggies. Its aggressive advertising campaign, showing Barbara Corcoran in various getups—a recent ad showed her in a beret leaning against a cartoon Eiffel Tower, touting her Web site—turns a lot of people off (especially competitors). But she claims it really works.

D. J. Knight & Company

101 Fifth Avenue (main office),
212-463-9880
654 Madison Avenue, 212-371-3400
295 West Thames, 212-964-4300
Although there are several offices, this company is known for its properties in Greenwich Village and environs.

Douglas Elliman

575 Madison Avenue (headquarters),
212-891-7000
575 Madison Avenue (rentals),
212-350-8500
980 Madison Avenue (gallery),
212-650-4800
2112 Broadway (West Side),
212-362-9600
103 Fifth Avenue (downtown),
212-645-4040
99 Battery Place (Wall Street),
212-898-4700
The biggest residential real estate company around, with more than six hundred sales agents in the company. Although they say they deal in apartments of every price, they tend to specialize in more expensive ones. Call Steven James, and he'll find someone for you to speak with.

Gumley Haft Kleier

415 Madison Avenue, 212-371-2525
Michele Kleier is the woman to see here, but the problem is that she usually is off handling multimillion-dollar listings.

Halstead Property Company

1065 Madison Avenue (main office)
212-734-0010
451 West Broadway, 212-475-4200
408 Columbus Avenue, 212-769-3000
776 Broadway, 212-253-9300
Halstead and Corcoran are the yin and yang of Manhattan real estate; they're about the same size, cover the city, and are known for their famous bosses. Way before Barbara Corcoran doffed her beret, Clark Halstead was out there in his British taxicab with HAL-STEAD on the side. Both agencies have all ranges of properties.

Stribling

Stribling and Associates (uptown)
924 Madison Avenue, 212-570-2440
Stribling, Wells & Gay (downtown)
340 West 23rd Street, 212-243-4000
A more refined image, perhaps, than others
have: Photographs of their apartments are dis-
played in ornate, custom-made gold frames
suspended from their shop-front windows.
Somehow, it doesn't make you think "bargain
basement apartments," does it? But maybe
that's the idea. . . .

Outfitting Your Apartment: Where to Find Stuff Worthy of a Connoisseur

Once you've found your cheap apartment, you're ready to furnish it. The real cheapskate millionaires can usually be found at auctions—city auctions and country auctions—poking through boxes of dusty tapestries and leafing through the leather-bound first editions of yore. Or they might be spotted in some backstreet antique shop, or backwoods flea market, ambling around in the early morning mist, on the *qui vive* for some priceless Roman bronze. Where to go, what to look for, and how to bid, unfolds below.

Occasionally—just occasionally—a place cries out for something new, something perfect for a certain spot. When that happens, it usually means you're in a hurry; you've done the place up as well as you can with wonderful *objets,* great paintings, and one-of-a-kind pieces, but now . . . you need a couch! Not only do you need a couch, but you need a pair of couches, one for each end of the living room. And you need them for your dinner party two weeks from now. So where do you go?

When just that happened to me a couple of months ago, I didn't have a clue. I just pounded the pavement. I went to all the big places: **Crate & Barrel** and **ABC Carpet & Home.** And if you like those enormous slouchy, slipcovered beige couches with the gigantic arms—couches for the Michelin man, in fact—you'll be overjoyed. But couches at these places surprised me; they're not even cheap. At

ABC Carpet, for instance, their smallest couch looked like a big white blob of linen-covered lard, and cost $1,200. It would have taken up my entire living room—and I wanted one at each end!

I went to **Palazzetti,** which is a fine store selling wonderful Jean-Michel Frank and Knoll and LeCorbusier reproductions for expensive—but fair—prices. But the small Jean-Michel Frank couches I wanted cost about $2,500 apiece. That was a killer. Not only that, they couldn't guarantee delivery for twelve weeks! Now, before I leave Palazzetti, I want to tell you to check out their warehouse sales, which take place in their showrooms twice a year. I was helping a friend decorate her office, and I found a hunter-green leather club chair and a matching loveseat in the same hunter-green nubuck—an absolutely smashing combination—both for $2,600! They were floor models, but in absolutely mint condition. Palazetti also had a canary-yellow leather Barcelona chair, for under $1,000. They also have delicious lamps and coffee tables.

Still searching for my couches, I went to SoHo, and I found them in **Nuovo Melodrom.** They were in the back of the store, Jean-Michel Frank knockoffs in simple unbleached muslin for $600 apiece. That's right. No discount, nothing. (I should have bought four.) Now here's a real caveat, and take it for what it's worth. This store is known in some circles as a Palazzetti wannabe without the high quality.

There are also tales of ordering furniture that it takes a year to get, and on and on. I can only testify that my couches took two weeks to be delivered to my apartment (they came in time for the party), and they arrived in perfect condition. They look as if they are stuffed with down, but true to the 1930s (when they were designed), they're not. They're stuffed with something that makes them feels like a futon, which kind of gives people a surprise when they throw themselves down on them and expect to sink in. They don't. Nevertheless, the couches have arms that are straight up and down, as sleek as a polished slab of marble.

Here's my advice, which applies here and pretty much everywhere else: Pay with a credit card. Most credit card companies have some kind of guarantee. If the items arrive, and they're not in perfect shape or aren't what you ordered, you can notify the credit card company and the company will fight it out with the merchant.

If you're already in SoHo, you might want to stop in at **George**

Smith, an English company that specializes in leather- and kilim-covered Chesterfield sofas. This is a great look, especially if you have at least one large room. The sofas here are tremendously expensive, even when they put them into their half-price sale, which they do a couple of times of year. But here's a tip: The same type of Edwardian sofas, chaise longues, and chairs often come up at country auctions. They usually can be bought for less than $200—sometimes for $10 or $15. I had to wait for hours at **Nadeau's Auction Gallery** in Windsor, Connecticut, all the way until the dead end of one of their "ironing board and antimacassar" sales, as a friend of mine refers to the midweek bric-a-brac sales where you can get the best deals, until they put up a down-filled sofa. The sofa was covered in the original linen velvet, but the color was a dated orangy gold. I was the only bidder. It went for $10. I took it to my favorite upholsterer (see Chapter 9) and had it done up in a wonderful mossy green antique velvet that cost $280. The upholsterer charged me $350, but it was well worth it. (I had already bought a couch very much like it, but more valuable—since it was an antique, not a reproduction—for $640.) A similar couch at George Smith's would be about $9,000. And now, speaking of auctions . . .

AUCTIONS

The best place to buy furniture, china, glassware, and all kinds of household goods—even washers and dryers—is at an auction house. If you have taste—and of course you do—you'll be able to find marvelous relics worthy of any millionaire for only a fraction of the cost of similar items in an antique dealer's shop.

And you're lucky. You're not *trying* to be a collector: someone for whom every object has to be the best money can buy. No, it doesn't matter to you that a back leg on a chest of drawers has been replaced. You can't see it—and nobody else can either—unless you tip it over and shine a black light on it, which is what dealers do. But because of that one replaced leg, you'll pay a fraction of what you might have if the piece were perfect.

And that's only one way to buy. You can also hope for a bargain on a true collector's item. Those happen too. Only last year, the antiques world was rocked by the tale of a postman who bought what turned out to be an $800,000 eighteenth-century tea table at a local auction (the name of the auction house where this reportedly took place is listed below) for $1,200.

Buying furniture at auction is not nearly as hard as buying, say, paintings, where there are expert fakes floating around. Now I'm not talking about buying a half-million-dollar bombé chest of drawers— then you need a connoisseur to help you. No, what you want to buy is great-looking furniture that looks as if it cost major money, but in fact was bought for next to nothing. That's easy, as long as you keep this checklist either in your head or on paper.

When you go to an auction, either in New York City or in the country, the exact same rules apply. *Look at the stuff carefully before you buy it.* Try to make notes. Figure an estimate. Buy a catalogue if there is one—lots of country auctions don't even have them. And if possible, go home and think and measure and visualize. If it's not possible because you just found out about the sale or the exhibition was a short one, make your list and your estimates and try to go somewhere quiet—even if it's only out to your car or to a coffee shop next door. Go through this list, being totally, painfully, ruthlessly honest with yourself.

Do you love this thing? If no, do you *desperately* need this thing? If the answer to both of these questions is no, cross it off.

If you love it, but don't need it, write down how much you love it—in dollars; for example, I love this cracked, eighteenth-century painting on glass. I love it $75 worth.

If you need it but don't love it, how much do you need it—in dollars? Also (very important), if you need it for a particular place, it must fit the place, in both style and measurements. Are you sure? If you're not sure about the size, can you call your super, girlfriend, boyfriend . . . and have the person measure the space in your apartment right away? (If you become an auction junkie like me, making the acquaintance of a person who can enter your apartment and measure things before the gavel falls becomes more and more vital.)

If you change your mind after you've bought it and try to sell it at another auction, will you recoup your money? (Just ask yourself. You probably aren't able to answer this one, but the question works wonders as a reality check.)

Figuring How Much to Pay

It is vital to put the amount of money you will pay for each item next to it in your catalogue or on a separate piece of paper. (Some auction-goers get paranoid and are afraid if they put it next to the item in the catalogue, somebody will peek and bid accordingly. I doubt it. Again, we're not talking about $2 million sideboards here.) Writing down the amount you will pay is probably the most important thing you can do because all the dishonest things you hear about auctions are true. Yes, there *are* dealer's rings. Yes, there are dishonest auction-eers who pick bids off the wall; in other words, nod to imaginary bid-ders. Yes, there are shills in the audience who are hired to bid you up. So that's why it's imperative to stick to your own prices and not to get into competition with some stranger who is sitting a few seats away from you.

If you "lose" the item, remember you never really had it. My mother used to tell me: "Don't worry. Another one will come along." I've found that's not true. There was the exquisite string of cultured pearls I let get away for $1,100 (the next week I went to Tiffany's and saw a similar set at $32,000!), the bronze by the famous sculptor that went for $1,800 at a country auction, the pair of eighteenth-century portraits for $500. And on and on. They never came again. But here's the real comfort. My father used to say: "You never know how high the other guy would have gone." And that *is* true. Maybe the jewelry dealer would have gone up to $5,000 for those pearls; the sculpture dealer, up to $20,000. So if you don't know the true value of the ob-jects you're bidding on—and I didn't at the time—*pay what they're worth to you.*

If the item has value (and you're willing to pay the extra as an in-vestment) because of the maker—say it's a painting or a piece of furniture—make sure the auctioneer will stand behind the identifi-cation. In other words, if you buy the pearls as cultured and they turn out to be fake, will he refund your money? Generally speaking, the rule is that if the object is identified in the catalogue as being by a certain craftsman or of a certain period and a respected curator or appraiser says the next week, not the next year, that it's a phony, the auctioneer will refund your money. But be careful. This book is about spending next to nothing on things that look great. If you're into investments, you'd better get an adviser: someone who really knows what she's looking at and its value.

Staying in the City

For great things at bargain prices, check out the auction houses in New York City that are my personal favorites. **The Tepper Galleries** are a lot of fun, even to just go look. It's always a fairly motley lot of stuff—the auctioneers take whole houses full of stuff, not one piece at a time from dealers. So in one sale, you might see a table that goes for $2,600—and a chair that goes for $5. Here are some of the deals I've gotten at Tepper's over the past ten years.

I found an English William and Mary chest of drawers in what is known as oyster veneer, complete with the original brass pulls. It was in fairly rugged condition: The veneer was pulling away from the drawer fronts and its bracket feet were questionable. (So would yours be if they were three hundred years old!) On a different week, I might not have been able to even get in a bid. But this was a big week for Art Deco, and all the Deco dealers turned out. So who wanted a William and Mary chest that needed repair? I got it for $425. I paid another $200 to have it repaired in Woodbury, Connecticut (see Sources, Chapter 9), and I had a piece that looked as if it was worth $5,000 or $6,000.

Another time, a zebrawood Art Deco sideboard, probably valued at around $10,000, was the only Deco piece in the sale. The rest of the stuff was for the gilt-chandelier-and-crystal-and-tufted-sofas crowd. The wood in this masterful sideboard was in perfect shape, but the knobs were 1950s. I can't explain why it went for $260—with a $60 delivery charge—except that I was just lucky. To be frank, I'm not sure it ever would again. But as long as you like things from a lot of periods, there will always be something. Like the eighteenth-century Chinese Export porcelain dishes I spotted inside a reproduction tureen in the back of Tepper's, off to the left side, in the glass-fronted showcase where they put the (cheap) household goods—different from the glass cases in the center of the rear, where they put the finer objects. I bought the lot for $10.

Tepper's is great, with one caveat: Beware of the paintings! The auctioneers warn you at the beginning of the sale. Except for certain specialized art auctions they hold, where the paintings are guaranteed to be authentic, Tepper's does not stand behind the signature. There are many bargains to be had—and of course, occasionally the signature does turn out to be right. But don't count on it. I once bought a painting here, an interesting 1950s still life with melons and a funky fifties frame signed by Brianchon. I bought it for $125 because I liked it (the only reason to buy art this cheaply). But then I mentioned the name to my friend J. J. Smith, an art dealer in New Haven. He started to get excited. The painting could be worth up to $35,000! (After all, we told each other, who would forge a signature by a painter no one ever heard of?) I took it to **Sotheby's.** They said it wasn't one of his best, but they thought it might fetch $7,000 to $10,000 and scheduled it for one of their Arcade sales. Well, I had pretty much spent that money when guess what happened. They had sent a photograph of the picture to Brianchon's relative in France, and he wrote back that he was not familiar with the painting. Death! Sotheby's withdrew it from the sale and told me to come and collect it. Humiliation! I showed up at the warehouse. They were surprisingly nice, but I slunk away with the painting, wrapped in brown paper and twine. It's still wrapped up, sitting in my attic.

I have had better luck buying from Sotheby's than selling there. Buying there is fun, as long as you pay attention to the same rules enunciated above. Both Sotheby's and their cheaper annex, **Sotheby's Arcade** (both located at York Avenue and 72nd Street), are great places to hang out and learn. The salespeople are, by and large, young and overeducated. As long as you're pleasant and appear serious, they will bend over backward to inform you about the things you're looking at. First of all, try to buy the catalogue if it's a period you love or an auction where you adore at least a dozen things. Even if the catalogue is $25, think of it as a textbook. If you buy the catalogue, they will send you the actual prices paid within a month after the sale. And now, you can telephone the day after the sale and punch in the numbers of the items you liked to see how much money they brought. Or check the Internet at www.sothebys.com for a complete calendar listing of events, auction schedules, auction results, and a helpful guide to buying and selling.

Contrary to popular belief, there are great bargains to be had here, especially in the Arcade. Again, don't forget—we are not necessarily talking about "steals," although those certainly exist. What we are talking about is finding wonderful things that will probably never depreciate in value (unlike new things, which are worth a tiny fraction of what you paid the second you plunk them down in your apartment).

When my friend Marcia Alazraki was decorating her apartment, I went to Sotheby's to buy her some turn-of-the-century cobalt blue Chinese rugs. Waving the paddle assigned to her, I was the successful bidder for an eight-by-ten-foot rug in excellent condition with a camel-colored Foo dog in the center, for $4,500. In a Madison Avenue shop it would have run closer to $10,000. She also bought a fanciful runner with what the curator called "Hee-Hee men" dancing across it, for $1,200. I don't pretend to know much about hundred-year-old Chinese rugs. But the difference between buying here and at Tepper's is that the men and women who work in the various departments really know—and share—information about their field. Thus, the head of Sotheby's rug department talked to me for about fifteen minutes about the two rugs before the sale and gave me a condition report and his own ballpark estimate (separate from that in the catalogue) about what the rugs were likely to bring. His opinion was amazingly accurate: The larger rug went slightly below the estimate, the Hee-Hee men right in the middle of the range.

If you need a set of sterling silver flatware, the Arcade is terrific. The silver goes to the Arcade when it's not considered important enough (rare and/or old enough) for the regular auctions. Thus, a set of George Jensen in the Pyramid pattern—my favorite—might go for $3,000 or $4,000, probably because it's still being manufactured. (What do you care? You're not a collector of rare silver—you want to use it to eat dinner! And the fact that it's still being made is great; you can add or replace pieces easily.) New, the set would cost closer to $12,000. The Arcade is also great for china and oriental carpets. Again, if you really like something and are serious about buying it, ask for advice from the staff. Build a relationship. (But don't ask for this favor if you're not considering bidding. They keep track. Even if they don't, if you do buy, you might want to send the staff person a thank-you note saying that you were successful and how much you appreciated the person's help. After you establish a relationship, you might find it easier to go to the exhibition, then go home and think about what you've seen. When you're sure, you can telephone and ask the staff person's opinion. It's more convenient, for both parties, than waiting in line on your lunch hour behind other advice seekers.)

For some reason, I've never bought at **Christie's.** But my friend Carol Prisant, who is both a writer and an appraiser, did a piece for *New York* magazine ("Let's Make a Deal," April 29, 1996, pp. 32–35) comparing Sotheby's, Christie's, and **William Doyle Galleries,** the three major Manhattan auction galleries. It's a wonderful article— she brought a series of her own *objets* to each and recorded the different reactions and estimates. In the end, Christie's scored the best, in terms of both knowledge and affability. And last year, Christie's had one of the most interesting Americana sales around.

GOING UP THE COUNTRY

There are dozens of country auctions within a couple of hours of Times Square, and everyone has his favorites. Part of the goal of this book is to outline methods to bid you can use anywhere. So if you get a strong recommendation from someone, just use the tips to your advantage—anywhere. For more information on specific auction sales, subscribe to *Antiques and Arts Weekly,* at 203-426-3141.

Among my favorites is **Brasswell Galleries.** Run by Gary Brasswell, this auction specializes in the more fancy-schmanzy stuff (faux neo-classical and Renaissance-look) and is a mecca for New York City decorators. But don't be deterred—they're cheapskates, too. And an occasional piece of early American painted furniture or a fun painting can slip by—right into your living room. Brasswell also has tag sales during good weather at the same time as some of their previews. The company specializes in cleaning out New York City apartments that are loaded with decorative things, so you never know. The bargains there, according to one expert, are in 1950s furniture: Charles Eames chairs, Italian furniture, pottery, and lots of good decorative lamps. You will find an exotic brew of designer stuff you can't find anywhere else: Some Peruvian guy might die or move on—and it ends up here.

Canton Barn Auctions, also in Connecticut, is best known for a rumor: that a tea table which sold at Christie's for hundreds of thousands of dollars a few years ago was bought here for about $1,200. I don't know if it's true—and I've never seen such quality here—but it's a good local auction that, like most of them, varies from week to week.

Like at many of the auction houses, you have to watch for the general merchandise sales at **Clearing House Auctions.** The big, well-advertised Americana sales are not exactly brimming with bargains. But the smaller sales may have a few steals, especially if you keep your eyes open for weird things: a brightly colored Art Deco painting of musical instruments, bought for $250 and worth about ten times as much; an early sugar bucket with the original luscious tomato red paint for $25; a pile of antique delft tiles for $15.

At the **E. S. Eldridge Warehouse Auction Gallery,** "Ernie" is amusing. Wearing his American-flag shirt, he addresses the women runners as "dear," while his wife looks on from the checkout table. If you can go to only one auction—and you want to go just for atmosphere—pick Ernie's. These Monday-night auctions can be worth the trip. (You'd have to stay overnight—it's about three and a half hours from Manhattan.) Not only is Ernie a character, but so are some of the customers—like the wild-looking individual with the gravy-stained suits who once bought an antique pack of Tarot cards for $200 and the rather smelly crowd that hangs out in the back, eating the greasy hamburgers that are sold on the premises. But there are some fascinating things here, and Ernie seems very fair and amiable. Each auction handles the dispersal of the items differently, though the usual thing is to pay for the items and then pick them up at some prearranged counter. But at Ernie's, they deliver the item to you at your seat—before you even pay. So one night—I think it was my first night (beginners' luck)—I was surrounded by a veritable treasure trove of junk! I sat on the country sofa I had bought for $100. Next to me was piled the early paper-covered hatbox with pictures of squirrels (bought for $200 and sold the next day for $400, when a dealer got my telephone number and called me with an offer). Next to that was a yellow-painted barrel chair I had bought for $15. Next to *that*. . . . Great fun—don't miss it—tell him I sent you. (Now that I have a full-time job, I never get to go . . . sob. My loss is your gain.)

Some cheapskate millionaires like sales at **James D. Julia**—rather than those of his closest competitor, Ronald Bourgeault—because they think you can still find a deal. But all the reputable auction houses in Maine have gotten ridiculously expensive these days, and even in the well-respected ones, you've still got to know what you're doing, especially when buying painted furniture. There's great stuff though. In a recent auction, Julia sold off eight hundred different gilt and painted frames, collections of playing cards, an old antique hatter's trade sign, a doll-size set of early blue Staffordshire, an early sawbuck table, and a rare needlepoint sampler with ascending balloons.

For some reason, Mr. Pari's logo at the **Joseph Pari Gallery** is "The Land of the Sleeping Giant." And while this auction house is certainly no giant, things certainly do get a little sleepy. But I recently saw a pristine landscape painting—a primitive gem—go for $600 here. It was bought by a prestigious Americana dealer, only to wind up in his booth for $2,400.

Ken Miller's Auction Barn attracts a lot of consignors who are known as "pickers," low-level antique dealers who mostly deal from the back of their car, usually to more-established dealers. But sometimes, when they can't make a sale, they like to put things in Miller's auction, because he pays them the next day. Great country stuff—quilts, primitive paintings, woodenware, interesting pottery—is found here, and the prices in this down-home kind of place are wholesale. Last summer, some customers flew down in a helicopter and landed on the lawn. They came in, bought a quilt, and took off. For the most part, though, it's a local crowd, and you can sometimes score.

Edward Nadeau—known locally as Eddie—at **Nadeau's Auction Gallery** is not your down-home humorist, the Will Rogers of the dinner party set. This guy looks like a grade B movie star and doesn't take any prisoners. If he doesn't like the way you bid—if you consistently bid low and then drop out, for instance—he may shut you out: not recognize your bid unless you stand up and shout. However, that said (and I have been frozen out from time to time), this is a place where you can really find great stuff. This is where I bought the down-filled couch for $10, as well as a wall of paintings for $40 (and left all but four on the wall). On a different night, I snagged a complete set for eight of new Ceralene by Limoges china, for $80. Still another Tuesday night, I found a rack of never-worn English suits for my cousin for $75, with a few Pratesi sheets and pillowcases thrown in, still in their cellophane wrappers. An antique dealer friend of mine bought an Adirondack kitchen table with birch legs for $125—and had it sold to a Maine dealer over the telephone before he even paid for it—for $650. One warning: Don't plan on buying Americana here or fine reproduction furniture. Those dealers watch Nadeau's like a hawk, and some records for high prices have been set here.

Paul McGinnis is a great place to buy refinished, early- to late-nineteenth century American furniture of a generally finer quality than that found at a lot of these country auctions—and the prices aren't bad! Like other auctioneers, Mr. McGinnis sometimes offers odd things as part of an estate sale: Recently, he was offering a 1996 Buick Roadmaster station wagon with only 1,800 miles, along with a 1972 Buick Skylark convertible with only 21,000 miles. (I guess the family liked Buicks—and didn't drive them too often.)

Paul Sage sometimes becomes irritated when the crowd at the **Sage Auction House** doesn't bid and exhorts these nonbuyers to "leave a dollar on the seat when you leave." But all kinds of great things have moved through here, although the sales have been kind of thin the last few years. One reason may be that Sage takes 30 percent of the selling price; other auctioneers usually skim off closer to 20 to 25 percent. One never knows what's here. Call and ask to be sent a postcard announcing upcoming sales. If the card is full of things like Hummel figurines and Cuisinart pots in harvest gold, it might be advisable to take a pass. (But don't forget, in sales like that, there might be a real sleeper.)

Winter Associates is referred to locally as "The Girls" because it was started by an elderly woman and her two assistants, who bought it after her death. Now only one, Linda Stamm, remains, but the sales haven't changed. By and large, the merchandise is not exciting and it's often expensive. But there are sometimes decent values, and the left bids—you fill out a form if you are not able to attend the Monday night auction—are fairly run, which is more than I can say about some of the others. Ms. Stamm lets the bidding begin from the floor—the correct way—and only then enters in from her list of written bids.

 Some auctioneers start with the left bidder's limit, which means if there is no other interest, the absentee bidder probably ends up paying a lot more than he had to. If the auctioneer starts with a bid from the floor and then—acting for the left bidder—just moves the bid up

one notch, the left bidder can wind up paying much less than his limit and saving hundreds of dollars. To the crooked auctioneers, running a fairly conducted auction is like losing money: The auctioneer knows he can set, say, $2,000 for a certain painting—the left bidder's limit—even though in fair bidding, the left bidder might get the painting for $1,500. Thus, to the auctioneer's way of thinking, he would "lose" $500. That's why some sleazy auctioneers go ahead and *start* the bidding at $2,000.

There are some interesting things at Winter Associates from time to time: an atticful of geometric abstract paintings by a virtually unknown Russian-American painter from the 1930s went for $300. (Cheaper than wallpaper—start a trend!) A pretty good, unrestored, late-eighteenth-century English tilt-top candlestand table went for $250. (Cheaper than at Ethan Allen—and about a hundred times better-looking, especially with a $200 restoration.) There is occasionally some excellent Americana, which, on a good night, you can buy reasonably. This is also a good place for estate jewelry.

THE OUTDOOR EXTRAVAGANZAS

There are three kinds of outdoor antiques shows: the extravaganzas, the antiques fairs, and the (more or less) antiques flea markets. Bargains can be found at all of them, as long as you know how to shop.

Right at the core of the Big Apple are the weekend antique flea markets around 26th Street and Sixth Avenue. There are three weekday parking lots around Sixth Avenue that, on weekends, become flea markets offering a wide range of nearly new stuff and antiques. There are also two indoor places on 26th Street called, appropriately enough, **The Garage** and **The Annex.** One summer, for a couple of Saturdays, I rented a spot on the second floor (it cost $125 a day) and sold stuff from my attic and my own garage, with mixed results.

There is no question that the best stuff goes fast. There is a man who sells furniture in the back of the northernmost Sixth Avenue lot; the stuff has included tubular furniture by Warren MacArthur and chests of drawers by Jens Riisom, for ridiculously cheap prices.

There are also straw skimmer hats from the 1920s for $20; cracked Quimper tureens for $25; ratty raccoon coats for $200; exotic samplers for $125; Mexican silver cuff links for $18; etc., etc., etc. It's okay to bargain, but don't think you're going to get something for nothing because these people are mostly professionals. (I was the exception—and my parents were antique dealers, so it's sort of in the blood!) If a Rookwood vase is marked $150, it's okay to offer $120. But offering $100 is not going to get you too far, and the dealer may well turn his back on you. That's okay. Just persevere; when he knows you're serious—just a little nervy—he'll counteroffer.

An assortment of separate outdoor shows line the main road through the town of **Brimfield,** Massachusetts, near Sturbridge. This is definitely worth going to, but bring your most comfortable shoes and try to get a motel room nearby. (Just try . . .)

Everyone has his favorite shows, and the Heart of the Mart is probably mine—at least partly because it doesn't open until 11 A.M.

This extravaganza really tests your endurance. There's too much stuff to see, and you end up walking around in a trance, brain dead or at least fried to a crisp. So how do you do it?

Pick *one* show and pretend the other ten don't exist—at least until you finish with the first one.

Don't race madly from booth to booth; take your time (but don't dawdle).

Try to learn to scan the booth from the grassy aisle and walk in only if you see an appealing target. You can usually tell a lot from the stuff the dealer chooses to put out in front. If you don't like his taste, why waste valuable time?

It is popular now to say there are no big bargains here anymore, and that may well be true. But again, let me repeat: You're not here to find a portrait by Ammi Phillips for $50 or a bronze by Gustav Doré for $10. That sort of thing probably did happen once, but it probably won't anymore. You're here to find some great things in order to furnish your pied-à-terre for a pittance. Oh, look! Here's a Jacobean-style (very stylish) low chest of drawers, complete with bun feet, for $85. Offer $75, which the dealer will take; pay for it (dealers love cash and it saves time). Get a receipt, mark down the location, and . . . leave it there. On to the next booth. Here are two brown, leather-covered Deco armchairs: $600 for both. Anything wrong? Yes, a tear in one of the seats, under the cushion. The chairs are great—they have a look. You can get the tear repaired, and it doesn't show. Offer $500. He won't budge. Take them anyway; they're a steal. What's this in two booths down? (Your friend has just called you on your walkie-talkie. . . .) A cornflower blue painted stepback cupboard straight from the Maine woods for only $800. It looks great, but . . . hmmm . . . There are entirely too many of these "antique" blue cupboards coming from Maine. Take a look at those backboards. Check the top. They look like they were sawed yesterday (and they probably were). Do not even think of buying painted furniture here unless you are a pro, and believe me, even pros can be fooled. Either that or buy it because it's cheap and just think of it as new. That way you won't be disappointed—and you might get a pleasant surprise although it's very, very unlikely.

You get the idea.

Renninger's, in Pennsylvania, is an enormous show, not a series of separate shows like Brimfield. The shows are held three weekends a year and are a lot of fun. Go only if you want to tour the Amish country, and stay at an adorable inn or bed and breakfast. I spent a couple of grueling Saturdays at these shows and came away empty-handed.

OUTDOOR ANTIQUES FAIRS

There are smaller antiques shows that are held outside during the summer, often on the grounds of a historic house, which gets a cut of the show manager's profits. These are definitely a step or two or three above the free-for-all flea market: The person running the show usually knows the dealer and his or her merchandise before letting him in the show. During the summer, each manager might put on ten or more shows, pretty much one a weekend.

These shows—run by **Linda Turner, Jacqueline Sideli,** and **Marilyn Gould**—are actually pretty great for bargain hunting. The dealers here usually have a pretty good eye for stuff—and they aren't so high-toned that you're paying extra for the provenance. At the Shaker Museum show in August, run by Jacqueline Sideli in Chatham, New York, I found a fabulous nineteenth-century small cabinet painted in a delicious dark blue-green (this paint was real) with paneled door and drawer below. This cupboard needed absolutely no work and had penciled inscriptions inside in some language I can't even begin to understand (Finnish? Latvian?). So it's clearly not American. But it was $200—a bargain in any language. The same dealer also had a marvelous gilt overmantel mirror for the same price. I didn't need it last summer, when I saw it, but I've bought another apartment and I do now. The Shaker Museum show also features—not surprisingly—Shaker baskets and chairs, at well below what you'd pay in New York City. There was also a primitive-style painting of strawberries for $35 that I should have bought. Bargaining is about the same as at other shows: some flexibility, but it doesn't pay to insult anybody.

ANTIQUES FLEA MARKETS IN THE COUNTRY

There are a lot of these, but avoid the ones in back of drive-in restaurants, the ones that bill themselves as antiques-laden but really sell primarily white cotton slouch socks and assortments of lug wrenches.

Stick to the better-known markets like **The Elephant's Trunk Bazaar,** Sunday mornings in New Milford, Connecticut, and the Saturday morning **Woodbury Flea Market,** also in Connecticut. The Elephant's Trunk is also a good place to unload an atticful of old stuff. Although both have their share of tube socks and paint brushes, there are some real antiques here—and potential deals galore. J. J. Smith, my New Haven art dealer friend, goes to Elephant's Trunk from time to time to just cash out. He pays $25 for a space, backs his van in, and sells great stuff really cheap—just to get rid of it and raise enough cash to go to the next auction. I love to bargain with J.J. If an item is marked $100, don't offer anything—just ask how much. A Mexican silver bracelet marked $125? He may say $50! And he's not the only one around doing the same thing. So play it by ear, and be polite. You never know what you'll end up with here.

I've also found interesting stuff at the side-of-the-road church flea markets, but they're very hit or miss. At a church fair in Haddam, Connecticut, I found one of my favorite things: an old silver salver with little paw feet and a family crest—for $5. (A general rule: You probably won't find anything at all at these affairs, but if you do, it may be the steal of the century!)

THE BIG(GER) TIME

Two times a year, **Stella Show Management** holds an antiques show on three of New York City's piers on the Hudson River. The shows are staged in March and November.

The pier shows are fascinating, as well as exhausting. The quality of stuff is quite high, especially in the Art Deco booths, which seem to be a specialty. But again, the price to show is expensive: By the time the dealers pay to have their lights hooked up and their colored-paper backdrop hung, the price for two days can easily top $2,000, plus hotel rooms and parking. So don't expect any $5 silver salvers here. But generally speaking, the prices are fair, and there can be bargains, especially for collectibles. (Even though the dealer knows what the object is, you may still get a bargain if you show real interest and knowledge and have practiced your negotiating techniques on the local level. If you're a collector, you may also get a swap going.) Textiles also seem to be very cheap here; I bought a superb set of flowered Deco draperies here for $60.

Then there is the **Winter Antiques Show at the Armory,** which, with all the add-ons, can run dealers $25,000. So what do you think you're going to steal here? Knowledge, that's what. This is a wonderful place to window shop, and by and large, if you're not a giggling fool, the dealers, unless they're frightfully busy, are amiable and helpful. If you don't know what you're looking at and have read the tag, ask politely. Fred Giampietro, of New Haven, Connecticut, and New York City, runs one of the best booths here. Giampietro was one of three dealers written about in the book *Objects of Desire* (a must-read, by the way: a real primer on the antiques business) and is a nice, knowledgeable guy who loves paint and patina and Americana.

But don't pay much attention to the prices. Just because a late nineteenth-century washstand painted yellow is marked $12,500 at the Armory doesn't mean *you* can get more than, probably, $1,000 for the same thing. And it certainly doesn't mean that because a nice red-and-green quilt—Ohio, mid-nineteenth-century—bore a price of $7,500, *you* could sell it for any more than about $800—on a good day. But it does mean that you will know what is "in" and what is considered good. Then you can take a taxi to . . .

Antiques at the Other Armory, held downtown, on East 26th

Street and Lexington. This show, not surprisingly, coincides with the uptown show: matching dates, but certainly not prices. The dealers downtown are all strong; they're just not in the $25,000-a-show league, which is all to your advantage. John Sideli, Jacqueline's ex-husband, usually shows here, and his things can be said to be on a par with the country's finest primitive Americana dealers. Mr. Sideli, a sculptor, is known for his "eye"—an overused description that is used by every big dealer to flatter every big would-be collector, but in this case it is true. Mr. Sideli's prices, while by no means cheap, are a lot less than they are on East 68th Street, and there are many interesting dealers, offering many wonderful bargains on highly decorative and fun things. Do check out the Armory, or East Side show, as it is called by some, and then head downtown—or to any of the other, smaller shows planned for the weeks around the poshest show in the country.

🍎 Sources

NEW FURNITURE

ABC Carpet & Home
888 Broadway (at 19th Street)
212-473-3000
Monday to Friday, 10 A.M.–8 P.M.;
Saturday, 10 A.M.–7 P.M.; Sunday,
11 A.M.–6:30 P.M.

Crate & Barrel
650 Madison Avenue (at 59th Street)
212-308-0011
Monday to Saturday, 10 A.M.–7 P.M.;
Sunday, noon–6 P.M.

George Smith Sofas and Chairs, Inc.
73 Spring Street (between Broadway
and Lafayette), 212-226-4747
Monday to Friday, 9 A.M.–5 P.M.;
Saturday, 11 A.M.–6 P.M.

Nuovo Melodrom
60 Greene Street (between Broome and
Spring), 212-219-0013
Monday to Friday, 9:30 A.M.–6 P.M.;
Saturday to Sunday, noon–6 P.M.

Palazzetti
515 Madison Avenue (at 53rd Street)
212-832-1199
Monday to Friday, 9:30 A.M.–6 P.M.;
Saturday, 11 A.M.–5 P.M.; Sunday,
11 A.M.–5 P.M.

152 Wooster Street (off Houston)
212-260-8815
Monday to Saturday, 9:30 A.M.–6 P.M.;
Sunday, noon–5 P.M.

Pottery Barn
2109 Broadway (at 67th Street)
212-579-8477
Monday to Saturday, 11 A.M.–9 P.M.;
Sunday, 11 A.M.–7 P.M.

1451 Second Avenue (at 76th Street)
212-988-4228
Monday to Saturday, 11 A.M.–8 P.M.;
Sunday, noon–6

600 Broadway (at the corner of
Houston), 212-505-6377
Monday to Saturday, 10 A.M.–9 P.M.;
Sunday, 11 A.M.–7 P.M.

AUCTION HOUSES

Most of the larger auction houses, and some of the smaller ones, have a Web site. Call for details.

NEW YORK CITY

Christie's
502 Park Avenue (at 59th Street)
212-546-1000

Sotheby's and Sotheby's Arcade
1334 York Avenue (at 72nd Street)
212-606-7000

The Tepper Galleries
110 East 25th Street (between Park and Lexington Avenues), 212-677-5300

William Doyle Galleries
175 East 87th Street (between Lexington and Third Avenues), 212-427-2730 or 427-4885
Exhibition hours are Monday, 10 A.M.–7 P.M.; Tuesday to Saturday, 10 A.M.–5 P.M.; Sunday, noon–5 P.M. Auctions occur on Wednesday mornings.

GOING UP THE COUNTRY

Brasswell Galleries
125 and 137 West Avenue (off I-95, Exit 14), Norwalk, Conn., 203-899-7420 or 203-838-6124
Previews are open Monday to Friday, 10 A.M.–4 P.M. Auctions are on Saturdays and Sundays. Call for details.

Canton Barn Auctions
75 Old Canton Road, Canton, Conn., 860-693-0601
Auctions are usually on Saturdays.

Clearing House Auctions
207 Church Street (off I-91, Exit 26) Wethersfield, Conn., 860-529-3344

Regular auctions take place every Wednesday. Previews are at 5 P.M.; auctions are at 7 P.M. The more important auctions take place on Friday nights, as scheduled. Call for details.

E. S. Eldridge Warehouse Auction Gallery
90 South Park Street, Windham, Conn., 860-450-0525
Auctions take place every Monday at 7 P.M.

James D. Julia
Route 201, Skowhegan Road, Fairfield, Maine, 207-453-7125

Joseph Pari Gallery
3846 Whitney Avenue, Hamden, Conn. 203-248-4951
Open Mondays.

Ken Miller's Auction Barn
141 Warwick Road (off I-91, Northfield exit), Northfield, Mass., 413-498-2749
Auctions take place one Saturday a month.

Nadeau's Auction Gallery
25 Meadow Rd (off I-91, Exit 34) Windsor, Conn., 860-246-2444 or 860-524-8666
Auctions take place almost every Saturday. Previews begin at 11 A.M., auctions at 1 P.M.

Paul McGinnis
356 Exeter Road, Route 88, Hampton Falls, N. H., 603-778-8989
Auctions are held on Saturdays.

Sage Auction House
221 Middlesex Road (I-95, Exit 69 to route 9 north; then Exit 6 to route 148, to route 154), Chester, Conn., 860-526-3036
Shop open Wednesday to Saturday, 11 A.M.–4 P.M.; closed Mondays and Tuesdays. Auctions are usually on Friday nights.

Winter Associates
21 Cooke Street (off I-84, Crooked
Street exit), Plainville, Conn.,
860-793-0288
Auctions take place once a month,
usually on Mondays; call for details.

INDOOR EXTRAVAGANZAS

"Atlantique City"
Atlantic City Convention Center, Atlantic
City, N.J.
For information call 800-526-2724 or
check www.atlantiquecity.com

**The Garage Indoor Antique
Show**
112 West 25th Street, 212-647-0707
Open Saturdays and Sundays, sunrise
to sunset.

OUTDOOR EXTRAVAGANZAS

**The Annex Antique Fair & Flea
Market**
Sixth Avenue (between 24th and 26th
Streets), 212-243-5343
Open Saturdays and Sundays, sunrise
to sunset.

Brimfield
Brimfield, Mass. (off I-84 east, Exit 3B to
route 20 west)
For information call the Sturbridge
Chamber of Commerce at
800-628-8379.
Shows are held in May, July, and
September.

The Grand Bazaar
West 25th Street (between Broadway
and Sixth Avenue), 914-273-1578 or
212-243-9124
Open Saturdays and Sundays, sunrise
to sunset.

Renninger's
610-683-6848 or 570-385-0104
Kutztown, Penn.
Extravaganzas in April, June, and September.
Generally on Thursdays, Fridays, and Saturdays. (Thursdays are reserved for dealer set-
up, but bargain hunters can pay a hefty
fee—this year it was $40 per car, up to three
people—for an early peek, and the fee pays
for subsequent entrances over all three days.)

OUTDOOR ANTIQUES FAIRS

Marilyn Gould
203-762-7357 for the Wilton Show.
Call for this year's shows—or read
about them in Antiques and Arts
Weekly.

Jacqueline Sideli
508-324-4900
Call for this year's shows—or read
Antiques and Arts Weekly.

Linda Turner
207-767-3967
Ms. Turner features shows between May and
October, usually at historic sites. Take in her
Bunker Hill Antiques Market in Charlestown,
Massachusetts, in May; the Dorset Antiques
Festival in Vermont in July; the Riverside Antiques Show during the big "Antiques Week in
New Hampshire" in August; the Bath (Maine)
show in late August; the Hildene show (held
on the grounds of Robert Todd Lincoln's home)
in Manchester Village, Vermont; and the well-
known Hartford Antiques Show in October, an
indoor show with dealers—and prices—more
than a tad above the open-field shows.

ANTIQUES FLEA MARKETS

The Elephant's Trunk Bazaar
New Milford, Conn. (route 7 off I-84,
Exit 2), 860-355-1448
Open Sunday mornings; $1 admission.

Woodbury Flea Market
Woodbury, Conn. (I-84, Exit 15)
203-263-2841
Open Saturdays.

THE BIG(GER) TIME

Antiques at the Other Armory
26th Street and Lexington Avenue,
212-255-0020
Takes place the same time as the Winter Antiques Show.

Stella Show Management, 147 West
24th Street, 212-255-0020
Shows, including the Triple Pier Expo, which takes place at Hudson River piers at 48th, 50th, and 52nd Streets.

Wendy Management
Holds eighteen shows a year, seven in New York City.
For information call Don Blauhaut, 914-5040.

Winter Antiques Show at the Armory
Seventh Regiment Armory
(at 67th Street and Park Avenue)
For show information, call Laura Latterman at 212-935-1033.

INTERNET AUCTION SITES

www.auctionuniverse.com
Advertises a money-back guarantee and an optional $3,000 insurance package.

www.ebay.com
The phenomenon: Lucky initial investors are now very rich. This site is easier to fathom than auctionuniverse's. I've both bought and sold here successfully.

For the Material Millionaire: Fabrics Galore to Make Your Cheap Apartment a Paradise

In New York City, there are three major places to find great fabric cheaply. My favorite are the stores around the aptly named Garment District. The next is along Orchard Street on the Lower East Side. The last is along Broadway north and south of Canal Street.

If you've got a car, there is another place to find *extraordinary* fabrics: the **Griswold Fabric Mill** in Westerly, Rhode Island. Very few people know that this is one of the mills used by Brunschwig & Fils and Clarence House, the most renowned fabric makers in the world. I have bought $125 a yard Chateau Landon by Brunschwig here for $7.99 a yard. I have bought Schumacher heavy document-printed linen (not their cheaper brand, Waverley) here for $5.99 a yard. It is catch-as-catch-can here: They bring out the styles bolt by bolt and you never know what will be offered, so buy *everything* you need now. If you buy a sample yard, say, and then come back for the remaining twenty-nine—vanished! A decorator could have bought the whole bolt, and there may never be any more. I also got a wonderful blue resist pattern made for Williamsburg here for $6.99. The saleswoman here is very helpful. She unrolls the amount you need from the bolt, and if there are any irregularities (bleeding or patterns that don't line up), she makes sure you see the problem. But a lot of the material is perfect; it's just overruns on an order. P. S. Bring *cash,* period. (They don't take any kind of check or plastic card. I've argued and it doesn't do any good!)

GARMENT DISTRICT

For city shopping, some of the best fabric bargains in the city are in the Garment District, along 39th and 40th Streets, between Seventh and Eighth Avenues. The stores are small in front, packed close together like their millions of bolts of linens and crepes, but they usually stretch way out in back, and some have second and third floors.

By and large, the service is friendly enough—they are used to retail customers, even though they advertise "Wholesale and Retail." To get the best attention, try to act decisive, even if you're just browsing. Formulate a list of three or four things you might be interested in buying. On one day, I chose a black-and-white checked linen, a good camel hair and an olive-colored silk taffeta—all of which could grace some project I have.

One of my favorite shops is called **U.S. Liberty Fabrics.** There, a clerk named Raman was friendly and helpful, but didn't hover. The turbanned owner in front graciously informed another shopper: "Looking is no charge!" There are some great buys here: black-and-white-checked acetate, 52 inches white, is $5 a yard; polished cotton and brushed cotton—there was a good beige-on-ivory stripe—is just $6 a yard. Cotton twill in a peaceful burgundy was $4 a yard. Perhaps the best deals were on linens: A dreamy Ralph Lauren navy blue pinstripe on a white ground, perfect for a summer shirtwaist, is only—get ready—$6 a yard. (Spectacular for curtains, too.) And there are also lovely beige-on-white stripes (choose either horizontal or vertical), plus the heavier linens in mostly solids. There is a closeout pile of pure wools for $4.99 a yard; nothing caught my eye.

Next door, at **Butterfly Fabrics,** the emphasis is on Indian fabrics, for saris, sheer blouses, or—maybe—some kind of delicious sheer curtains. In the sheers, there is an intense deep purple—the most intensely colored fabric I've ever seen—with an exquisite gold-embroidered geometric pattern: little gold lines and squares. Then, in the same sheer stuff, there are gold medallions on a navy-black and on an emerald green—take your pick. The price? $10 a yard. There is also a heavier Tussah silk for $12 a yard: The orange-and-champagne stripe is particularly yummy. Draperies that fall to the ground like a waterfall? Yes, please. Or how about whipping up an evening bustier and skirt like the similarly striped silk set Yohji Ya-mamoto designed this season, both for $7,685 in Bergdorfs?

Across the street is **E and M Fabrics,** a temporary-looking store with simple hanging rods displaying bolts of lush drapery and uphol-stery tapestries for as little as $9.75 a yard. Then there was an Ital-ian-made brick red stripe with gold and champagne—*très élégant*—for $27 a yard, and worth every cent, as well as 100 percent camel hair, very thick, for $35 a yard. A delicious black blend that is 65 percent wool, 15 percent nylon, and 20 percent angora is only $14.99 a yard. E and M will also make your curtains. They charge $165 for a swag and two jabots, plus the cost of the material, and you can see what it will look like: One is stapled to the side wall of the shop.

Another good place to check is **Art-Max,** a block away on West 40th Street. They have linings in every hue for $2.50 a yard; swell-looking satins for $10 and $15; luscious pale strawberry-colored cashmere and wool for $25 a yard; and divine silk taffeta (real silk, not polyester) for $30 a yard, which isn't bad.

As long as you're browsing, drop into **A & S Quality Fabrics** and **Felsen Fabrics,** both also on West 40th.

FABRICS ON LOWER BROADWAY

There used to be many fabric stores in SoHo, but because the area has gotten so trendy (to the people who come from New Jersey) or touristy (to the people who live here), they have been replaced by jeans stores and patisseries. But Canal Street is still an amazing array of $10 watches (mine's still running after a year), glazed ducks hang-ing in the windows of Chinese restaurants, art supply stores, and elec-tronics warehouses, so it's worth at least one visit. And if you're looking for fabrics, you should venture into the **Fabric Warehouse** at Broad-way and Canal, where no prices to speak of are marked. When you ask how much anything is, Maria will tell you one price—and then quickly reduce it. "This velvet you asked about?" she whispered, hold-ing a piece of my favorite color (pond-scum green) material. "It's $15 a yard—but I'll sell it for $11." How about that wonderful wide navy blue grosgrain ribbon with the tiny white polka dots? "It's $1.50 a yard, but if you see me, I'll give you a different price!" (Meaning: When you're serious about buying, ask me for real.)

As their fellow merchants are getting squeezed out by the Levis, some of these fabric shops are getting militant. **Du Kane Fabrics** on Broadway has a sign that says "No Retail." Usually, you can ignore that, but it appears they mean business. In another window, a sign says "500 Yard Minimum." Instead, stop into **Rae Trading** at 452 Broadway and **Jacob Wiesenfeld** nearby. JOBBER-TEXTILES-EXPORTER, the sign says.

BACK TO ORCHARD STREET

Within the last few years, my own interest has shifted to Grand Street, in the blocks on both sides of Orchard Street—and best of all, to the shops creeping up Orchard Street itself, as if pushing out the older clothing shops, their passementerie strangling the old phony-discount shops selling hideous bright red acrylic blazers and similarly undesirable items.

Frankly, I'd just as soon skip the fabric shops along Grand Street, although the best of them are listed at the back of the chapter, and head right over to Orchard Street.

Of all the shops, there are two that definitely must be seen, for completely different reasons: **Beckenstein's** and **Joe's.**

"Joe's Fabric Warehouse" is the name on the card, with the following description written underneath the name: "Two Full Floors of the Most Current Designer and Imported Upholstery Drapery Fabrics and Trimmings in Stock!"

And it's all true.

Joe's, at both 102 and 110 Orchard Street at the corner of Delancey, offers some of the city's greatest bargains for cheapskate millionaires.

Don't be fooled by the little showroom at 102 Orchard. I almost didn't walk a few doors down—and up the stairs—although I was certainly attracted to the elegant little silk taffetas on rolls in the showroom. So were two Asian women, who handled the silks lovingly, whispering admiringly in a language I didn't understand. Two other women announced they were from the Yale Drama School and were looking for material for costumes. We are all directed upstairs.

Ah, upstairs! For a material girl like myself, this place is nirvana—and if you think I'm overhyping the place, go there and see. It's not the size of the place—I've seen bigger rooms of fabric at the **Colchester (Connecticut) Mill Fabrics.** It's the quality. There's hardly a piece of cheap-looking fabric here.

Here's a sampling: a Richie-Rich stripe of black sateen, embroidered with deep mossy-yellow bees and small olive circles, next to a black-on-beige weave of—what?—olive branches, sandwiched between a narrow mossy-yellow Greek key design with a pinstripe of terra cotta. Hard to envision? I suppose so, but trust me: On a Federal sofa, there's nothing better. (In fact, I'm thinking of buying a Federal sofa just so I can use this heavenly fabric.) Oh, I forgot to mention: It's only $25 a yard, although if someone told me they paid $175, I wouldn't bat an eyelid.

Then another stripe: this one in tomato red sateen with an equally sized, three-inch stripe of a light chocolate brown, with tiny dots of maize all over it, for the same price as the bee tapestry.

Then there's heavy cotton one-and-a-half-inch taupe-and-cream, for $15 a yard; a waffle-weave white piqué for $20; a wonderfully hued, tiny herringbone in a kind of olive-mustard, also for $20; and finally a cheery silk taffeta in a cobalt blue, white, peach, and yellow stripe for another $20 a yard.

Joe's also does custom-ordered material and keeps dozens of fabric books in the back of the second floor. They found an antique velvet I was looking for to cover an old down-filled couch, in exactly the right tone: an intense (and indescribable) muddy olive. It's $25 a yard, and I ordered 14 yards.

WANDERING THROUGH THE D&D BUILDING: NOT A DAY TRIP FOR AMATEURS

Now here's the first thing you have to learn about working the **D&D Building,** the famous designers' and decorators' galleria on Third Avenue: The showrooms here are strictly to-the-trade, with no exceptions. So in order to just browse here, you need to have entrée. Entrée itself is not hard to gain, especially if you have friends who are interior designers, architects, shopkeepers, or building contractors. Just tell them you're going, and grab a fistful of their cards. That way, in the event that some snippy saleswoman decides to check up on you, you're covered.

In most cases, you'll have to produce the card even to be admitted to browse. I went recently in an attempt to see what would happen if I did not produce my card. In many of the showrooms—including Boussac of France and Sanderson and Gretchen Bellinger—I just strolled in. It was late in the day (I'd advise this), and the clerks were in the back room or somewhere else. But at Brunschwig, the woman was right there at the front of the showroom foyer. I said I had my own business and wanted to browse. She asked if I had an account. I said no, but I'd like to fill out an application. She gave it to me—all the while staring into my eyes—and decided to let me look. But buying was out of the question—as it is in any showroom here.

In order to buy something at the drastically reduced prices that designers get, you have to line up one of your friends who has an account with the supplier, or persuade him or her to get one. The account can be what is known as a *pro forma* account: That means you are billed for each order. This type of account is relatively easy to get because the companies figure you can't abuse it. If there is any question, or if you fail to pay the first time, they don't have much liability. When I was working as a general contractor restoring antique houses, a friend of mine, an interior designer in Avon, Connecticut, allowed me to use her account. It was great fun—I ordered dozens of rolls of Brunschwig wallpaper for a fraction of the retail cost—and paid her back when she got the bill.

If your project is big enough—say, a whole house or a huge apartment—you may decide to go into business seriously. This, of course, is up to you and your accountant. But if you think you'll save enough money to make it worthwhile—and if you absolutely must save thousands on that Clarence House chintz—I know a lot of people who have done this successfully. Then you can browse and shop here to your heart's delight. But be careful: Make sure you fill out all the applications accurately, pay your taxes, and do whatever you have to do honestly. These things have a way of catching up with you—and it might be better to persuade a friend to order the material for you, as a business transaction, rather than get into something that will backfire. Nevertheless, if you *do* start your own business, make sure you register with plumbing supply houses, too! (They're the *most* fun places to browse around.)

WALLPAPER

There are only two places I go to get great wallpaper really cheaply. The first is the **Ocean State Job Lot** stores. The second is England.

Let's take the first. Ocean State Job Lot stores are a Rhode Island chain, and now there is even one in Clinton, Connecticut, less than a mile from my favorite designer outlet center (Clinton Crossing), both only two hours from Times Square. It might be worth the trip just to go to Ocean State—only *might* because like any of these outlet stores, it depends on the day you go. But on any one day, these are the things you might find at prices that will amaze you:

> Charming wooden crates containing four candles in the shape of acorn squash and red-and-orange gourds, nestled in beds of straw—for only $5.99 per crate.
> A West Bend electric bread maker that is easy to use and bakes great bread—for $29.99.
> Bread mix to go with it—multigrain, sourdough, wheat, and country French—for $1.29.
> Great-looking mugs with pea pods or hot peppers painted on them—for 49 cents.
> More little crates with sets of four spatter-painted Chinese cereal bowls or plates—$3.99 (per set) for the bowls and $4.99 for the plates. They also had matching ovenproof casserole dishes for $2.99.
> Good-looking iron butcher's racks with plain finial-ends—not those clichéd curlicues—for $39.99.
> English, American, and Canadian wallpaper—for $2.49 a roll.

Yes, the store recently had some really great wallpaper for the price of a six-pack of toilet paper. There were a couple of huge tables—the kind they have at church suppers—set up, and hundreds of rolls were laid upon them, all brand new. They weren't that kind with the ghastly vinyl coating, either. One pattern was a white background, with some simple cobalt-blue shells on it. Another had an aubergine background with a kind of simple Gothic diamond pattern on it. One had tomato-red-and-ivory stripes. Others were the more familiar flowery prints. And they had enough of each pattern to more than cover a room or two—a problem with some of the sample sales for wallpaper I've attended (where you can buy only enough to cover half of a very small closet). Last time I went, they had plenty of Robert Allen (a well-known American designer, with headquarters in the D&D building) paper in a delicious mossy green *strieé* and another in a kind of beige-on-beige stripe (I bought ten rolls) and some Laura Ashley in small quantities. They also had plenty of wallpaper that bore the Victoria and Albert Museum imprimatur. These were, not surprisingly, small Victorian prints in traditional colors, very appealing if that's what you're looking for. P. S. I just found some of the same York wallpaper selling at the **Janovic Plaza** store on West 72nd Street near Broadway—for $37.95 a double roll. (Compared with $2.49, it suddenly seemed expensive. . . .)

You always need more wallpaper than you think. To cover a small (8-by-10-foot) bedroom, you may need twelve rolls! So measure carefully: One 20-inch-wide roll usually covers only 15 feet. This means the roll will cover a 40-inch-wide piece of wall in a room with normal-height ceilings.

For places like the Ocean State stores, call before you waste a trip. They can't describe the patterns, but at least they'll tell you if they even have wallpaper, and if you ask, maybe they'll tell you whether they've still got a good selection or whether it's pretty well picked through. If the clerk who picks up the phone is uncooperative, either call back or ask to speak to the manager.

Now, the wallpaper at the Ocean State was pretty nice—nicer than a lot of the stuff at **Home Depot,** for instance. But if you want something *really* nice, it's a lot easier to send away to London for a William Morris print (made by Sanderson) or a Cowton & Towt or one of the great English papers. You can save hundreds of dollars doing this, and it's all perfectly legitimate.

Here's what you do: Either find the pattern you want in a book borrowed from Janovic Plaza, or if it's not available there, go to the D&D Building. Although you must be a registered designer to order from the shops here, many will not mind if you come in to look at patterns—especially if you look chic and confident. (Or you could ask a decorator friend to take you, but it probably won't come to that.) Anyway, just jot down the name of the pattern, the color, and any other information you think might be helpful.

Then run home and dial up a wallpaper shop like **John Oliver** in

London, check the price, and place the order. Two weeks later, your paper will show up. I recently ordered three of the William Morris designs: "Fruit," "Willow," and "Acorn." They cost about £22 per double roll, or about $35. In the United States, the double rolls list for $96. For ten rolls of wallpaper, I just saved about $600.

BLINDS

Now what can I buy for all that money I saved on wallpaper? What about some of those natural-colored, two-inch wood blinds by Hunter-Douglas? I've used them everywhere: not too fussy, but they go with every period. They were used in the eighteenth century; they were used in Thomas Jefferson's study at the University of Virginia. The only thing is, you say, they're expensive. Well, I thought so too—before I discovered **National Blind & Wallpaper Factory.**

Noooo, you moan. Not those awful ads in the back of every not-so-ritzy shelter magazine? Yes, one and the same. One day I was so aghast at the prices at my neighborhood paint and wallpaper shop—one that advertises 60 percent off on all blinds, by the way—that I telephoned the 800 number (800-477-8000) just for laughs. I figured that it would be like dealing with a company that advertises on the inside of a matchbook: a puff of smoke and there's nothing there. I figured there would be countless add-ons and shipping costs and that it would end up costing double what my local hardware store charged.

Wrong. Here are the comparisons on Hunter-Douglas two-inch wood blinds in natural, measuring 36 inches wide by 60 inches high:

Janovic Plaza **$181.86**
(a New York City paint chain, with advertised deep discounts)

**American Blind and
Wallpaper Factory** **$103.50**
(a competitor of National's, also with an 800 number: 1-800-735-5300)

**National Paint &
Wallpaper Factory** . . . . **$ 94.97**

Both mail order companies offer free shipping and no tax. And I have ordered from both of them, with entirely satisfactory results.

🍎 Sources

ANTIQUE TEXTILES

Bryony Thomasson
283 Westbourne Grove (corner of
Portobello Road), London, England
011-44-171-731-3693
She specializes in antique linen sheets, old
toiles, and embroidered silks; perfect for making draperies, pillows, and bed hangings.

FABRIC

A & S Quality Fabrics Corp.
250 West 39th Street (between Seventh
and Eighth Avenues), 212-921-5072
Monday to Friday, 9:30 A.M.–6 P.M.;
Saturday, 9:30 A.M.–5 P.M.; closed
Sundays

Art-Max Fabrics
250 West 40th Street (between Seventh
and Eighth Avenues), 212-398-0755
Monday to Friday, 8:30 A.M.–5:45 P.M.;
Saturday, 8:30 A.M.–5 P.M.; closed
Sundays

Beckenstein Home Fabrics
130 Orchard Street (between Rivington
and Delancy), 212-475-6666
9 A.M.–5:30 P.M., seven days a week

Butterfly Fabrics
256 West 39th Street (between Seventh
and Eighth Avenues), 212-575-4744 or
800-275-4097
Monday to Saturday, 9 A.M.–5:30 P.M.;
Sunday, noon–5 P.M.

Colchester Mill Fabrics
120 Lebanon Avenue, Colchester, Conn.
860-537-2004
Monday to Friday, 9 A.M.–6 P.M.;
Thursday, 9 A.M.–8 P.M.; Saturday,
9:30 A.M.–5 P.M.; Sunday,
10 A.M.–5 P.M.

Du Kane Fabrics International
451 Broadway (between Grand and
Howard Streets), 212-925-8400
Office open Monday to Friday,
9 A.M.–5:30 P.M.

E and M Fabrics
257 West 39th Street (between Seventh
and Eighth Avenues), 212-391-9232
Monday to Friday, 9 A.M.–6 P.M.;
Sunday, 11 A.M.–4 P.M.; closed
Saturdays

Fabric Warehouse
406 Broadway (at Canal Street)
212-431-9510
9 A.M.–6 P.M., seven days a week

Felsen Fabrics Corp.
264 West 40th Street (between Seventh
and Eight Avenues), 212-398-9010
Monday to Friday, 9 A.M.–5:45 P.M.;
Saturday, 9 A.M.–4:45 P.M.; closed
Sundays

Griswold Fabric Mill
White Rock Road, Westerly, R.I.,
401-596-2784
Monday to Friday, 8 A.M.–2:30 P.M.
Take Exit 92 off route 95 in Connecticut; turn
right onto route 2; go to the second light (gas
station on left side). After the light, take the
first left onto White Rock Road; go over the
bridge. Go to the stop sign and take a left. The
old brick factory and shop are on the left.
Cash only.

Jacob Wiesenfeld Textiles
450 Broadway (at Grand Street)
212-431-6010
Monday to Friday, 9 A.M.–5 P.M.

Joe's Fabric Warehouse
102 and 110 Orchard (at Delancey
Street), 212-674-7089
Monday to Thursday, Sunday,
9 A.M.–6 P.M.; closed Fridays and
Saturdays

Rae Trading

452 Broadway (between Grand and
Howard Streets), 212-966-1414
Monday to Friday, 9 A.M.–6 P.M.;
Saturday, 10 A.M.–6 P.M.; Sunday
11 A.M.–6 P.M.

U.S. Liberty Fabrics

250 West 39th Street (between Seventh
and Eighth Avenues), 212-354-9360
Monday to Friday, 9:30 A.M.–6:30 P.M.;
Saturday, 9:30 A.M.–6 P.M.;
Sunday, noon–4 P.M.

HARDWARE

J. Shiner & Sons

8 Windmill Street, London, England
011-44-171-636-0740
Call for a catalogue; prices can be one-third
the price of comparable knobs, hinges, and
locks here.

WALLPAPER AND BLINDS

American Blind and Wallpaper Factory

Call for a catalogue or to speak with a
sales rep at 800-735-5300.

D&D Building

973 Third Avenue (at 57th Street)
212-759-2964

Home Depot

There are many branches of this
popular hardware chain. Here are three
of the best: 131-35 Avery Avenue,
Flushing, Queens, 718-358-9600
Open 24 hours

541 Kings Highway (off I-95, exit 23)
Fairfield, Conn., 203-254-3888
Monday to Saturday, 6 A.M.–11 P.M.;
Sunday, 8 A.M.–7 P.M.

55 Weyman Avenue (off I-95, exit 15)
New Rochelle, N.Y., 914-235-7575
Monday to Saturday, 6 A.M.–midnight;
Sunday, 8 A.M.–7 P.M.

Janovic Plaza

1150 Third Avenue (at 67th Street)
212-772-1400
215 Seventh Avenue (at 23rd Street)
212-645-5454
159 West 72nd Street (between
Columbus and Amsterdam Avenues)
212-595-2500
1555 Third Avenue (at 87th Street)
212-289-6300
125 Fourth Avenue (at 12th Street)
212-477-6930
292 Third Avenue (at 23rd Street)
212-777-3030
2475 Broadway (at 92nd Street)
212-769-1440
771 Ninth Avenue (at 52nd Street)
212-245-3241
161 Sixth Avenue (at Spring Street)
212-627-1100
All stores are open Monday to Friday,
7:30 A.M.–6:30 P.M.; Saturday,
9:30 A.M.–6:30 P.M.; Sunday,
11 A.M.–5 P.M.

John S. Oliver

33 Pembridge Road, London, England,
011-44-171-221-6466
Pick out that expensive wallpaper here—and
then call London to check out the price plus the
shipping costs. It may amaze you!

John Lewis

Sloane Square, London, England
011-44-171-730-3434
See above. Even more variety.

National Blind & Wallpaper Factory

To speak with a sales representative, call
800-477-8000.

Ocean State Job Lot

90 West Main Street (off I-95, exit 62)
Clinton, Conn. 860-664-9446
Monday to Saturday, 9 A.M.–9 P.M.;
Sunday, 9 A.M.–5:30 P.M.

9

Having Them Made: Curtains, Upholstery, Cabinets; Finding the Raw Materials; Light for All

DRAPERIES

Now here's the best tip of all: Draperies are out. Yes, those big, pleaty, chintzy draperies that pool on the floor are more or less passé. Which is good for you, dear shopper, because the thousands of yards of expensive material they take—even if you know a place to get it—cost the earth to make.

Instead, think simple, elegant. Think sumptuous, thin, gauzy swags and basic rectangles that just cover the window. Think delicious fabrics: silks and skinny wools in tomato red. Think beautiful hand-blocked linens gathered up into Roman shades. This is a time for creativity, which, lately, is admired more than all the passementerie in Paris. So even if you're not particularly handy, you can often come up with something yourself.

Last time I was in London, I bought the most delicate red-and-white antique toile valences with the original red-and-white ball fringe hanging from them. I bought them from a wonderful woman named Bryony Thomasson, who has a stall at the Portobello Road market (see Sources, Chapter 8). The scraps of toile cost me about $20. I stapled them to a piece of plywood cut by a lumber yard to exactly the width of the inside window frame (no, this is not turning into a Martha Stewart book) and voilà. Believe me, this was incredibly easy. I've also bought some antique linen sheets from Bryony—

thick beige stuff that can be transformed into swags or shower curtains or do-it-yourself slipcovers. Or you can call one of the cheap slipcover services listed each week in *The New York Times* House & Home section. I've had some upholstering done by one of these one-price-fits-all services, and it was perfectly decent.

When dealing with an upholsterer for the first time, bring photographs from magazines, not only of the style you want, but of the detailing. Many upholsterers, especially cheap ones, like to use cording (the round roping around the seat cushions and the rest of the seams) as thick as your pinky finger. No, no, no. The smaller the better, especially if it's for cotton or linen or thin wool. The best thing is to visit a sewing supply place and buy a sample piece to show them. This serves two purposes: showing them the right size and, more important, showing them you really care.

That said, it might be better to do slipcovers. First, slipcovers have a wonderful old devil-may-care country-house look, and second, they *are* devil-may-care, i.e., you can unzip them and wash them, whether the problem was an awkwardly balanced glass of Beaujolais or Fida and her puppies cavorting. You should be able to get a well-fitting slipcover for an average couch for about $250. And if you've bought the couch at auction for under $100, you're way ahead. A decent slipcovered couch, even those bulbous monstrosities in Pottery Barn, is apt to cost close to $1,000—and often more.

If you decide to have curtains made too, they will run about $75 for a pair of simple to-the-windowsill or to-the-floor if there are no trims or elaborate detailing. The slipcover people will probably be able to do them, or will give you a recommendation.

If you are looking for a seamstress to make your curtains, post a "Wanted" notice on the bulletin board at your job or in your local Manhattan laundromat—anywhere there is a notice board. This may seem risky, but

it really isn't. Curtains, and perhaps pillows as well, aren't that tough to make. When you visit the woman's home or shop, just ask to see other things she's made; she'll be glad to show you. Using this method, I've gotten excellent pillows made for $15 (my material, of course); shower curtains for $20—and, incidentally, found someone to alter my jackets, sew on my buttons, and cuff my pants, all for a pittance. New York is a very friendly city once you figure out how to find people to do things for you.

FINDING THE RAW MATERIALS: PAINT AND LUMBER

Paint

What I've always done in the past still works: Go to **M. Schames & Son** on the Lower East Side, or to **B. Cohen & Son** on the Upper West Side, or any of the "wholesale and retail" paint dealers in New York, and order in quantity. In other words, instead of going to your local hardware store and buying one gallon at a time—for close to $30—call these places and place the whole order at once. If you can use five gallon cans, you will save at least 20 percent, and sometimes more.

Order oil-based primer and the top grade of any paint. *Don't* buy the "landlord" or "value" grade of Benjamin Moore; it will look like watery chalk.

The clerks seem to be pushing semigloss for walls in bathrooms and kitchens. I don't like shine—anywhere—so I still get flat. If it's a good brand of flat paint, it will still be washable, and hey, how much of a slob are you, anyway? (If you really need the washability or like a little sheen, buy eggshell finish. If you must.)

Recently, I've discovered Martha Stewart paint at **Kmart**. Okay, at first I just thought I was a sucker for all those delicious names—

Sandcastle and Goat's Beard and Tea Bath and Ursa Minor and Heirloom Rose—but then I saw the price: $11.99 on sale per gallon, even for deep colors like Flower Pot that are usually more expensive. What a deal! The stuff is great—and despite the rumors that it doesn't cover very well, I think it does fine. (It's the Ralph Lauren Suede finish that takes about five coats to cover—but that paint, while expensive, will camouflage a bumpy plaster wall better than any paint I know.) Another paint that's supposed to be fantastic is the paint at **Wal-Mart,** which may be even cheaper. I haven't tried it yet.

Lumber

There is no place I know of where you can buy lumber cheaply—outside of a sawmill. (I once bought raw hemlock boards for a floor in a country kitchen; the wood was almost free, and I sanded it myself and pickled it. Not bad.)

But in New York City, there are two top-notch lumber yards that are fairly priced and offer an excellent selection. **Rosensweig Lumber** in the Bronx is a well-run place and offers a wide selection of woods: teak, mahogany, cherry, and so forth. If you want to pick out the boards as I do, you can take the subway out and spend all day choosing exactly the right piece of quarter-sawed oak—or you can telephone your order and leave it to them.

Dykes Lumber has a terrific catalogue showing the profiles of all their moldings along with the rest of their stock: a full range of doors and mantles and ceiling rosettes and more. They have elaborate rules: Delivery is free for orders over $200, otherwise they charge $50; they won't take a credit card over the telephone, but they will if you bring it in—that kind of stuff. They will accept COD orders. If you're ordering baseboard or door moldings to paint, you might want to try ordering the moldings made from resin, which are about 20 percent cheaper. Some folks think they actually look better than the solid wood when they've been painted.

FINDING THE PEOPLE TO WALLPAPER, PAINT, AND BUILD

Now, New York City is full of craftsmen and women, who can make your life a lot easier. The trick is to find them: wallpaper hangers, painters, tile men, carpenters, electricians, and plumbers. Almost everyone who has renovated an apartment has them. At the end of this chapter, I will give you a list of those craftsmen I have used personally, or those who are recommended by friends I really trust. But to be honest, these people are hard for me to snag now. If they become much more in demand, they will have waiting lists of a year or more, so don't be surprised if they're busy. But here's how to find others like them.

From Friends

This is by far your best source. So many people are getting work done on their apartment. Ask for the names of the people they like the best. Then interview them. Ask to see their samples. Ask to visit their jobs. Interview their customers.

From Other Craftsmen

If you get a great floor sander, he'll probably be able to direct you to a competent painter and maybe even a carpenter, since they'll see each other on so many jobs. This is a fabulous way of finding people. The guy making the recommendation won't want to give you anyone bad because it reflects on him professionally; you would probably never use him again if his recommendation turned out to be no good.

From the *Village Voice*

I've found a great carpenter, a great painter, and some great and not-so-great movers from the *Village Voice*. You never know, so check references, visit other jobs, and get contract prices in writing.

No matter where you get the workers, watch them carefully—check in at least every day. If anyone is not doing exactly the job you want, give him one day to straighten it out. If he doesn't, settle up with him as soon as possible and get someone else. Believe me, you won't regret it, even if you have to pay him a day's wages on the way out the door.

LIGHTING

If you need a guiding light—or two—head for the Bowery, where the drunken bums of yore have been replaced by lighting stores.

There are a million. Do you prefer glitzy, Trumpesque chandeliers? Or high-tech lamps that look like plastic eggshell crates—on wheels. Painted puce. It doesn't matter. It's all here, and usually, the windows tell the story.

At **Sovereign Lighting,** at 138 Bowery, tiny hand-blown globes of raucous red, gritty green, and daffodil yellow are dangling from their tiny cords (tiny, by the way, seems to be chic now for lighting fixtures . . .) in the window—and just about everything, even the tiny Italian glass globes, is marked down. There is no particular sale—this is the way it always is.

The Italian lights range around $200—not exactly dirt cheap, but you'd have to see them; they're irresistible. Some of the big lamps look as if they're made out of shoji screens: They're $499. But Sovereign has cheap stuff too: floor lamps marked down from $165 to $99 and torchères for $119. Some outdoor bulkhead lamps are marked down to $69 (in case you don't have a bulkhead to light, they're great and gutsy for loft bathrooms). Sovereign also has some intriguing coffee tables: made by Palecek, one particularly Heywood Wakefield-esque example is $399, down from $699. I liked their new take on a Shaker candlestand, now $159.

My old standby is **Lighting by Gregory,** a few doors down. At first, this place looks too dismally ordinary, and the vast room-to-room layout isn't really conducive to browsing; but the persistent shopper will eventually stumble into the Closeout Wall-o'-Sconces: Anything for $49, "with values up to $349," intones Kimberlee, the salesclerk. From the wall of cheap sconces, we amble over to the most delicate little (45-inch-tall) floor lamps I've ever seen. These floor lamps, made by Holtkötter, are certainly not bargain basement: they're around $280 apiece, but really, they're worth the trip. They are divine! They are so miniature, with their superb Teutonic craftsmanship; their enameled shades that appear dark, deep oceanic blue when turned off. Then switch them on and—presto!—an indescribable light cornflower blue (or emerald if you so desire). And the body of the lamp . . . it's not brass, it's not chrome, it's not exactly bronze . . . it's the greatest. And Kimberlee, sensing a real customer, comes out of her trance and pulls over a chair for me to sit in. She beckons, and moves the floor lamp over to the chair. I sit. "See, it's the perfect height for reading!" she proclaims. And she's right. (When I win some jackpot, I'm buying one of these lights in every color, and the wall lights that bend out from the wall and . . . Can I have a brochure, Kimberlee? "There aren't any." Aw shucks, she's gone back into her trance.)

At **Bowery Appliance,** in between Sovereign and Gregory, the do-it-yourself lampmaker can really score everything to make a shade into a lamp. Or you can buy it whole. "Promotion" signs dot the place, and there are complete sets of track lighting—the track, the switches and stuff, and three track heads, for $49.99. Little candlestick lamps with beaded shades in silver and gold could be yours for $29.99. There are stainless-steel floor lamps for $109, along with a selection of plain floor lamps from $64 to $79, and a few are downright handsome.

🍎 SOURCES

GENERAL CONTRACTORS

General contractors will give you a bid for everything you want done—plumbing, wiring, and carpentry—and will include their own fee for managing the whole thing. I have had some experience with the following small companies and, in addition, have checked out their references, men and women who spoke well of their competence and attitude.

Tom Breslin
718-361-1708

J. Nap Construction
2010 Lurting Avenue, Bronx, N.Y.,
718-931-1491

Rooney Contracting
43-19 56th Street, Woodside, N.Y.,
718-899-5132

CABINETMAKERS

Little Wolf Cabinet Shop
1583 First Avenue (between 82nd and 83rd Streets), 212-734-1116 or 734-2120 or fax your sketch 212-628-1966
This is a really big shop, and you can smell the sawdust from the street. The elder Wolf is the one with the personality—talk to him if he's available. The prices are fair, and the craftsmanship can't be beat. Take these custom-built cherry cabinets: two upper cupboards with raised panel doors (each 2 feet wide by 3 feet tall), plus one 3-foot-wide upper cabinet with glass doors (also 3 feet tall), plus one 30-inch sink cabinet with raised panels and a false drawer. All would cost $3,400 to have made here, using extra-thick 5/4-inch cherry—a great price for a New York City cabinetmaker.

FURNITURE REFINISHER

Patina
Glenn Allard
228 Southbury Road, Roxbury, Conn.
860-355-9382 or 203-888-5310
Okay, so it's a trek. But Glenn's good—he doesn't do museum quality French polishing, but he does a nice hand-rubbed finish. As examples, he charges $300 to $500 for a round table; $600 to $900 for a chest of drawers.

LIGHTING

Bowery Appliance
144 Bowery (between Grand and Broome), 212-343-3499
10 A.M.–7 P.M., seven days a week

Lighting by Gregory

158 Bowery (between Delancey and
Broome), 212-226-1276
Monday to Friday, 8:30 A.M.–5:30 P.M.;
Saturday, Sunday, 9 A.M.–5:30 P.M.

Sovereign Lighting

138 Bowery (between Grand and
Broome), 212-966-5644
9:30 A.M.–5:30 P.M., seven days a week

LUMBER, NEW

Dykes Lumber

348 West 44th Street (between Eighth
and Ninth Avenues), 212-246-6480
Monday to Friday, 7:30 A.M.–5 P.M.;
Saturday, 8 A.M.–1 P.M.; closed Sundays

Rosensweig Lumber

801 East 135th Street, Bronx, N.Y.,
718-585-8050
Monday to Friday, 7 A.M.–4 P.M.; closed
Saturdays and Sundays

LUMBER, ANTIQUE, OR JUST
PLAIN USED

North Fields Restoration

Hampton Falls, N.H., 603-926-5383
Monday to Friday, 7 A.M.–4 P.M.;
Saturday, 11 A.M.–4 P.M.
Specializes in antique wide board flooring in
oak, southern yellow pine, and chestnut. Also
marvelous eighteenth- and nineteenth-century
paneled walls.

PAINT

B. Cohen & Son

969 Amsterdam Avenue (at 107th
Street), 212-222-6289 or 212-666-
4516
Monday to Friday, 7:30 A.M.–5:30 P.M.;
Saturday, 9 A.M.–5 P.M.; closed Sundays
Deals on paint, especially if you buy in quan-
tity.

Kmart

1 Pennsylvania Plaza (at 34th Street
and Seventh Avenue), 212-760-1188
Monday to Thursday, 7 A.M.–9 P.M.;
Friday, Saturday, 9 A.M.–9 P.M.;
Sunday, 9 A.M.–8 P.M.

770 Broadway (at 9th Street)
212-673-1540
Monday to Friday, 9 A.M.–10 P.M.;
Saturday, 10 A.M.–9 P.M.; Sunday,
11 A.M.–8 P.M.

M. Schames & Son

3 Essex Street (between Hester and
Canal Streets), 212-673-3860
Monday to Friday, 6:30 A.M.–4:45 P.M.;
closed Saturdays and Sundays
Discount paints, especially if you buy in quan-
tity.

Wal-Mart

None in Manhattan. Lots outside of it.

UPHOLSTERERS

Jaime Diamint Upholstery

324 East 59th Street, 212-754-1155
I've done business here for years. They would
prefer to come and see the piece before giving
an estimate, but sometimes they will accept a
Polaroid. A club chair will run $420 to $480;
a Lawson couch with six cushions costs
$1,480 to upholster—you supply the material.
The problem here is not the work—it is excellent—but with the timing: They are so popular
that the wait is usually at least two months. But
if you can spare the time, delivery and pickup
are free if you live on the East Side between
50th and 70th Streets, and not a great deal
more if you live elsewhere in Manhattan.

Upholstery By George/George
Cyr

1451 New Britain Avenue, Farmington,
Conn., 860-678-7763
An alternative to the Big Apple backup. Upholsterer to the trade in the Hartford area. A
wingchair will cost $210 to 250 to upholster;
a couch can run $490 to $610. Those prices
are COM (customer's own material.) Time is
usually measured in weeks here—not months.

WALLPAPER HANGING, SPECIAL

John Nalewaja

170 West 74th Street, 212-496-6135

For routine jobs, get a routine wallpaper hanger—or do it yourself. But for special jobs like hanging fabric, grasscloth, and scenic murals, call Mr. Nalewaja. He's certainly not cheap, but even a cheapskate knows you've got to spend sometime, especially to protect your investment in the Zuber murals!

Kitchens and Baths Worthy of a Millionaire: Most Important Is Strategy

Everybody throws around extravagant prices to do over kitchens and baths. *House Beautiful* has called a $45,000 budget for a closet-sized kitchen in a New York studio apartment "modest." Marble bathrooms with polished-nickel faucets can run to $60,000—or at least that's what you'd think if you spent a lot of time talking with architects and interior designers as I do.

Sixty thousand dollars for a bathroom?

You can create that same bathroom for less than $15,000 if you know how and where to shop.

First of all, let's analyze what's in a $60,000 bathroom. There has to be a new one-piece toilet and, of course, a double sink with undercounter-mounted oval nickel sinks, set into a solid piece of white marble. Then there might be a Kohler "Steeping Tub," an extra deep tub with a whirlpool. Then—hey, why not?—give it a honed limestone floor. Then let's add some paneled wainscoting around the room and some William Morris wallpaper and trim it up with nickel-plated sconces. The experts say there's no way can you do this bathroom for $15,000.

Let's just try.

First of all, there's only one ground rule in New York City apartments or you'll pay a lot more than $60,000: None of the fixtures can change their location; in other words, the toilet goes where the old one did; so do the tub and sink. Otherwise, you have to get a building permit, permission from the co-op board, and on and on. So keep the stuff in the same spot and be creative.

GATHERING PRICES AND BIDDING THE JOB

Once you have your design, call a good plumber and ask him to bid the job as labor only. And tell him that if he uses his professional discount to get the tub, toilet, sinks, and faucets (usually around 30 percent off the retail price), you'll give him 10 percent of his costs for his troubles. This is a good deal for both you and the plumber, and while some plumbers will refuse to go along, there are plenty who will. (There is absolutely nothing unethical about this. The plumbing supply house doesn't care what deal the clients make with the plumber—they only want to make sure the plumber is a real plumber and not some handyman with a $5 set of business cards, working on his own house.)

But even if this does not work out for some reason—like you're too shy to ask—you can still save a lot of money.

Here are the prices of the tub, sinks, and toilet, including the plumber's 10 percent add-on:

Kohler "Steeping Tub," grip bars, trim, and drain $3,775.07
Kohler one-piece toilet 311.00
Oval nickel undermount basins 1,180.00
Nickel wideset faucets for the basins 754.66
Nickel faucets for the whirlpool tub 600.00
   So far. $6,620.73

Here is the cost of the honed limestone tile for a 5-by-9-foot bathroom—the retail price—from **Tiles-A-Refined Selection,** one of the nicest tile stores in New York. (Ask for Janet. She's the best.)

$540.00

Now here's where you're really going to save the most money. Go to a lumber store, and get some 1/4-inch Luan plywood that is exactly the size of your double sink (or single if you have a typical New York City bathroom). Take that and your nickel sinks over to **Colonna & Company** in Long Island City, or to almost any other marble yard in the area. Pick out the exact slab of marble or granite you want—it's fun! Show them exactly where you want the sinks to go, and pick out what kind of edge you want. To save money, many people pick ¾-inch stone with a 1½-inch bullnose, but for the extra $100 or $200—since you're going to see the thickness above your sinks—it might be wiser to go for the extra-thick stone. (This also depends on who's carrying it from the car!) As this book was going to press, I asked Maria at Colonna how much she'd charge for such a thick slab, a luxurious 40 inches wide with a fluted front edge, including the sink hole. She gave me an estimate of:

$900.00

Now you're going to need a good carpenter, to make the paneled wainscoting and the paneled front of the tub, as well as the frame to hold up the whirlpool tub and the base for the sink vanity. Good carpenters are worth a fortune, but they usually don't charge one. I once got the best carpenter in the world, a New Zealander named John Dunstan, from an advertisement in the *Village Voice*. Another great carpenter—who could saw through an 8-foot two-by-four with a handheld jigsaw at a 45-degree angle, straight up the whole board—I got from the guy who was fixing up his loft a few floors up in a building in SoHo. Another great trim carpenter I got through my real estate agent.

If you show the carpenter a photograph of what you want in a shelter magazine, he should not act flummoxed, but will ask intelligent questions, take out his measuring tape, and immediately start to sketch something. If he doesn't do that, there is something wrong. Find someone else. A good estimate for this job is $3,000, including all the clear pine necessary. (If you're trying to save even more money or, like some people, don't want wood in your bathroom because of its proximity to water, the paneling is good item to skip.)

Now the estimate from a plumber friend of mine: no more than $2,000. Add that to the estimate to tile the floor and install marble on the walls and—presto—$13,060.73! You haven't lifted a trowel or a plumbing wrench. You just called in some people and drafted your own design, without using any special tools. And there you have it.

NEXT: THE UN–$45,000 KITCHEN

Now on to the $45,000 kitchen. The kitchen I once wrote about was only 5 X 7. Let's make it bigger.

Let's say you have a typical New York City kitchen. It's a one-sided Pullman kitchen, 5 or 6 feet wide and 10 or 12 feet long, with a window at the end. You know the type, whether it's in the cheap rental you just leased or the cheap apartment you just bought. Sure, it's got potential—but right now, it's also got those ghastly wood-grained Formica cabinets with the very faux black borders embossed in it, and maybe it has cheesy faux-brick linoleum and a dented old stainless steel sink and an ancient dishwasher that still works. It's got a refrigerator standing out on the end that should have a CONDEMNED—NYC DEPARTMENT OF HEALTH sign on it and an enameled stove that was last cleaned when Lucy was married to Ricky.

Okay, guys, what do you do?

First, you get out the scrubbing bubbles and the Top Job. Look at the stove. It's white enamel, standard issue, gas. Figure out what else you want. The tall refrigerator, especially if it's harvest gold or avocado, may have to go. Get a 24-inch GE undercounter fridge—bending down is good for you—or if you want to splurge, the way I did recently, get matching stainless steel Sub-Zero undercounter freezer and refrigerator. You still have to bend, but you do it in style. Or if the fridge looks okay, move it toward the window, out of your face. Play around with the plan.

Now look at the dishwasher. Is it an okay brand, like Whirlpool, GE, Kitchenaid? Even if it's avocado, these companies all make black, white, or stainless fronts (GE's costs about $30). Some even make kits so your carpenter or cabinet company can make you a pan-eled front to match your new cabinets. (No, we're not fussing with Formica.) You may decide to keep both the dishwasher (let's say it's an old Kitchenaid, and looks downright vintage but somehow cool) and the stove—at least for now. I hope you'll replace the tall refrigerator, but most people swear by the tall ones, the ones that wreck the line of the counters and the view toward the window. But that's your choice—and everything will certainly look better with those scrubbing bubbles! (And, of course, in a rental, it's always tempting to do the least amount possible, a temptation I've always resisted, especially if I'm paying hundreds under market value—every month.)

Three things you absolutely must change: the cabinets, the floors, and the countertops.

In one of the last renovations I did, for a kitchen exactly this size, I chose top-of-the-line cherry cabinets at **IKEA.** Yes, it *is* a bore to have to take that dumb shuttle bus to New Jersey, but it turned out to be worth it: a row of cherry-veneered cabinets, some with glass doors, uppers and lowers, cost $1,600. I paid a carpenter $500 to assemble them, which wasn't particularly cheap, but he did a good job.

For the renovation I just finished, in the penthouse of a 1914 landmarked apartment building on the Upper West Side, I had a cabinetmaker make solid cherry cabinets with raised paneled doors from scratch, to my design, rubbed with Watco Danish oil. He charged $6,000—and people gasp when they walk in.

For both of these jobs, I chose granite countertops: a Luna Pearl salt-and-pepper fleck for the first job; a wonderful pure black granite for the next job. The first cost $700; the second, because it was bigger and more intricate, $2,000.

Now for the floor: In the first job, I laid some charcoal gray, textured paving tiles by **American Olean** (about $165—I laid them myself and so could you, but someone else might only charge about $200 for such a simple job). In the second, I had my favorite floor guys put down some random-width oak planks throughout the entire apartment. They charged $5,000 for the whole apartment, so it's difficult to say how much they would've charged for the kitchen. But most people like to have tile in a kitchen, and if you buy the tile yourself and have it delivered, your kitchen floor—even with installation—won't cost much more than $900.

The appliances included a new GE dishwasher; a new 30-inch Magic Chef brushed-chrome gas stove (great value—looks a lot more than $699); and an undercounter Sub-Zero refrigerator and separate freezer with stainless steel doors. If two undercounter refrigerator units don't work for you, add a Jenn-Air, Kitchenaid, or GE Profile double-door refrigerator with built-in icemaker in the front door, and subtract about $600. (See Appliances, below.)

So here are the prices for a 6-by-12-foot kitchen, with all new appliances and a splurge for the twin Sub-Zeros—and the custom-made cherry cabinets. If you are renovating a larger kitchen, just add a proportionately larger amount for counters, floors, and cabinets:

Maximum cost of appliances	$3,400
Sink and garbage disposal	600
Floor, including labor	900
Granite countertop	2,000
Custom-made cherry cabinets	6,000
Labor to install cabinets	500
Paint for walls and ceiling	400
Total	s$13,800

These prices, dear reader, are not pie-in-the-sky. I've renovated five apartments in the last three years and acted as my own general contractor. The figures above were gathered for an identical kitchen I'm doing in a co-op apartment on East 86th Street. The bathroom figures were also gathered at press time.

HARDWARE AND FAUCETS: NOW THE FUN BEGINS

For cabinet and door hardware, it's worthwhile to visit **Simon's Hardware.** In fact, it's a treat! The place is often mobbed, and the service is erratic, along with the moods of the various clerks—some are wonderful; others are arrogant; others are just plain frantic. But look around by yourself first. Everything is pretty much on view. Because the place is so hectic, steel yourself to be calm and make a list, noting down the section of the store where you found the different things. Giant rosehead showerheads? Sand-blasted pewter shell cabinet knobs? Reeded chrome bath curtain rods? Baldwin knobs and Italian knockoffs of Baldwin knobs? They're all here. The prices are reasonable—not bargain basement—but this is stuff you can't get anywhere else in New York City, and it's solid stuff.

There *is* an alternative to Simon's, and that's sending away to a little shop named **J. Shiner & Sons** on Windmill Street in London. For a house I was restoring in Chester, Connecticut, I bought superb Legge locks and big, bulbous, reeded brass spherical doorknobs—about twenty-four of them. I also bought dozens of brass H-hinges for the cabinets at the end of the family room. Right now, a pair of the Legge beehive-design knobs, plus spindles, goes for about $30—far less than the $75 you'd pay at Simon's.

I've also gotten some wonderful plumbing fixtures at the Portobello Road and Islington flea markets in London. The kind they sell now in **Waterworks** for thousands of dollars are only about $300 in the flea markets, all reconditioned and (almost) ready to install. Be careful to line up a good plumber before you bring them back, though. The English fittings are not exactly the same as ours. A good plumber can get adapters to fit the size of the threads inside their pipes, or he can fabricate something.

Even buying vintage American faucets can be a problem. I've bought plenty of faucets from **United Housewrecking** in Stamford, Connecticut, a wonderful trove of vintage bathroom and kitchen supplies only an hour from Times Square. General rule: You can't just buy an antique fixture and bring it home and expect it to work. It may or it may not. If you need a cartridge that will fit your old spigot or some other repair, the place to go is **George Taylor,** late of SoHo, now of TriBeCa. You may never leave. In fact, you might want to stop here *before* you go to Stamford or to **Urban Archaeology.** Taylor's not only has antique fixtures, but they have the best quality reproduction fixtures around. Again, it might be wise to pick out what you want and have your plumber snap up the discount.

If you're looking for a pedestal sink, you might try **Home Depot.** (Surprise!) In past years, Home Depot has done this cheesy thing: When they opened, there were knockoffs of the overpriced big brands here. You could find, for example, small, egg-shaped brass cabinet knobs here for under $2: exact imitations of the $8 Baldwin knobs. But no more. Now Home Depot handles Baldwin itself—and the cheap (but high-quality) imitations are gone. *But,* as of this minute, Home Depot still carries a superb $99 pedestal sink that looks very much like ones for four times as much—wholesale—in your favorite plumbing supply house. I must have used three or four of these sinks. Then, if you put on a really fine faucet, it looks like a much more expensive sink.

SOAPSTONE SINKS

Every tightwad millionaire wants a soapstone sink, but where to get one without breaking an already minuscule budget is a sticky problem. Well, there's only one good place to find one: at the **Vermont**

Soapstone Company in Perkinsville, Vermont, where they've been mining the stone and making the sinks since 1850.

Because they are custom-made—you give them the dimensions and where you want the hole for the drain—prices for the sink vary. But they do stock two sinks, so you can get an idea from that. The first sink is called "The Wright," presumably after Frank Lloyd, because they date it at 1907. It is 30 inches wide and 24 inches deep, with a rear deck. The price is $949.62. The other model, called the "Williams Sink" (Boston, circa 1835) is even plainer: a 26-by-18-inch open box that costs $705.

The company also can make stone tops for vanities and counters, and can cut the stone into any size tiles. An inch-and-a-quarter-thick countertop costs $57 a square foot—which may be an even better deal than a sink. A 2-by-10-foot countertop will cost $1,140 and make a lot more of a splash (no pun intended) than a sink. They can ship anywhere—just call for an estimate.

THE MILLIONAIRE'S ACCOUTREMENTS

That brings me to the subject of where and how to spend your renovation dollars. To make a renovation look like you've spent way more than you have, it's important to sometimes pay more. The whole strategy, though, is to pay more on a few scattered items—which will then, by their obvious merit, elevate the perceived value of the rest of the stuff.

In a bathroom, this is particularly important—and easy. Buy Ralph Lauren towels in a delicious Breton red (bought at the outlet store, they are only about $7 apiece), put them on the towel rack and maybe stack a few on the little Chippendale-esque stool next to the tub, or roll them and stack them in one of the shelves of the bookcase. Buy a wonderful antique mirror at an auction, rather than an ugly medicine chest (hide the medicines in a drawer of your bureau). Or splurge and buy a great-looking medicine chest (is there one? I had one made once by a carpenter; it had a raised panel on the front; the mirror was glued into the recess of the panel on the back. The price: $200). *Buy good faucets.* I was shocked at how much the cheap-looking Pfister faucets cost at Home Depot: $169! Spend $350 and get Chicago faucets, which look sturdy and elegant. Buy a big old engraving for $125 at the 26th Street flea market and hang it on the wall. Buy a double roll of Hinson wallpaper in an elegant stripe. (This paper feels like a heavy brown paper bag—not at all what you'd expect to find in a bathroom, which is usually coated in some horrible vinyl stuff. It's practical, but who cares? The Hinson is washable anyway.) The wallpaper is expensive, but you'll probably only need one double roll, or two at the most. Maximum: $250—and what a difference. Or order it from London, as described in Chapter 8, and save hundreds of dollars. Add your silver baby cup and a couple of other ones—the older and more dented the better—that you got in a box lot at an auction, and stick toothbrushes and razors and cotton balls in them.

You have just created a millionaire's bathroom—far better than any *cheapskate* millionaire would commission. But it doesn't hurt to flaunt it every now and then.

In the kitchen you have designed and built, the same rules apply. Buy an oil painting of melons at Brimfield (see Chapter 7). Hang it over the cheap round plywood table covered (to the floor) with Clarence House fabric. Buy an old wall faucet in London and have it replated with nickel and reconditioned. Splurge on ivory- and mustard-colored Mexican tiles for the backsplash: It doesn't require very much square footage to make one, and it looks great! Then, buy your big floor tiles at **Bergen Tile** in Brooklyn for $2 a square foot. No one looks at the floor tile; their eyes go straight to the backsplash and the wonderful funky faucet. If you have room, stick a bar sink in an alcove; it doesn't cost much more if the plumber's there already, and it is so convenient!

Voilà! A millionaire's kitchen—or close enough.

APPLIANCES: SHOULD YOU SHOP WHERE THE DECORATORS SHOP?

It seems as if everybody in New York City goes to Gringer's Appliances on First Avenue between 1st and 2nd Streets. "It's where the decorators go," they say, breathlessly. The problem is that I've never had much luck there. This must be because every time I've gone there, and it is a terrible schlep—or worse, every time I've telephoned—it seems that the world *is* there. The service is dreadful! The other day, researching this section, I waited on the telephone for twenty-three minutes. And it's not as if the prices are so great. Every time I've compared their prices to anyone else's, Gringer's has been higher! That said, one of the reasons why the decorators use the place is that the store does carry all the top lines: Miele, Gagge-nau, Viking, Wolf, and, of course, Sub-Zero. And if you want to see at least a few of these top brands on display, take a trip downtown. But if you don't have about three hours to go there and fight to be waited on by the sometimes downright surly help, there are other, often cheaper alternatives.

My favorite way to buy appliances is by telephone. I've ordered perhaps a dozen times through an 800-numbered service and never had any problem. It's kind of like buying mail-order window blinds. The services I've used are fast and efficient. (I can only tell you my experience with the companies listed below.) They deliver when they say they will. Some figure the delivery charges into their quoted prices—and tell you so.

The key to the shop-by-phone companies is that you have to know exactly what model you want. Either you can find the appliance at your local store, or you can telephone the manufacturers' special help lines (GE's, for example, is 800-GE-CARES). They will fax you a picture and description of the type of appliance you want if you de-scribe to them the features and size and color. The only thing they won't tell you is the price, because they don't want to undercut or overprice their distributors.

I knew I was looking for a four-burner gas stove with a brushed-chrome top. Charles at **Dial-A-Brand** told me that Magic Chef made a good one. He kindly gave me the Magic Chef–Maytag Hot-line. The company faxed me a picture of a terrific new product—Model CGR3765, a stove that is actually all brushed chrome, with four gas burners (two of them the bigger, higher-heat burners) and a self-cleaning oven.

With that number, and the model number of the undercounter Sub-Zero refrigerator I wanted (245), I started calling the appliance shop-at-home services, including **Eba's Appliance & Electronics World** and Dial-A-Brand. As a backup, I also asked about a much cheaper GE undercounter fridge, the TAX6SNX.

These were the best prices. Since I have ordered appliances from each of them, I can testify that their track record—on-time delivery and good condition of product—have all been good in the past.

Here is the comparison:

Company	Magic Chef Range	Sub-Zero Fridge	GE Fridge	Delivery
Dial-A-Brand	$749	$1,215	$323	$ 0
Eba's	710	1,259	374	30
Gringer's	829	1,265	329	35

Oh, and just for fun, I decided to ask one of the services—Dial-A-Brand—to price out a 48-inch, six-burner stainless-steel Viking restaurant-type stove. According to Barbara, the stove would cost $3,500 without the convection feature and $4,200 with convection. At Gringer's, the same stove was $4,947 without convection and $6,000 with convection.

Discount Appliance Stores

If ordering over the telephone makes you nervous, and you have time to browse and bargain, go to one of the big chain stores that have come to Manhattan. My two favorites are **Circuit City** and **Tops,** both on 14th Street around Union Square. Tops surprised me; it looks like a typical low-end bargain basement store like P. C. Richards, just another chain store merchant. But they had a great-looking, white-on-white, Italian 20-inch range—perfect for my tiny apartment. Very chic, $347, and the only good-looking 20-inch stove I've found.

At Circuit City, I bought a handsome Amana double-door refrigerator with both ice crusher and cuber in the front door—for only $849. And when the same refrigerator went on sale the next week (wasn't it already cheap enough?), they credited my charge account with a $100 refund for the difference. I still can't believe it! They also offer to give you six months—without any interest—to pay for major appliances you charge. But keep track of that six months; if you let it go a day past, you'll pay all the interest put together, at some exorbitant rate! And Circuit City has constant sales on "scratch and dent" merchandise, floor models, and overstocks. I just saw a very handsome, white-on-white, GE slide-in range for $399 in what they called an "open box" sale. No scratches or dents, and a full guarantee, but in this case, no instruction manual. But how much do you need to know? Just plug it in and save about $400. So if you have the time, you may save a lot of money by haunting this place.

Restaurant Equipment

Right now, the trend for gigantic six-burner restaurant stoves, stainless-steel refrigerators, and gargantuan toasters (which nevertheless still toast a maximum of four pieces of toast) is raging. Rich bachelors who barely microwave their hot chocolate are buying $6,000 Viking stoves (I think they just like the name).

But if they would just go down to the Bowery, they could at least find their mega-stoves for a fraction of the price—plus a lot of other cool stuff like two-foot whisks and giant colanders and stainless steel cooking pans that are one-fifth the price of similar ones in Williams-Sonoma. And if (heaven forbid) they're willing to put up with somebody else's grease (or their cleaning lady is), they can save even more buying used equipment on the same block.

First, the used equipment. Go to **A&P Restaurant and Deli Equipment,** at 215 Bowery. There, a wag named Alex gives funny answers to dumb questions and generally acts as master of ceremonies to a bunch of used stuff that looks like it just came off the truck from their Brooklyn warehouse, which it undoubtedly did, because they have one. One of those larger-than-life toasters costs $200; Alex told me that, new, they cost $500. Big brown sugar cookers—heavy solid copper, about 18 inches across and very decorative—go for another $200. If you want to add on a six-burner stove, that'll set you back about $750, more or less.

But in a way, it's the new things that are the bigger bargains. For instance, across the street at **Matas Restaurant Supply,** a brand-new South Bend restaurant stove, very chic in its total lack of glamour, costs $1,500 for the six-burner and $1,300 for the four-burner. (Quite a far cry from the Viking.) These stoves are gas pilot, without electric ignition, according to Brian Wells, the manager, and because of that, the South Bend stoves need three-inch clearances on either side. "So it can't go flush into a counter unless you fireproof it," he said. But for that much money's difference, it bears investigating. The stores carries Hobart appliances and a very neat-looking Victory refrigerator, for $1,600.

For those who don't care about spending thousands to have their kitchens look like the back end of a high school cafeteria, the restaurant supply companies carry smaller bargains too. Gutsy stainless-steel saucepans with bolted handles were $14. An enormous strainer was $13. And the biggest whisk known to man, a full 24 inches, was $11.95. Ladles were $4.50, and terrific rubber floor matting was $45 for a 3-by-5-foot "rug."

◉ SOURCES

KITCHENS AND BATHROOMS

American Olean Tile Company
150 East 58th Street, 212-688-1321

Bergen Tile & Linoleum
215 Flatbush Avenue, Brooklyn, N.Y.,
718-789-9000
Monday, Thursday,
8:30 A.M.–8:15 P.M.; Tuesday to
Wednesday, Friday to Sunday,
8:30 A.M.–5:15 P.M.

Colonna & Company
34-46 Vernon Boulevard, Long Island
City, N.Y., 718-274-1111
Monday to Saturday, 8 A.M.–5 P.M.;
closed Sundays

George Taylor Specialties
100 Hudson Street (between Franklin
and Hudson Streets), 212-226-5369
Monday to Wednesday,
7:30 A.M.–5 P.M.; Thursday,
7:30 A.M.–6:30 P.M.; Friday,
7:30 A.M.–4 P.M.

Home Depot
541 Kings Highway (off I-95, exit 23)
Fairfield, Conn., 203-254-3888
Monday to Saturday, 6 A.M.–11 P.M.;
Sunday, 8 A.M.–7 P.M.

55 Weyman Avenue (off I-95, exit 15)
New Rochelle, N.Y., 914-235-7575
Monday to Saturday, 6 A.M.–midnight;
Sunday, 8 A.M.–7 P.M.

IKEA
Exit 13A on the New Jersey Turnpike,
Elizabeth, N.J., 908-289-4488
Monday to Saturday, 10 A.M.–9 P.M.;
Sunday, 10 A.M.–6 P.M.
Shuttle bus hotline: 800-287-4532. Buses
leave from Port Authority (42nd Street and
Eighth Avenue), Gate 5 on the lower con-
course, every half hour from 10 A.M. to 2:30
P.M. and return every half hour from noon to 6
P.M. Buses are free on weekends.

J. Shiner & Sons
8 Windmill Street, London, England
011-44-171-636-0740
Monday to Friday, 6:45 A.M.–3 P.M.

Simon's Hardware
421 Third Avenue (at 29th Street),
212-532-9220 or 212-378-4142
Monday to Wednesday, Friday,
8 A.M.–5:30 P.M.; Thursday,
8 A.M.–7 P.M.; Saturday, 10 A.M.–6 P.M.;
closed Sundays

Tiles-A-Refined Selection
42 West 15th Street (between Fifth and
Sixth Avenues), 212-255-4450
Monday to Wednesday, Friday,
9:30 A.M.–5:30 P.M.; Thursday,
9:30 A.M.–8 P.M.; closed Saturdays and
Sundays

United Housewrecking
535 Hope Street, Stamford, Conn.,
203-348-5371
Monday to Saturday, 9:30 A.M.–
5:30 P.M.; Sundays, noon to 5 P.M.

Urban Archaeology
285 Lafayette Street, 212-431-6969
Monday to Friday, 8 A.M.–6 P.M.; closed
Saturdays and Sundays

239 East 58th Street (between Second
and Third Avenues), 212-371-4646
Monday to Saturday, 9 A.M.–5 P.M.;
closed Sundays

Vermont Soapstone Company
248 Stoughton Pond Road, Perkinsville,
Vt., 802-263-5404
Visit Monday to Thursday,
10 A.M.–4 P.M, or call for an
appointment.

Waterworks
469 Broome Street (at the corner of
Greene), 212-966-0605
Monday to Friday, 10 A.M.–6 P.M.;
Saturday noon–6 P.M.; closed Sundays

237 East 58th Street (between Second
and Third Avenues), 212-371-9266
Monday to Friday, 10 A.M.–5 P.M.;
closed Saturdays and Sundays

DISCOUNT APPLIANCES

Circuit City
East 14th Street, 212-387-0730
Monday to Saturday, 10 A.M.–9 P.M.;
Sunday, 11 A.M.–6 P.M.

Tops Appliance City
1400 Third Avenue, 212-744-0470
34 West 14th Street, 212-645-5530
138 East 34th Street, 212-532-6667

APPLIANCES BY PHONE

Dial-A-Brand
800-237-3220
Monday to Friday, 9 A.M.–5:30 P.M.;
Saturday, 9 A.M.–noon

Eba's Appliance & Electronics World
800-380-2378
Monday to Friday, 9 A.M.–8 P.M.;
Saturday, 9 A.M.–5 P.M.

RESTAURANT EQUIPMENT

A&P Restaurant and Deli Equipment
215 Bowery (at Rivington Street)
212-477-6130
Monday to Friday, Sunday,
9 A.M.–5 P.M.

Matas Restaurant Supply
219 Bowery (between Prince and
Spring), 212-966-2251
Monday to Saturday, 9 A.M.–5 P.M.;
closed Sundays

You Knew You Wanted It–But You Didn't Know You Could Afford It: Those Sybaritic Extras

After you've outfitted yourself in every way, there may still be a few little extras. You've always wanted them, but you didn't know where to find them cheaply. As practically their birthright, millionaires always seem to know exactly where to go. Now so will you.

THE BALLET

You can go to the ballet every night—just about—if you join the Fourth Ring Club at the **New York City Ballet.** It costs $15 to join, and then it costs only $12 a ticket—a few dollars more than a movie—to see Ballanchine's and Jerome Robbins's best works performed by the world's great dancers.

New York City Ballet at Lincoln Center
New York State Theater, 70 Lincoln Center Plaza, 212-870-5570

CRYSTAL WEDDING PRESENTS

Where else but Tiffany's? Ah, I know you're laughing. But the *cheapest* cheapskate millionaires know that you can make the biggest impression by sending off one of those distinctive baby-blue boxes from this famous jewelry store—for only $50. How? By purchasing one of Tiffany's beautiful wine (say "champagne") buckets, in crystal. It's stunning and practical; you can use it for flowers, too. There's only one problem: Now they'll all know how much you paid!

Tiffany & Company
727 Fifth Avenue (at 57th Street), 212-755-8000

CUBAN CIGARS

Cuban cigars are, alas, illegal in the United States. But the men and women who must have them fly to London to smoke them, and Davidoff is one of the best places to find the real Montecristos (a Number One costs £10.60), Cohibas (a Panatela costs £6.75), and H. Upmanns (a Corona costs £8.25).

Davidoff of London
35 St. James's Street, London, England, 011-44-171-930-3079

CUSTOM-MADE BOOTS

One of the easiest—and cheapest—ways to feel like a millionaire is to have your shoes or jodhpur boots made for you. For either $385 or $395—depending on whether you choose the standard leather or the French calf—you can have the best-looking pair of trouser boots in town.

Not only that, but you'll enjoy the trip downtown. **E. Vogel** is located at 19 Howard Street in SoHo, a tiny street just below Grand Street, off Broadway. Not only do these boots and shoes—they make regular shoes only for men—look terrific, but they last forever. I had a pair of heavily grained brown leather boots made for working on a construction site. Some might think this was the ultimate waste, but in fact, I'm still using them, and I always get a kick out of putting them on to haul sheetrock! But the French calf boots, particularly, are divine for hunting anything from antiques to foxes. (Although for serious riding, you might want to order a pair of high boots—"dress" or "field"—for $591 in standard leather.)

The basic men's shoes are more expensive than the jodhpur boots are. I'm not sure why, but they too look as if they wear forever, and with John Lobb shoes going for $660 in Hermès, handmade, molded-to-your-own-individual-feet shoes for $565 (for the model called the "Midwest") seem like a bargain. The men's shoes come in a variety of styles, from the regular wing tips to monkstraps.

For an additional charge, you can further customize your shoes. How about an extra sheepskin insole ($15)? Or zippers to the calf for your riding boots ($40)? Or a ribbed sole ($15)?

Take a trip down here and talk with Vince Dittmer, an affable young man who will also tell you about Vogel's affiliation with a custom shirtmaker, Newell's Custom Shirts. They also represent L. R. Ermilio, a Philadelphia tailoring shop, Lock & Company Hatters, and Sawyer of Napa shearling coats.

Oh—the boots normally take twelve to fourteen weeks. (That's right, weeks!) But for a little extra "grease"—like $60—they can cut that time in half. They can also ship them to you, via UPS ground service, for $11. If you want them the day after they're finished, that will cost you $37. (P. S. For those who aren't ready to spring for the boots, a can of Vogel's Polish goes for $5.)

E. Vogel
19 Howard Street, 212-925-2460
Monday to Friday, 8 A.M.–4:30 P.M. Saturdays by appointment only.

DESIGNER EYEGLASSES

If you need prescription glasses, doesn't it make you furious to have to pay $200 for something decent—and that's just the frame!

Try this (I've done it about half a dozen times): Find a pair of designer sunglasses you like in a discount place like Syms. Buy a pair of Ralph Lauren or Perry Ellis or whatever you happen to see and like. Make sure they are made sturdily and are optical quality. They usually are. You'll probably pay something like $19.99. Then take them to your local optician or Vision Corner chain to have the lenses replaced with your prescription lenses. They may not particularly like it—they always say they have to check with the doctor or something—but so far, no frames have been refused, and this pair will last just as long as the $200 Ralph Lauren or Perry Ellis ones do as long as you take reasonable care of them. Most recently, I bought a pair of $28 ready-made reading glasses—fabulous tortoise-type frames—at Lord & Taylor and had them converted to prescription glasses. They, too, are working out very well, and I get a lot of compliments. The stores usually charge between $60 and $90 for the lenses when they use the frames you provide.

You can also buy frames at flea markets. There are some wonderful clear frames with a greenish tint that resemble the English National Health Service glasses of the 1930s so beloved by collectors, on display every weekend at several of the downstairs booths at **The Garage** (see the listing in chapter 7). They, too, are easy to convert.

And while you're snooping around, check out the clip-on shades that can be picked up for between $5 and $10.

DESIGNER HAIRCUTS AND HAIR COLORING

Cheapskate millionaires want the best—but they won't pay for it. So they branch out and run towards any of the great hair salons on "bargain nights." Didn't know about them? Well, the great hair salons have to train their new recruits—who served their residency somewhere else, no doubt—*sometime*, don't they?

So on Tuesdays at 6 or Wednesdays at 7—whichever—you can get your hair cut in the best places for as little as $20. Call the salon you've always wanted to go to and get all the details. Also make an appointment—one is imperative!

Here is a list of the best:

Frederic Fekkai
15 East 57th Street, 212-753-9500
Tuesdays at 6 P.M.; $30 for a service that routinely averages $100 for a haircut.
Call to sign up. The wait is now about six months. The good news: You can get your hair colored, too, and a makeup lesson is free!

Pierre-Michel Coiffeur at the Plaza
131 East 57th Street, 212-593-1460, 753-3995, 755-9500
Tuesdays at 7 P.M.; $20 for a haircut, $35 for color.
The current wait is three months.

Louis Licari
797 Madison Avenue, 212-327-0639
Wednesdays at 5:30 P.M.; $30 for hair coloring. Calls taken Friday mornings from 8:45 to 9:15 *only*.

Peter Coppola
746 Madison Avenue, 212-988-9404
Tuesdays at 6:30 P.M.; $40 for a haircut.
At press time, there was only a two-week wait.

ENGRAVED STATIONERY

In an undistinguished warehouse building on West 39th Street, **Ross-Cook Engraving** has the most varied and beautiful engraved stationery this side of, well, Cartier's, for whom they do business.

I don't remember where or how I first heard about them, but I had my wedding invitations done here and from then on, everything else. The atmosphere is amazing—a wonderful, almost frighteningly brisk woman named Barbara will help you make your choice in record time. But what to choose? The tiny engraved navy blue yachts? The green squirrels? The great and simple Chinese red block initials (my favorite)? They use mostly Crane's stationery, and the combination of Chinese red on heavy ivory stock makes my heart beat faster when I use it. I have giant sheets, fold-over notes, and correspondence cards. (It's definitely millionaire-worthy, if not billionaire.)

This place is a great secret. The price? Oh, I forgot to tell you—about half of what you'd pay at Tiffany's or Cartier's or any of the elegant stationers—who may very well send their orders to Ross-Cook!

Ross-Cook Engraving
135 West 29th Street, sixth floor, 212-563-2876
Monday to Friday, 8 A.M.–4:45 P.M.

GROUNDSKEEPER

To need a groundskeeper cheap, you have to have grounds. But if you do, you can advertise in the local shopping gazette. Ads are sometimes free or, as in my local paper in Connecticut, cost $5. Here's the ad I ran last summer: "Wanted: Someone with car to tend my five gardens, mow the lawn, and occasionally paint the fence. Experience required. $7 an hour, with a flexible schedule." Believe it or not, the telephone rang off the hook. I ended up with a middle-aged Scandinavian fellow, a former seaman, who loved the job. I trust him completely, so he can come to work whenever he deems it necessary, which in summer is perhaps two or three times a week. The place looks better than ever, and the bill is never more than $75.

LIMOUSINES

One of the best deals in town—which practically no one knows about—is to hire a chauffeur-driven car for only $20 an hour through one of the major car services. This is really a cheap way to travel, and you'll save the cost of countless taxis, plus the aggravation of finding them in midtown or on the Upper East Side or wherever you want to be. Recently, I visited sales at no fewer than sixteen shops scattered from the East 80s to West 57th Street, for only $60. It's peaceful, especially if you get a great driver like Pavel at **Allstate.** You can chat on the cell phone, catch up on your reading—and he'll always be waiting for you just outside.

Allstate Limousine Service
212-333-3333

Carmel Limousine
212-666-6666

MERCEDES AND JAGUARS

Ever had a hankering for a Mercedes? Or just a Jag? But how could you possibly afford one of those, you might ask. Well, for a price less than a new Honda, you can buy one. Oh, yes, of course there's a catch: They're used. But wait—everybody knows the old cars have far more class than the new ones. The new Mercedes? Who can tell them from the new Hondas, anyway? Take the 1974 Mercedes sports car, the 450SL. These cars, with their crisp styling, their chrome, their leather seats, still look like a million. Who cares that the new SL costs $120,000? They look plastic! Uncool! Like you're just plain rich.

Look in the *New York Times* or the *Bargain News*, a great shopping gazette that sells for $1.75 and is full of useful stuff. How much are the 450SLs? Check out this ad: "1975 450SL convertible. 2 tops. Auto, air, p/windows, 40K miles on rebuilt motor, new seats, brakes, exhaust, Becker stereo, Euro headlights, red with tan interior, stainless steel fender trim, no rust, undercoated $10,900." Or this 1983 Jaguar XJS (yes!): "55,000 miles, white with tan leather $3,500." There are even Rolls Royces for sale—cheap. (Although I hear the problem is the astronomical service bills, so beware.)

I own a 1959 Mercedes 190SL myself, and I've bought countless old cars for ridiculously low prices. And yes, of course, you can get really taken. Don't be: Learn to ask good questions on the telephone—people will surprise you with their honesty if you ask them straight out what needs fixing or what's going to go next or whether the car will pass inspection. Depending on what they say, go visit— and bring a mechanic, or ask if they will let you take it to your (hopefully nearby) garage for a checkup. I bought my 1986 Volvo station wagon for $2,000—it looks great and I've gotten 40,000 miles out of it so far.

Hemmings Motor News
The bible for car collectors. This catalogue has absolutely every car, especially the vintage cars you're looking for. And at surprisingly low prices. (Two Mercedes 450SLs were less than $10,000 in a recent issue.) On sale everywhere for $4.95. Web site: www.hemmings.com.

The Bargain News
203-377-1808
This is a great resource for everything from cars to restaurant stoves to armoires. On sale everywhere in Connecticut for $1.75.

MINK

For furs, one of the best places in town is **Revillon Furs** at the corner of 58th Street and Fifth Avenue. This is a shop with a superb reputation—and during the winter sale, their exquisite furs are as much as 60 percent off. These midwinter sales are the absolute best time to buy—even better than the summer!

Revillon Furs
717 Fifth Avenue (at 58th Street), 212-308-0003
Monday to Saturday, 10 A.M.–6 P.M.

MUSEUM MEMBERSHIP

Membership in the **Museum of Modern Art** is one of the great cultural deals in New York City. For $75 for a single membership—$120 for a family or two-person membership—you get free admission (normally $10, and there's no pay-as-much-as-you-wish, as at the Metropolitan Museum of Art); invitations to exhibition previews (meet interesting people, if you can survive the crush at these events); a 10 percent discount at the museum store (great deals on reduced books; when they reduce them, they *really* slash prices); a free subscription to the museum magazine; guest tickets for $5; advance tickets to screenings; and hotel and parking discounts. How can you lose? (Also check out the $15 membership deal at the **American Museum of Natural History.**)

American Museum of Natural History
79th Street and Central Park West, 212-769-5606

Museum of Modern Art
11 West 53rd Street, 212-708-9400

ORCHIDS, DELPHINIUMS, AND OTHER CUT FLOWERS

Every cheapskate millionaire I know pays wholesale prices for cut flowers. And where do these savvy buyers head? Straight to the flower district on 28th Street between Sixth and Seventh Avenues. Not every store sells retail, but some do; and it doesn't hurt to ask in the ones you like the looks of. If you find one, make friends with one of the employees. That way, you can call in advance to find out about the new shipments, and plan your decor accordingly. Along this block, there are also places to buy great ribbon at bargain prices, along with vases, baskets, candles, and galvanized tin buckets.

The Flower District
28th Street between Sixth and Seventh Avenues

PEDIGREED PUPPIES

Don't be embarrassed if you're a pet snob, and want a dog that's as carefully bred as yourself. You can buy great pets cheaply, and I'm not talking about the ASPCA or a shelter, although that's certainly the nicest way to adopt them.

Go into a Manhattan pet store. There's a Wheaten terrier. He looks great. Look at those big eyes. You want to "save" him from that disgusting cage. But the price is $2,000. Think again.

Look in any regional newspaper out of New York City. A Wheaten terrier or a Dalmatian, or whatever breed you choose, is probably going to be $400 or $500—a lot cheaper. The dog will also be AKC-registered and may well have a more distinguished ancestry—not that you care unless you're going to breed him or her. And a lot of people I know believe that a farm-raised dog is healthier than a "puppy factory" dog bought in a pet shop. Most of these newspapers have Web sites, so you don't even have to leave the city to find the paper. (Alas, you do to get the dog!)

But just look at the *Hartford Courant.* There are some Chinese shar-pei pups: "AKC, champion bloodlines, parents on premise"—all good things—$400. Cairn terriers are $400 and $450. Samoyeds are $350. Standard poodles are $500.

The *Hartford Courant*'s Web site is www.courant.com. The telephone number is 1-800-842-8824—but any local paper will do just as well.

PERFUME

Do women still use perfume? I guess they must, because the perfume makers aren't going out of business, are they?

You can get great deals on perfumes in all the discount clothing stores: Check out **T. J. Maxx** and **Syms,** particularly. (See the listings in Chapter 1.) Here is an informal price comparison between some of the most in-demand perfumes found at T. J. Maxx recently. For the comparison, we went to Sephora at 555 Broadway between Prince and Spring Streets, a lovely perfumery.

	Sephora	T. J. Maxx
Yves St. Laurent "Opium," 1 oz.	$ 40	$19.99
Burberrys "Weekend," 50 ml.	39	24.99
Jean Patou "Joy" eau de parfum spray (note different sizes)	122 (45 ml.)	24.99 (25 ml.)
Christian Dior "Diorissimo" eau de toilette, 50 ml.	42	19.99
Versace "Blonde," 50 ml. spray	55	19.99

PERSONAL SHOPPER

I thought I'd experienced everything having to do with shopping, but until recently, I'd never seen a personal shopper in action. I didn't even know that, like travel agents, they work without charging the customer; the store pays their commission. Personal shoppers don't work for just anyone. Although spokespeople for the stores say there is no minimum, presumably you have to want more than a $5 pair of socks. I went with my friend Regina Norman to see **Connie Burke,** who has a large private dressing room on the fifth floor of Saks Fifth Avenue. Ms. Burke, who does not like the title "Personal Shopper," works mainly as a wardrobe consultant for soap opera stars. But she also takes regular people as her clients.

The experience is sublime. When you arrive, you are escorted to your huge private dressing room. Ms. Burke asks you if you'd like a cup of coffee or a pot of tea. You sit on a leather couch as she shows you the outfits she's selected for you. You try them on. Ms. Burke counsels you about what looks best. But the cheapskate millionaires wait for sales. That's when it's *really* good to have a personal shopper. During the winter sales, Ms. Burke found my friend a whole of rack of luscious items: blazers, dressy skirts, and suits that were 50 percent off the existing marked-down prices. There was an embroidered Edwardian jacket from Favourbrook, the English firm that makes jackets for Mick Jagger and other pop stars; the jacket had started out at about $1,200. During the sale, you could buy it for about $475—and your personal shopper could have it ready for you! (Ms. Burke had it on the rack, waiting for some other client, and I tried it on—alas, too small!)

Many of the large Fifth Avenue stores, like **Bergdorf** and **Saks,** offer this service. At Saks, the Fifth Avenue Club requires an advance appointment; the 101 Club does not. Both are primarily for women. Then there's the Men's Club, which does not require an appointment, but if you do make one, you probably won't have to wait. A spokesman said there is no fee, no minimum, and you don't have to buy anything. Once you are known to a particular salesperson, he or she can pull clothing from the racks before you arrive, further reducing your shopping time. This is a great idea for a birthday or Valentine's Day present from husband to wife or wife to husband—especially since men notoriously hate to shop!

At Bergdorf's, the personal shopping service is strictly by appointment, and there are ten women and one man who work only as personal shoppers. Again, there is no fee or minimum. The same service is available at Barneys on Madison Avenue; the store's two personal shoppers are available only on weekdays.

Personal shoppers are not confined to clothing stores. **Tiffany** has one. (But at Cartier's, a spokesman said haughtily: "Every salesman is a personal shopper." Not quite.) A friend of mine called Tiffany's for help in selecting an anniversary present for his wife. He made an appointment, and over the telephone he gave the shopper an idea of the type of gift—some distinctive earrings—and a budget of under $150. When he arrived, he said a charming, dark-haired woman already had selected a handful of things, and he happily selected some great-looking (and wildly appreciated) sterling silver starfish earrings with ebony centers. He handed her his American Express card and was escorted to a small lounge with leather chairs and soft lights. When she returned, the jewelry was beautifully wrapped in the company's trademark blue paper, and he was on his way.

Barneys
660 Madison Avenue (at 61st Street), 212-826-8900
One shopper each available for women's and men's clothes. They work only during the week. Appointments are required; they want to discuss what you're looking for before they take you on. Then they will pull clothes for your perusal.

Bergdorf Goodman
754 Fifth Avenue (at 58th Street)
Personal shopper number: 212-872-8757

Connie Burke
At Saks Fifth Avenue, 611 Fifth Avenue, 212-753-4000
Personal number: 212-940-4560

Tiffany & Company
727 Fifth Avenue, 212-755-8000

PERSONAL ASSISTANT OR INTERN

Want someone to type your letters, make your business calls, and generally straighten out your chaotic life? You can find someone cheap—but only if you have an interesting job yourself. If you do, you can put an ad in the *Village Voice*—or register with the placement office at your neighborhood college. Depending on your own job, you can even get an intern to help you for nothing, but I'd advise against it: If you're paying someone, even if it's next to nothing, you feel freer somehow to offer constructive criticisms or—heaven forbid—fire them. But for $10 an hour, or less if you dare, you'll come up with a plethora of candidates. Why would anyone want to work like a navvy for $5 an hour? Simple. For the reference. If young people can say they worked for a publisher or a lawyer or a clothing manufacturer, it's a lot better than saying they washed dishes or baby-sat.

PLANTS

Once you have your pied-à-terre with a terrace, you'll need some plants—and hundreds of daffodil bulbs to plant in your whiskey half-barrels.

Call **K. Von Bourgondien** and request their wholesale catalogue. You have to order at least $50 worth at a time, but you'll be amazed at some of the prices, especially when you order in bulk. You can buy one hundred pink tiger lilies for $48.50 and twelve hosta plants for $18.75. Their best deals are probably for tulips and daffodils. You can get hundreds of top-size daffodil bulbs for about 25 cents apiece; in a garden shop, you'd pay at least $1. I've been ordering from them for more than ten years now, and although their prices have gone up faster than I wish they had, they're still cheaper than the competition.

K. Von Bourgondien & Sons
For wholesale catalogue, call 1-800-552-9996.

SILVER PICTURE FRAMES

Forget Tiffany's. Their cheapest silver picture frame is $100 and feels as thin as tin. Instead, go to Fortunoff's. They have larger, more substantial-looking ones for $60 and $70. You can also try auctions, where they sometimes sell piles of them for an average of $25 apiece. But not only are they often tarnished and dented, they're almost certain to have somebody else's initials on them!

SILVER PLATING

Join New York City's fanciest dealers in line here. Transform those attic losers, with their dark pits and unsightly black spots, into something an Astor would covet. Or pick up something in a $5 box at a flea market and make it gleam. The minimum is $55, and they have to see it before they give an estimate.

Paramount Silver Plating
1509 129th Street, College Point, Queens, N.Y., 718-358-8100

SWEDISH MASSAGES

If you buy a package of ten, you can get hour-long Swedish massages by students here for $20 apiece—the cheapest massage in town! (The other licensed massage therapists charge upwards of $60.) You can't pick the student you want, and you usually stay with the same student for all ten massages.

The Swedish Institute School of Massage
226 West 26th Street, 212-924-5900

Flying Down to Rio or Over to London: The Best Travel Deals for Our Favorite Millionaire-to-Be

Now that you've outfitted yourself and your new apartment, found the gourmet nibbles for your first party, arrayed yourself in diamonds, emeralds, and Joy perfume, where do you go from here?

That's easy. London. (Or, if you happen upon a charity auction like the one described at the end of this chapter, you'll be on your way to Kuala Lumpur or Mexico City or Milano—to stay for just a fraction of what you'd expect to pay.)

Because not only is travel broadening, there's great stuff there! And what could be better than to attend the theater in London every night, seeing all the best shows—which, incidentally, will come to New York, where you can say, wearily: "Ah, yes, wonderful play; I saw it in London last season"—and shopping the antiques markets every day.

As you may have noticed, I use London as a sort of offshore flea market and wholesale distribution center. Not only do I find shops that will send me exquisite English fabrics, wallpaper, and brass hardware for about one-third the price of the same stuff here, but I find great bargains in the once-a-week antiques markets like Covent Garden, Bermondsley, Islington, and yes, even the touristy Portobello Road.

One time, I found the most charming, small oil painting, circa

1840, of an English gentleman writing a letter. The dealer, manning one of the booths off the main road (the impromptu tables are always better than the ones run by the many shopkeepers along the road), told me it came from a house in Wiltshire that had been bought by some Kuwaitis. The Arabs, the dealer explained, had purchased the stately home and proceeded to paint the garden sculptures garish colors. The neighbors protested, according to the elderly woman, and the house mysteriously burned down—but not, she added shrewdly, before she had bought this painting. Great story! Who cares if it's true? The painting cost the equivalent of $60—the story is worth at least $75!

Another time, I bought a larger painting of a horse and two Irish aristocrats, picnicking on a summer's day. I paid $125 for it and was chased down the street by two dealers who wanted to buy it for $400. I didn't sell it but instead bore it home—and after I had gotten sick of it, put it in an auction and got . . . $150. Ah, well, maybe it was the spirit of the whole thing. I also bought wonderful antique prints of blue parrots and other creatures for $8 apiece and saw a tiny tortoiseshell (real tortoiseshell) frame with sterling silver mounts at the corners for $40. I passed it by, strolled down the street and saw another one, polished up, for $450, and ran back, but it was gone. That gives you some idea. At Portobello Road (Saturday mornings—be there by 8 A.M. at the latest), there is sometimes a dealer selling antique brass faucets, both single hot-and-cold and the elaborate tub spouts with the porcelain-handled telephone shower attachments. The faucets average about $45 for the pair, and the tub apparatus sells for under $300.

The Covent Garden market is on Monday mornings and is my second favorite; one can find almost anything here (except furniture, which you couldn't carry anyway) from tarnished silver Georgian candlesticks for $30 to a miniature Irish crystal decanter for $15 to an elegant Asprey leather clutch purse for $10. The prices are excellent, especially if you bargain; the same rules apply here that are valid at Brimfield or 26th Street in New York City. (See Chapter 7.) The Covent Garden market also has vintage clothing dealers; I got a hacking jacket that looks right out of Ralph Lauren's fall catalogue: an auburn herringbone, thick Harris Tweed, according to the label, fitted at the waist, for about $40. People envy it wherever I go.

It's also fun to go to the London auction houses, which, since you're already familiar with the Manhattan ones, will not faze you in the least.

GETTING TO LONDON—CHEAP

The best time to fly to London is in late March. The plane fares are the cheapest from January to March, and by taking the last month available, you get the best weather. In late March in London, the weather is more like late April in New York: Jonquils and primroses are blooming their little heads off, and the streets are not yet clogged with tourists.

There are four main ways to buy tickets to London, listed in order of my preference. Use the last three ways for just about any destination.

British Airways

If you can get a bargain deal on airfare, fly **British Airways.** Not only are the service and the food both pretty decent, but you get the absolute best deal on accommodations. If you bought your tickets by a certain day in January 1999, the fare was an incredible $228— round-trip—and you could fly until the end of March!

For another $25 per person, British Air offered a room at the Royal National hotel in Bloomsbury. *This is really cheap!* In London, it's tough to get a decent room for less than $100 a night. And even if you don't get the $25-a-night hotel—which BA offers in a number of European cities—you can still stay in dozens of other hotels for far less than you'd pay if you walked in off the street. You can get a clean, very serviceable double room at the Tavistock Hotel, near Russell Square, for about $37 a person, or less than $75 a night for the room.

And let me tell you about the Tavistock: It's an Art Deco Hotel where the rooms normally go for close to $200, but this room is part of a block of rooms reserved by British Air in the off-season. The lounge and lobby are terrific-looking—right out of *Poirot* on the BBC—there's a complete breakfast thrown in, and the bathrooms are, unlike in most bed and breakfasts, private and, in fact, bigger than the ho-hum room. (Also unlike in B&Bs, there is room service and there are hair dryers in the rooms.) If the Tavistock is full, as it so often is, the President and the St. Giles are good value.

As you will see, this deal works best if you travel with somebody. The single rates are not anywhere near as great, although they're still okay. For the Tavistock, you'll pay $79 for a single room.

Courier Services

Unlike the regular airlines, whose rates *rise* as they get closer to flight time, prices at the courier services grow cheaper. At **Now Voyager,** trips to London are usually $299 round-trip in the off-season. (They've even been $199 round-trip if you wait until a few days before the flight to reserve.) Obviously, the deals: like any airfare, change by the season. But on one snowy Sunday in January, Now Voyager had the following last-minute deals: If you were prepared to leave within a week, you could fly to Dublin for $259; London for $259; Paris for $338; Rome for $399; Bangkok for $499; Hong Kong for $426; São Paulo for $299; Caracas for $199; and Rio for $359, all round-trip. In February, prices had dropped to $199 for Dublin and $299 for Rio, just to pick two destinations. Now Voyager has a host of noncourier discount flights too—including flights throughout the United States. Just listen to their recorded announcement of last-minute specials.

If you do decide to fly courier, it's important you understand what it means. The most important thing is the concept: The courier service is, in effect, giving you a big discount because you're giving back your allotted check-in baggage space. They, in turn, are selling that space to someone who needs to send air freight at the last minute. These services will not make you carry anybody else's luggage or freight; they just use your allotment. (Don't worry about being asked to carry contraband, they say. You never touch the freight, and they've been doing business a long time.) *But because of this, you usually will be allowed to bring carry-on bags only.* If you're one of those would-be millionaires with trunks like a first-class passenger on the QEII, forget about this service. There is also a $50 annual charge you pay to Now Voyager—each courier company has its own rules and fees. (And usually, there is only one ticket available per flight; a companion can probably fly the next day.)

Not exactly a piece of cake. But if it's the late spring or summer and you want to go to London, all the British Air deals will be over. So a $199 Now Voyager flight may be your answer.

Bucket Shops

The one I've used is called, appropriately enough, **Cheap Tickets.** You may visit them at the Galleria condominium complex at 117 East 57th Street, or they will mail you the tickets. In either case, check the tickets *immediately;* some tickets I bought to Savannah had the wrong date for the return flight, and I didn't notice it. The whole thing was a disaster, as one might imagine. But the prices are very good—they have deals with a bunch of airlines and offer some really good prices. While I can't vouch for this company or any other, my experience with the actual flights has been good. (And it *was* my own mistake not to catch the error.) Undaunted, I chose them again for my flight to Los Angeles in October. The rate on Continental Airlines was about 33 percent less than the lowest fare I was quoted through the American Express travel people, who are usually very thorough and good. But that's why it pays to check several agents.

The Internet

There are dozens of Web sites touting cheap tickets. From what I've experienced, they vary wildly in terms of accessibility and quality of service. Some I tried were almost impossible to figure out. Others promised to e-mail me information—and didn't. Two that were easy enough to access were Air Fares and travelnow.com; the former gave me the information right on the screen, and I was able to print it out. Bravo! The other did, in fact, e-mail the fares the next day. Interestingly, both offered very similar fares—but their lowest fares to London ($315 on Continental) did not beat out the $228 British Air fare I stumbled upon by calling the airline directly to inquire, and the Internet services didn't even mention the BA fare. These services might be more useful in the high season. One Web site that monitors cheap travel (http://www.cs.umass.edu/ckc/people/kim/cheapair) came to the same conclusion: "There is a flood of information on the web for finding cheap airfare. Much of it is duplicate information or useless. . . . I mean, do you really want to surf the web for three hours to shave $25 off your fare?"

This particular site mentions **Cheap Tickets, Expedia Travel,**

Internet Travel Network, One Travel, Preview Travel, Traveler's Net, and **Travelocity** as personal favorites. The site also recommends calling two discount travel agencies: **1-800-AIR-FARE** and **1-800-FLY CHEAP.**

The airlines themselves also have Web sites and offer their own last minute specials. To sample the service, go to www.twa.com or almost any other major carrier. There are usually buttons that say "Hot Deals" or something like it. **TWA,** for instance, will e-mail you last-minute specials—largely starting on the next weekend—every Tuesday if you give them your e-mail address. **American Airlines NetSAAvers** (at www.americanair.com) lets you know every Wednesday.

There are also standby services—**Air-Hitch** and **Air-Tech** on the Web—and two Internet auction services—**Priceline** and **Travel Bids**—that let you name the itinerary and how much you want to pay. Then they try to fix you up. Priceline demands that to use the service, you agree to make at least one stop.

CAUGHT IN LONDON WITHOUT A HOTEL RESERVATION?

Then head to the British Tourist Centre at Victoria Railroad Station. (Buy a one-week ticket for the Underground—the "tube"—right at the airport; it's really the best deal of all.) The tourist center has all kinds of deals on places to stay. One March, I got a double room at the Marlborough Hotel, a three-star hostelry with the most wonderful French bistro and a private guest bar, for just less than $100 a night, a room that might be compared to one at least double that amount. It was heaven! Chocolates on the pillow and a fluffy white terry cloth robe. Other times, I've found just plain bed and breakfasts, for about half the posted rate.

Ask for something around Russell Square. It's a great area, close to theaters and shopping and the British Museum, and there are plenty of places to stay. (Don't take Earls Court unless you're truly desperate. It's not your kind of place.) And don't be afraid to negotiate. The representative behind the counter will call the hotel to ask if there is a vacancy. While she has them on the telephone, offer less—with the "carrot" of a whole week's stay. Follow Mr. Goldberg's advice: Be nice. See what happens. But don't leave without someplace to stay. Otherwise, you'll end up paying a lot more in a dreary place. (Once you arrive, feel free to see rooms different from the one they've assigned, which will be, if my experience means anything, the smallest, meanest, most uncomfortable room on the front—where all the noise is. Don't worry. It's a gambit. They know you'll ask for another one.)

HOW TO BUY LONDON THEATER TICKETS

Although they have a half-price tickets booth in Leicester Square, similar to the one at Broadway and 47th Street in Manhattan, I prefer not to use it unless I'm desperate. They don't seem to offer the shows I want to see, and anyway, when I've been there, they have offered only the most expensive tickets.

Instead, this is what I do: Before I leave New York, I try to find a current copy of *Time Out London.* On the unbearably tedious flight over, I make my theater choices, circling them happily as the inevitable infant or infants scream in my ear. Then, as soon as I get to London, I buy a £10 phone card and find a nice telephone situation, where I can hunker down and make some calls. I pick the most interesting plays, which, to my discredit I suppose, are *not* musicals. Because I don't want to see *Phantom* or *Cats,* I usually have luck. I saw *Skylight* and *Art* in London before they went to Broadway, and they were memorable. In London, you can usually see plays for ten, fifteen, or, at the very most, twenty pounds, and you can charge tickets over the telephone. I go right through the week, booking plays at the Royal Shakespeare, the Old Vic, and anywhere else there's a good play.

THE REST OF THE WORLD:
ANOTHER SUGGESTION

Although Now Voyager and all the Net sites listed here can fly any cheapskate millionaire anywhere in the world—more or less—there's one more place to find travel bargains: a charity auction.

Many silent auctions run by charities across Manhattan have great bargains. Pick your favorite group and give them a call. If they're not running one themselves, they will gladly tell you who is—people who work for charities seem to be more than usually generous with information about their competitors.

Let me tell you about my favorite, the **Heart & Soul Auction,** which holds its event, not surprisingly, in February. (The advertising has pictures of hearts and cupids.) The auction, which is run by the All Souls Unitarian Church on the Upper East Side of Manhattan, benefits a wide range of programs for troubled or at-risk youths and for the homeless.

There is a cocktail reception (with fabulous food, by the way) and both a live and a silent auction. The price for admission is $50, and if you call beforehand, the charity (the church has set up a foundation) will send you a list of the items open for bids.

At Heart & Soul, the best deals are in the silent auction. Fifteen-day trips to India—without the airfare—including all hotel accommodations and some meals went for around $1,100 last year. Trips to exotic places are particularly cheap—the trips to London, Paris, and San Francisco are never a bargain.

For those who have never bid at a silent auction, it's easy: They list the various trips separately, with a description of where you are staying and in what type of room ("dbl rm w/sea view" for instance, or my favorite, "superior/taj [or garden] facing"). There is also an estimate, but the key thing is not to pay any attention to the estimates. Although these are the real prices of the rooms, at the auction these packages may well go for one-third of the estimate. Then there is a lined sheet of paper under the glossy picture of the hotel or vapid travel magazine shot of the country. Just start at the minimum bid and watch the prices go up. If yours is the last, highest price, you win the trip. So obviously, once you find the trip you want, you've got to stay close to the lined sheet. When the bell rings (or whatever), you've got to be right there, to make sure no one else sneaks in and ups your bid. And let me tell you from personal experience, no matter how well these charitable souls are dressed, they go for the jugular! So don't lose sight of your lead for one second.

Among some offerings at the 1999 auction:

Four nights at the Château Grand Barrail near Saint-Emillion, France
Four nights in the Santa Marina Hotel on Mykonos, in Greece
Fifteen nights at seven different hotels in India, with views of the pool, the taj (palace), or the lake, depending on the city
Seven nights at the Mazzaro Sea Palace Hotel in Taormina, Italy
Four nights at The Orchid at Mauna Lani, Hawaii

And it's not just a handful of hotels. In the 1999 auction, Heart & Soul had eighty-seven different hotel packages alone: in Vienna, Brussels, Canada, Ecuador, Germany, Ireland, Peru, the Philippines and . . . well, you get the picture. (And don't forget—these are rooms for two.)

So with your cheap airfares, and your cheap hotel rooms, all any cheapstake millionaire has to spend cash on is just . . . food and the fun stuff!

● Sources

TICKETS BY PHONE

1-800-AIR-FARE

1-800-FLY-CHEAP

British Airways
530 Fifth Avenue or World Trade
Center, 800-247-9297

Cheap Tickets
117 East 57th Street, 212-570-1179
www.cheaptickets.com

Now Voyager
74 Varick Street, 212-431-1616

TICKETS BY WEB

Air-Hitch
www.airhitch.org

Air-Tech
www.airtech.org

American Airlines NetSAAvers
www.aa.com

Cheap Tickets
www.cheaptickets.com

Expedia Travel
expedia.msn.com or www.expedia.com

Internet Travel Network
www.itn.com

One Travel
www.1travel.com. or
www.onetravel.com

Preview Travel
www.previewtravel.com

Priceline
tickets.priceline.com or
www.priceline.com

Travel Bids
www.travelbids.com

Traveler's Net
www.trv.net

Travelocity
www.travelocity.com

TWA
www.twa.com

CHARITY AUCTIONS

Call your favorite charity. Several suggestions follow.

The Cooper-Hewitt Auction
2 East 91st Street (at the museum),
212-849-8400
In 1999 this auction took place in June. A nonmember pays $250 and bids on mostly design items, but there are usually some trips, which, most recently, included airfare and a stay at the Connaught in London as well as trips to Los Angeles and Ireland.

Heart & Soul Auction

1157 Lexington Avenue,
212-535-5530 or fax 212-535-5641
In 1999, the event took place on February 25;
it's always around Valentine's Day. Admission
to the cocktail reception, and both silent and
live auctions, is $50.

Museum for African Art Gala Benefit and Silent Auction

For information, call 212-966-1313.
Sponsored by the museum. In 1999, the event
took place on May 24; guests first drank cocktails
at the museum at 593 Broadway and
then walked a block to the Puck Building,
where the auction took place. Besides African
art, opera tickets, and brunches, ticketholders
could bid on a holiday in Anguilla, a weekend
in Brussels, and trips to the Hamptons on Long
Island and Litchfield County in Connecticut.

Conclusion: Thinking Cheap

Now that you're back from London, let's talk.

You've done over your new $150,000 apartment on Park Avenue. It's scheduled for next month's *Met Home*. You've thrown your parties and dressed to kill. You've instructed your fiancé (or fiancée) on where to pick up the ring you want. (One of the reasons you're loved is that you know where to get it for about one-third the price of Tiffany's.)

Ho, hum.

There is, of course, the temptation to tell your friends and business associates of the coups you pulled off, the bargains you found, the fact that the material for those watery silk draperies cascading all over your impeccably stained parquet floorboards cost $5 a yard. But you must resist this temptation—although you might want to let out a word or two to only your closest buddies. Or not. Better yet to adopt a Mona Lisa smile and just say "Thank you."

Now that this book is written, I fear I'll never again be able to look my suppliers in the eye. Never again will I be able to call that shop in London and order that William Morris wallpaper. But wait—there are plenty of other shops in London. And plenty of other projects to carry out in New York City.

Now that you know all the good sources—and the strategy for developing more—your own future projects are limitless.

So what does a cheapskate millionaire do next?

You could buy a wrecked apartment or a weekend house for an investment and do it over for fun and profit. You could open a shop—selling anything from antique quilts to English wallpaper to pedigreed puppies. You could spend your time meeting friends in nightclubs. You could always start an interior design firm, like so many unemployed millionaires do.

But the best thing, in my experience, is to just keep on doing whatever it is you do—and live very, very well indeed.

Good luck.

Acknowledgments

My editor for this book, Philip Turner, a patient and noble man and a fine editor, talked me through the completion of this book like a famous pilot speaking to a complete novice who suddenly finds herself at the controls of a 747. My editor at the House & Home section of *The New York Times,* Barbara Graustark, has been receptive to my doing just about anything and has been a really supportive friend and colleague through the whole process. Dylan Landis and Carol Prisant, both far more experienced at this sort of thing, have been wonderful and even shared some of their best sources; so did Pat Ross, Jill Kirschner, and Jill Herbers. And where would this compendium be without Hally Burak's dogged pursuit of details? Thanks to them all, and to all the cheapskate millionaires—you know who you are—who inspired me!

Index